SOUTH SUDAN STATE FORMATION:

Failures, Shocks and Hopes

FIRST EDITION

JACOB DUT CHOL RIAK

A Note from the Publisher

The publisher wishes to acknowledge and thank Dr Douglas H. Johnson for his invaluable help and support for Africa World Books and its mission of preserving and promoting African cultural and literary traditions and history. Dr Johnson and fellow historians have been instrumental in ensuring that African people remain connected to their past and their identity. Africa World Books is proud to carry on this mission.

© Jacob Dut Chol Riak, July 2021

Softcover 978-0-6452105-5-2
Hardcover 978-0-6453010-2-1

Cover design, typesetting and layout : Africa World Books

DEDICATION

This book is dedicated to all innocent South Sudanese people who lost their precious lives due to South Sudan's state failure and shocks, despite its celebrated independence from Sudan. This is equally dedicated to the innocent citizens who lost their lives through state machinery while advocating for the prosperous South Sudanese State.

CONTENTS

ACKNOWLEDGMENTS

I WANT TO POINT OUT that the success of this academic work cannot be solely accredited to an individual's hard work, but it is the collection of many efforts of various persons and institutions.

I want to especially thank almighty God for the many blessings he showered upon me in my academic sojourns; particularly, the gift of good health of both body and mind. May the Good Lord's name be praised: Amen!

Special gratitude goes all those who helped me to write this book. I appreciate Professor Ambassador Joram M. Biswaro for accepting to write the foreword.

I thank the Africa World Books Press, Australia for accepting and publishing this manuscript, and to Tyler Fleming for editing my book.

I am extremely grateful of my friends, both academic and non-academic, for their moral support and encouragement to accomplish this tremendous task despite major hiccups in the country. Your sincere inspirations helped me to achieve this work on time.

My acknowledgements section would be incomplete without recognizing my relatives and siblings. I pay special gratitude to my lovely wife, Rechoh Achol Dau for allowing me to spend time away from her as I write this book. She is the rock of my life! Our first-born son Deng is a blessing as he was born during the time of completion of this book.

I would like to thank all my siblings for giving me the opportunity to learn and train thoroughly in Political Science as a profession. I owe my father, brothers and sisters, cousins and distance relatives the credit for their numerous help in my academic voyage. I acknowledge with great humility the moral assistance they have accorded me during the time of writing this book.

Finally, I would like again to reiterate and appreciate every single service provided for the success of this book. I do regret not being able to list all of them in this acknowledgement. To all of those I have acknowledged and those I have forgotten, you are in my heart forever!

ABOUT THE AUTHOR

JACOB DUT CHOL RIAK was born on 3ʳᵈ May 1983 in Malakal, the Upper Nile State, in South Sudan. His father is Abraham Chol Riak Akoi, a retired Police RSM Sergeant, and his mother is late Daruka Aguet Ajang Duot. Both parents come from Twic East County of the Jonglei State. Riak attended primary school in Narus, South Sudan, a displaced camp near the Kenyan border at the time in 1992. When the war raged on in South Sudan, his family moved to Kakuma Refugee Camp located in Turkana District, North-Western Kenya. It is there in Kakuma Refugee Camp that Riak completed his Kenyan Certificate of Primary Education (KCPE) in 1998. Having been amongst the top six best refugee pupils, he won a merit-based scholarship, which was offered by Jesuit Refugee Services (JRS). That scholarship took him to Kakuma Boys High School in 1999. He attended boarding for four years and subsequently completed secondary education and sat for the Kenyan Certificate of Secondary Education (KCSE).

In 2003, right after high school completion, Riak worked with JRS as a Scholarship Desk Officer to give back to community through community services, especially the Society of Jesus, for the award of the scholarship. In the same year, he engaged as a youth leader in the camp where he offered a lot of help to so many fellow refugees through community mobilization, peace education initiatives, inter-community conflict mitigation programmes, and women empowerment. In 2004, he worked with the Lutheran World Federation (LWF) as a primary school teacher and later an editor of the Kakuma News Bulletin (KANEBU), a refugee-based newsletter.

After all these services to the community, Riak won another scholarship to study an Advanced Diploma in Social Work and Community Development for two years (2005-2007) at Kobujoi Development Training Institute in Nandi Hills, Eldoret, Kenya and graduated with Distinction. In August 2007, he won another scholarship from JRS to study a BA in Social Sciences with double majors in Political Science and Sociology at the Catholic University of Eastern Africa (CUEA) in Nairobi, Kenya. He later graduated with Summa Cum Laude (First Class Honours) on 1st October 2010 for both Sociology and Political Science Degrees. While at CUEA, Riak served as student leader for both Sudanese Students' Community and University Guild.

Having appeared in Kenyan newspapers as the Best Student in the Faculty of Arts and Social Sciences in October 2010 graduations, Riak secured another prestigious scholarship in September 2011 from Africa Educational Trust (AET) that took him to London School of Economic and Political Science (LSE) to study a MSc in Comparative Politics at the Department of Government and later graduated in 2012. He returned and commenced teaching at the University of Juba where he excelled in research and academic works. In 2014 he enrolled in a PhD programme in

Political Science (Comparative Politics) at the University of Juba and graduated in June 2018.

Dr. Jacob Dut Chol Riak is a renowned international comparative political scientist and seasoned political analyst who is an Assistant Professor of International and Comparative Politics and the former Head of Department of Political Science at the University of Juba.

Dr. Riak has researched, published and extensively consulted on political theory, democratization and governance, ethnic politics, violence and spiritual mythology, peace building, mediations and negotiations, regional integration, particular RECS, secessions and secessionist movements, comparative hydropolitics, politics of petroleum, State building and failure in Africa, institutional design in divided societies, human rights as well as small arms surveys in South Sudan.

His work has appeared in *African Review Journal, Third World Quarterly, Journal of African and Asian Studies, Journal of East African Studies (JEAS), East African Journal of Social Sciences and Humanities (EAJSSH), APCG newsletters* and other *international peer-reviewed academics journals.* He is a scholar of the Study of U.S. Institutes (SUSI) on American political thought. Above all, he is the author of the book '*The Birth of States: Successful and Failed Secessions: A comparative Analysis of South Sudan, Somaliland and Western Sahara*'. The book was published by Africa World Books Press, Australia in March 2021.

Dr. Riak is a life member of the Development Policy Forum (DPF), Greater Horn Horizon Forum (GHHF), Council for Development of Social Science Research in Africa (CODESRIA),

African Peace Building Network (APN), Institute of Security Studies (ISS), Nordic African Institute (NAI), American Political Science Association (APSA) and the International Political Science Association (IPSA) amongst others. He is currently the advisor of South Sudan Accession to Regional Economic Communities (RECs).

Dr. Riak is the founder and the Executive Director of the Centre for Democracy and International Analysis (CDIA) registered as a research cum academic think-tank in Juba. CDIA does policy design and research on Good Governance and Democratization in South Sudan and Africa.

FOREWORD

I AM DELIGHTED AND HUMBLED to write the foreword for this book, which is a thought-provoking one on the state's formations, failures and shocks in contemporary Africa. It details the understanding of South Sudanese State formation, failures, shocks and hopes. The book covers ten chapters: Chapter One covers historical and modern theories of state formation, Chapter Two discusses South Sudan independence, Chapter Three analyses South Sudan and the tasks ahead, Chapter Four traces back to the 15th December 2013 political crisis and its shocking consequences, Chapter Five interrogates the role of the international community, Chapter Six analyses the 2015 and 2018 peace agreements and their implementations, Chapter Seven appraises the role of civil society as the purposed voice of the voiceless, Chapter Eight discusses the women of South Sudan as the 'rock in the mud', Chapter Nine discusses the youth of South Sudan as 'the young lions', and Chapter Ten reveals the hope for South Sudan and the institutional engineering in the deeply divided society.

The book argues that the political parties, political elites, UN (UNDP & UNMISS), troika countries, women, youth, civil society have contributed to South Sudan State failures and shocks through institutional deficits and direct intentional influence. This book also argues that re-institutional engineering through federalism with quality leadership in the divided society is a hope for South Sudan.

Nonetheless, the book acknowledges the role UN (UNDP & UNMISS), troika countries, women and civil society have played to move South Sudan into a prosperous state. A notable example is the provision of humanitarian aid at the time South Sudan greatly needed help, and further still, the capacitation of the police and state authorities. On the other hand, troika countries such as the United Kingdom, Norway, and countries within the United States of America have helped in the South Sudan State formation through continued donations in support of provisions for social services to the South Sudanese people. These monetary donations have been earmarked to the R-TGoNU as direct budgetary support in education, health, sanitation, water, women and youth programmes. Huge donations have also been pumped in the NGOs and INGOS in rendering of educational, health sanitation, water, and women and youth services.

Above all, women have played the greatest role in supporting the South Sudan State formation. This has been demonstrated in the critical support women gave to the ARCSS and R-ARCSS. Women were seen in the forefront convincing their husbands both in Juba, Addis Ababa and Khartoum to sign the peace agreements. The same role should continue for the full implementation of the R-ARCSS.

Moreover, Civil Society Organisations (CSOs) through their members have contributed to the building of South Sudan. This has been done through their advocacy work as well as engagement with the country's leadership and their citizens. While CSOs members have constantly voiced their concerns on the safety of their members, they have endeavored to support the citizens and urge the leaders to implement the R-ARCSS in letter and spirit.

While Dr. Jacob Dut Chol Riak, a renowned international comparative political scientist and theorist, argues that political parties, political elites and youth should have heavily contributed to South Sudanese state failures and shocks, he also acknowledges that political elites agreed and inked the R-ARCSS and that they are determined to implement it. However, he also recognizes that UN has contributed to South Sudanese state failure and shocks by UNMISS failure to protect citizens during conflicts and violence period, particularly, December 2013 and July 2016. UNMISS was tainted also in March 2014 when a truck labeled 'UN' was purported to be carrying UN goods was impounded in Rumbek, the capital of the Lakes state, and found ferrying machine guns and ammunitions destined to arrive in Bentiu. This oversight was viewed as intentional and an act of sabotage to fail the South Sudanese State through sustenance of violence.

With state failures and shocks, Riak premises the construction of the South Sudanese State on the resilience of South Sudanese citizens and further argues this resilience stems from the acceptability of the situation of the country without citizens complaining and demonstrating against the government.

With the failures and shocks on South Sudanese State formation, a rethinking of institutional engineering was thoroughly discussed using institutional theory. It has emerged that establishing strong institutions is very important but not respecting these institutions is as bad as not having established them in the first place. A further rethinking on the type of the governance system is very paramount. Riak has helped us to understand that decentralisation is no longer popular in South Sudan. What has emerged strongly from his book is a federal concept of the government that should be implemented through territorial-based federalism. This territorial-based federalism should be implemented immediately, particularly when the constitutional review process has taken place. South Sudanese citizens should confirm this type of federalism to govern South Sudanese State through a referendum.

Riak, has rigorously unpacked the theoretical and empirical underpinnings of the State and what happens when the State is absent. The book is very useful and timely to scholars and practitioners in understanding the State's building processes of South Sudan as well as where South Sudanese actors stumbled in realizing prosperity in the nascent State.

The book captures the present era of unique political and socio-economic transformation in South Sudan, Africa and the world that continues to unfold. I sincerely commend the author for this excellent work that challenges the contemporary and the generations to come as a great source of inspiration in their endeavor to contribute to this debate.

Prof. Amb. Joram M. Biswaro, PhD
Head of African Union Mission in South Sudan, Juba.

ACRONYMS AND ABBREVIATIONS

AU: African Union

ARCSS: Agreement on the Resolution of the Conflict in the Republic of South Sudan

SSES: School of Social and Economic Studies

CSOs: Civil Society Organisations

CDC: Constitutional Drafting Committee

CMC: Crisis Management Committee

CNN: Cable News Network

CPA: Comprehensive Peace Agreement

CSOs: Civil Society Organisations

DCP: Democratic Change Party

DDR: Disarmament, Demobilization and Reintegration

ECE: Equatoria Council of Elders

EO: Executive Order

FPDs: Former Political Detainees

FSI: Failed States Index

GDP: Gross Domestic Product

GRSS: Government of Republic of South Sudan

IDPs: Internally Displaced Persons

IOs: International Organisations

IGAD: Intergovernmental Authority on Development

J1: Juba 1 (State House)

JIA: Juba International Airport
JCE: Jieng Council of Elders (JCE)
NCC: National Constitutional Conference
NCP: National Congress Party
NCE: Nuer/Naath Council of Elders
NLC: National Liberation Council
OoP: Office of President
PoCs: Protection of Civilians Site
PSC: Preparatory Sub-Committee
SPLA: Sudan Peoples' Liberation Army
SPLM: Sudan Peoples' Liberation Movement
SPLM-IG: Sudan Peoples' Liberation Movement in the Government
SPLM-IO: Sudan Peoples' Liberation Movement in Opposition
NGOs: Non-Governmental Organisations
R-ARCSS: Revitalised Agreement on the Resolution of Conflict in the Republic of South Sudan
RPF: Regional Protection Force
R-TGONU: Revitalised Transitional Government of National Unity
SSDM/A: South Sudan Democratic Movement/Army
SSLM/A: South Sudan Liberation Movement/Army
TGoNU: Transitional Government of National Unity
UNDP   : United Nations Development Programme
UNHAS: United Nations Humanitarian Air Service
UNMISS: United Nations Mission in South Sudan
UNOCHA: United Nations Office of Coordination of Humanitarian Affairs
UNSC: United Nations Security Council
SOFA: Status of Forces Agreement
USAID: United States Agency for International Development
U.S.: United States

MAP OF SOUTH SUDAN

INTRODUCTION

STATE FORMATION, FAILURE, SHOCKS and consolidation has been a topical concept for the modern political scientists who have toiled to assess the emerged States' performance in offering political, social and economic liberties to their citizens and to ensure stability in regional and international system. Many states emerged after the World War II and Cold War periods to find their debuts. After some of these states were formed and they consolidated themselves to prosperity, others wasted institutional opportunities for effective formation, consolidation and thus became failed and collapsed states.

Upon independence, South Sudan delved into a lot of malpractices such as corruption, tribalism, nepotism, personal rule and political apathy to mention but a few. These issues led the state to be viewed as a cry that has not been nurtured well. However, the state survived and continued to stand despite the challenges.

Given this startling decline in the state formation, the Washington based Fund for Peace Research Think-tank in 2020[1] on Failed States Index (FSI) categorized South Sudan as the 4th most failed state and its 2018[2] report on fragile States ranked South Sudan as the most fragile

---

1   Fund for Peace-Fragility State Index Report for 2020
2   Fund for Peace-Fragility State Index Report for 2018: Best and Worst by Indicator

state in the world based on social and economic indicators, such as demographic pressures, group grievance, uneven economic development, refugees and IDPs, brain drain & human flight and poverty & economic decline. On the other hand, South Sudan state failure was also gauged on political and military indicators such as state legitimacy, human rights & rule of law, factionalized elites, public services, security apparatus & external intervention, replacing the long-collapsed state of Somalia in 2019's fragility index report. This state-of-affairs required critical study to understand South Sudan's state formation, failures, shocks and hopes.

This book therefore seeks to critically examine the processes of state formation in South Sudan. It analyses the achievements, failures, shocks and hopes for South Sudan. The book is organised in the following chapters: Chapter One deals with the historical and modern theories of state formations, Chapter Two discusses the independence of South Sudan, Chapter Three analyses South Sudan and the tasks ahead, Chapter Four discusses 15th December 2013 political crisis and it consequences, Chapter Five appraises the role of the international community, Chapter Six evaluates 2015 and 2018 peace agreements and their implementations, Chapter Seven discusses the civil society as the voice of the voiceless, Chapter Eight analyses the women of South Sudan as the 'rock in the mud', Chapter Nine discusses the youth of South Sudan as 'the young lions' and Chapter Ten analyses the future and hopes for South Sudan through institutional engineering in the divided society. Finally, this book concludes with the recommendation for future research.

CHAPTER ONE
HISTORICAL AND MODERN THEORIES
OF STATE FORMATION

STATE FORMATION IS THE DEVELOPMENT of a centralised government structure where one did not exist prior. State formation has been a study of many disciplines of the social sciences for a number of years, so much so that Jonathan Haas writes 'one of the favourite pastimes of social scientists over the course of the past century has been to theorize about the evolution of the world's great civilizations.'[3] The study of state formation is divided generally into either the study of early states (those that developed in stateless societies) or the study of modern states (particularly the form that developed in Europe in the 17th century and spread around the world). Academic debate about various theories is a prominent feature in fields like Anthropology, Sociology, Economics and Political Science. State formation can include state building and nation building.

---

3   Haas, Jonathan. Class Conflict and the State in the New World. In Grant D. Jones; Robert R. Kautz (eds.). The Transition to Statehood in the New World (Cambridge University Press, 1970) pp. 80–104.

Following Max Weber, most researchers tend to define a state as a 'set of individuals or organisations holding the monopoly of coercion over a given territory and population in a stable manner'. However, this definition does not go uncontested. Part of the literature on state-building in modern Europe defines the state in a more restrictive way. Strayer Joseph (1970) sees the modern state (characterized by having absolute sovereignty over relatively large populations, normally using compact, impersonal institutions) as a different construct from the pre-modern states (city-states, empires, city leagues, feudal arrangements) and hence places the former's emergence in the late middle-ages.[4]

Skinner Quentin (1988) locates the birth of the modern state and defines it as one in which the ruler does not just maintain his position of power but where he has a duty to defend and govern a separate legal and constitutional order in the philosophical and conceptual debates of early modern Europe.[5] Most realists in international relations literature take the Peace of Westphalia as the point of departure of a system of sovereign states.[6] As I point out later, these conceptual choices affect our coding of the dependent variable and therefore have important implications for the study of state-building processes (at least in modern times).

A state can be defined as a political system with a centralised government, a military force, a civil service, an arranged society, and literacy. Though, there is no clear agreement on the defining

---

4   Strayer, Joseph. On the Medieval Origins of the Modern State (Princeton University Press, 1970), 4
5   Skinner, Quentin. The Foundation of Modern Political Thought. New York (Cambridge University Press, 1988), 6
6   Osiander, Andreas. Sovereignty, International Relations, and the Westphalian Myth. International Organisation (2001), 55: 251-287.

characteristics of a state and the definition can vary significantly, based upon the focus of the particular definition. A state is considered to be territoriality bound and is distinct from tribes or units without centralised institutions.

According to Herbst Jeffrey (2000), there are 5 distinctive features of the modern state:

i.   They are ordered by precise boundaries with administrative control across the whole;

ii. They occupy large territories with control given to organised institutions;

iii. They have a capital city and are endowed with symbols that embody state power;

iv. The government within state creates organisations to monitor, govern and control its population through surveillance and record-keeping;

v.   They increase monitoring over time.[7]

Additionally, Herbst holds that there is another relevant characteristic of modern states-nationalism. This feeling of belonging to a certain territory plays a central role in a state's formation since it increases citizens' willingness to pay taxes.

Voluntary Theories of State Formation

Voluntary theories contend that diverse groups of people came together to form states as a result of some shared rational interest.[8] The theories largely focused on the development of agriculture,

---

7   Herbst, Jeffery. States and Power in Africa: Comparative Lessons in Authority and Control (NJ: Princeton University Press, 2000), 9

8   Norton. Bates & Robert H. When Things Fell Apart: State Failure in Late-Century Africa (New York: Cambridge University Press, 2008), 15

and the population and organisational pressure that followed and resulted in state formation. The argument is that such pressures result in integrative pressure for rational people to unify and create a state. Much of the social contract philosophical tradition proposed is a voluntary theory for state formation.

One of the most prominent theories of early and primary state formation is the hydraulic hypothesis, which contends that the state was a result of the need to build and maintain large-scale irrigation projects. The theory was most significantly detailed by Karl August Wittfogel's argument that, in arid environments, farmers would be confronted by the production limits of small-scale irrigation.[9] Eventually, different agricultural producers would join together in response to population pressure and the arid environment, to create a state apparatus that could build and maintain large irrigation projects.

In addition to this is what Carneiro Robert calls the automatic hypothesis, which contends that the development of agriculture easily produces conditions necessary for the development of a state. With surplus food stocks created by agricultural development, as well as a creation of distinct worker classes and a division of labour would automatically trigger the creation of the state's formation.[10]

A third voluntary hypothesis, particularly common with some explanations of early state development, is that long distance trade networks created an impetus for states to develop at key locations, such as ports or oases. For example, the increased trade in the 16th

---

9   Karl August Wittfogel. Voluntary Theories of State Origin: Hydraulic Hypothesis (Oxford University Press, 1826), 11
10   Carneiro, Robert L A Theory of the Origin of the State. Science Journal 169 (August, 1970): 733-738.

century may have been a key to state formation in West African states such as Whydah, Dahomey, and the Benin Empire.[11]

Conflict Theories of State Formations

Conflict theories of state formations regard conflict and dominance of particular populations over another population as key to the formation of states.[12] In contrast with voluntary theories, these arguments believe that people do not voluntarily agree to create a state to maximize benefits, but that states form due to some form of oppression by one group over others. A number of different theories rely on conflict, dominance, or oppression as a causal process or as a necessary mechanism within certain conditions and they may borrow from other approaches. In general, the theories highlight: economic stratification, conquest of other peoples, conflict in circumscribed areas, and the neo-evolutionary growth of bureaucracy.

From Stateless Societies to Political Institutions

Discussions on the formation of state institutions were limited, until very recently, to two strands of research: a) a normative approach, mostly cultivated by political philosophers working within the contractarian tradition (Hobbes, Locke, etc.); b) a broad, structural sociological literature, devoid of any analytical/formal foundations and generally imprecise about the origins of the state. The second strand includes three approaches: a Marxist one that

---

11   David, Elaine. 1977. A Theory of the Size and Shape of Nations. Journal of Political Economy (1977), 85: 59-77.

12   Becker, Gary. Conflicts and the Birth of the Nation State. Journal of Economic History 33 (March, 1985): 203-211.

sees the state as an instrument of class domination (for a relatively modern version see Wallerstein's concept of 'world-systems').[13]

A literature is something that thinks of the state as a functional response to certain collective or economic needs. Wittfogel's conception of Middle Eastern states emerging to coordinating vast hydraulic works would fit here; the closest in the political economy literature to a functionalist argument would be Olson's discussion of the state as a solution to collective action problems in large groups (1993); as well as a literature that emphasizes the role war plays in the formation of the state, as the latter has developed mostly to study modern state formation. In the last two to three decades, the literature on the formation of the state has both expanded considerably in volume and adopted a more rationalist perspective based on the principle of methodological individualism. Drawing on contractarian theory and neoclassical economics, the first generation of this research modelled the process of state formation as the outcome of a contract between two parties (producers and soldiers), each specialized in different activities, whereby the producers exchange material support for protection against external threats. Contractual approaches presented at least two problems: the ruler has little or no incentive to abide by the terms of the contract after he acquires the monopoly of coercion; and a simple contractarian theory cannot account for any asymmetrical or unequal relationships between the ruler and the ruled (unless it brackets the question of the initial inequalities of the parties in the contract). As a result, the literature in state formation has given way to a second generation of theories that insist on modelling

---

13   Wellerstein, Immanuel. The World-System Theory (Cambridge Academic Press, 1974), 1

explicitly the problem of violence and predation to understand the formation of the state.[14]

These theories offer a synthesis between pure contractual and predatory-Marxist models of state formation. Although the precise structure of the second generation of state formation models varies across authors, the basic components of that approach are as follows. In a world populated by income-maximizing agents, some individuals specialise in violence and the rest specialise in production, according to some underlying personal characteristics or endowments. The 'specialists in violence' may either expropriate the producers or offer their protection in exchange for some permanent transfers. If the latter, the specialist in violence moves from being a 'roving bandit' to becoming a 'stationary bandit' or monarch/ruler. As a result, a state (in the Weberian sense of the word) is born. The emergence of the state as a stable equilibrium depends on the benefits of receiving a continuous stream of revenues (as opposed to engaging in one-time looting followed by systematic conflict); the discount rate of the bandit; and, arguably (although less discussed in the literature), the military skills/technology of the bandit (vis-à-vis producers and other potential bandits).

Given the structure of the model, empirically we should observe that the stationary bandit equilibrium tends to collapse (and conflict reappears) in the aftermath of sudden price shocks, the discovery of new types of assets and shifts in military technology. Overall, the empirical validation of this model has been sparse. Little has been said about the underlying factors behind different

---

14   Konrad, Kai A. and Skaperdas, Stergios. The Market for Protection and the Origin of the State. (Princeton, 2010), 12

discount rates, about the types of assets that affect the intertemporal calculations of bandits and about the ways through which military technologies affect them. Boix (2010) provides a historical review of these theories, which turns out to be mainly located in classical contractarian theories plus some Hume and Smith; economists using pure exchange models look more at lobbying and policy making than state building.[15]

Process of State Formation

The literature on civil wars may be the closest empirical work we have to see the problem of state formation – seen, however, from the point of view of institutional collapse. From a theoretical point of view, the existing models of state formation are imprecise about the conditions under which non-enforced cooperation is feasible (the closest condition relies on size and the ability of groups to overcome collective action problems, but then size - generally, not endogenized - is at most explained by the explanandum; the state). They do not entertain the possibility of states forming as self-governing polities. They say little about the distributional effects of state formation. David Laitin (1998), offers a model in which all individuals cooperate without permanent political institutions provided that their economic conditions are relatively equal.[16] However, as soon as inequality rises (due to a biased technological shock), their spontaneous coordination around peace becomes unfeasible. Agents sort out into different types (productive

15 Boix, Carles. A Theory of State Formation and the Origins of Inequality. (Princeton University, 2010), 8

16 Laitin, David. Identity in Formation: The Russian-Speaking Populations in the Near Abroad (Ithaca: Cornell University Press, 1998), 19

or predatory). Three outcomes are then feasible: a permanent situation of conflict; the formation of monarchies, where the more productive agents make a transfer to the less productive ones in exchange for permanent protection; or a self-government or republican system, where the producers invest directly on some defensive structures to deter the latter from looting them. For the 'republican' solution to be stable, the producers must be relatively homogeneous (this has a strong connection to the democracy-inequality literature). All the political solutions to violence, which are strongly affected by military technology and the opportunity costs of not producing, lead to distinct distributional outcomes (in conjunction with the nature of technological shocks). For the sake of simplicity, state formation models assume a single 'stationary bandit' (and therefore a single ruler). However, states generally form when a set of several bandits forms a coalition to rule over the rest of the population. Hence, a central factor behind the creation of political order (and its breakdown) is the construction of mechanisms (normally via institutions) to make sure that the coalition of bandits remains stable over time.[17] In other words, the process of state building cannot be easily disassociated from the investigation of its governing institutions.

Modern Theories of State Formation:
State Formation in Modern Europe

War and state-building was a response to Marxists theories of the state as an instrument of economic domination; the historian Otto

---

17   Posner, Dan. Institutions and Ethnic Politics in Africa (New York: Cambridge University Press, 2005), 23

Hintze characterized war as "the great fly-wheel for the whole political enterprise of the modern state" (as quoted in Ertman 1997)
in his 1902 essay "*State Formation and Constitutional Development*".[18]
Max Weber (1968) followed suit in his book *Economy and Society*.
Nonetheless, interest in war-making and state-building would
only take off with a series of conferences of SSRC's Committee
on Comparative Politics in the late 1960s, finally published in an
edited volume in 1975 (Tilly 1975). The best, more elaborated
exposition of this 'historical sociology' approach is Charles Tilly
(1990). In Charles Tilly's book *Coercion, Capital, and European States*
(1990), war makes the state and state makes war.[19] In an anarchical
system, where states need to accumulate power simply to pre-empt
any offensive actions of their neighbours, technological shocks determine the size (and type of state). In late medieval Europe, the
invention of the cannon forced rulers to look for resources and to
expand their armies. That in turn triggered the creation of modern bureaucracies, the introduction of systematic taxation, and, in
response to the resistance of the population, the deployment of
state institutions to maintain political order at a domestic level.
Operating under a Darwinian logic of competition (survival of the
fittest), the growing sophistication of military technology and the
intensification of interstate warfare led to the gradual (sometimes,
sudden) merger of units into larger states in Europe: from 200
states, principalities and city states in 1450 to about 25 in 1830.[20]

---

18   Otto Hintze. The Historical Essays of Otto Hintze. Edited by Felix Gilbert,
with the assistance of Robert M. Berdahl. (New York : Oxford University Press, 1975), 2
19   Tilly, Charles. Coercion, Capital, and European States. (Cambridge, Mass.: B.
Blackwell, 1990), 18
20   The Formation of National States in Western Europe. (Princeton: Princeton
University Press), 5

The process of political 'mergers and acquisitions' proceeded at different speeds across Europe: states became territorially large early in time in the Western and Eastern tips of the continent. The European core (stretching from the low Countries and Denmark to Central Italy) remained quite fragmented, at least until the Napoleonic wars. With the Italian and German unifications of 1870, almost all states became territorially large. Charles Tilly attributes this variation in the impact of war on state-making (both in territorial size but also on type of constitutional structures) to a 'coercion/capital' ratio across Europe: areas rich in capital could arguably remain small for a longer period of time.[21] Although Tilly's argument is relatively compelling, it suffers from at least three problems: (i) 'coercion' is not a resource – akin to money – to be employed by the ruler to build a state but rather a mechanism to muster compliance (a solution to this problem is to replace Tilly's ratio with a land/capital ratio); (ii) it does not specify why capital-rich areas remained small and did not expand; (iii) England, which Tilly treats as rich in both coercion and capital, fits uneasily with the predictions of her failures.[22] Tilly also associates the capital-coercion ratio with the constitutional type: capital-rich countries maintained medieval constitutional structures (unless until the Napoleonic wars); coercion-rich countries became absolutist. Roger Myerson (2008) explains that particular variation as a function of a type of military (navy-based versus land army).[23]

---

21   Ibid, 7
22   Ibid, 8
23   Myerson, Roger. The Autocrat's Credibility Problem and Foundations of the Constitutional State. American Political Science Review 102 (February, 2008): 125-139. McNeill, William H. 1982.

Samuel Huntington (1968) expands this to distinguish between Anglo-American institutions and European continental political development.[24] For a critique that stresses endogenous institutional formation, Charles Tilly discusses the effects of state-making (notably the creation of large standing armies, universal conscription, etc.).[25] On national identity creation, nonetheless, the literature on the emergence of modern national identities, which is extensive, mostly stresses non-war factors. For example, Ernest Gellner (1983) sees nationalism as a functional response to the needs of economic modernisation in a mostly historical study, which emphasizes the role of territorial elites constructing 'imagined communities.'[26]

Olson Mancur (2000), who has extended the argument that war and war technology affects state type (in territorial size and institutional structure) to pre-modern Europe, argues that Italian cities survived for purely technological reasons – i.e. the invention of the so-called 'trace italienne'.[27] The closest thing to war and realpolitik accounts are pure instrumental models where political elites employ a national identity strategically to rule.[28] Daniel Posner (2005) reviewed former colonies and found that their assumptions of non-elite actors as gullible individuals ready to accept any elite-constructed story is problematic and the measurement of

---

24   Huntington, Samuel. Political Order in Changing Societies. (New Haven: Yale University Press, 1968), 17
25   Tilly, Charles. Coercion, Capital, and European States. (Cambridge, Mass.: B. Blackwell, 1990), 18
26   Gellner, Ernest. Nations and Nationalism. (Ithaca: Cornell University Press, 1983), 3
27   Olson, Mancur. Power and Prosperity. (New York: Basic Books, 2000), 7
28   Migdal, Joel S. 1988. Strong societies and weak states: state-society relations and state capabilities in the Third World. Princeton, NJ: Princeton University Press.

identity unconvincing.[29] On the impact of nationalism on state stability, there is well-known literature on ethnic fractionalization and
governmental efficiency and on ethnic civil wars. Patrick Bolton
and Roland Gerard (1997) shifted the emphasis from strict ethnic
fractionalization to the existence of imbalances (resulting in colonial legacies) in the participation of different ethnic groups in state
institutions.[30]

Institutional Theory in State Formation

Institutional theory is one product of political engineering within
the discipline of political science. It looks at how institutions once
well-established could enhance strong and successful states. John
R. Commons defines institution as 'working rules of collective actions in restraint, liberation and expansion of individual action.'[31]
Jack Knight emphasises Commons' argument by noting institution as 'a set of rules that structure social interactions in particular
ways.'[32]

States fail when they have weak and non-working institutions
coupled by a lack of rule of law and respect to the institutional culture. Coined as a constructivist paradigm by multi-scholars, such as
Mary Douglas, Aron Wildavsky and Pierre Bourdieu, institutions
determine the power relations between the state and citizens, the

---

29   Posner, Dan. Institutions and Ethnic Politics in Africa (New York: Cambridge University Press, 2005), 26

30   Bolton, Patrick and Gerard Roland. The Breakup of Nations: A Political
Economy Analysis. Quarterly Journal of Economics 112 (November, 1997): 1057-90.

31   John R. Commons, Institutional Economics And Its Place in Political
Economy, 1st Vol. New Brunswick and London. Transactions Publishers (London,
1934a), 73

32   Jack Knight, Institutions and Social Conflicts (Cambridge University Press,
1992), 2

equity distribution between citizens, as well as having an indirect effect on social and economic livelihoods.[33] Douglas and Wildavsky envisioned the role of institutions as problem-simplifying devices arguing that individuals delegated their decision-making processes to the institutions.[34] Hence, for Douglas, institutions will succeed when they are based on natural structures. However, Bourdieu argues that institutions will succeed when they are based on practice.[35] The two worlds for Douglas and Bourdieu could be used to analyse the institutions desire for South Sudan.

Let us begin with Douglas's view; South Sudan immediately after the Comprehensive Peace Agreement (CPA) of 2005 established various institutions in executive, judiciary and public service with numerous laws passed by the National Parliament and the states Parliaments. The guide to laws was the Interim Constitution (2005) that stipulated the system of governance as decentralisation. After independence in 2011, various institutions were also added to the lots of the existing institutions with additional laws and amendments from the Interim Constitution to the Transitional Constitution (2011) as amended. The Transitional Constitution (2011) as amended also stipulated that the system of governance was based on decentralisation. On natural structures, South Sudan had established institutions, however, these institutions had not aided in the promotion of good governance, rule of law and

---

33   Mary Hobley and Dermot Shields, The Reality of Transformation of Structures and Process: Forestry in Rural Livelihoods, Overseas Development Institute, WP (London, 2000). 11

34   Mary Douglas and Aron Wildavsky, Risk and Culture: An essay on the Selection of Technological and Environmental Dangers (Berkeley: University of California Press, 1983), 80

35   Pierre Bourdieu, 'Structures, Habitus, Practices', in Bourdieu, Pierre, The Logic of Practice'. Polity Press (1990) 52-65

democratisation. Corruption and impunity thrived with the deepening of personal rule and violation of human rights, thus stifling the efforts of democratisation and good governance. Quite the conundrum; how has 'natural structures' failed to improve institution's effectiveness?

In response to such a pedagogy question, Bourdieu's view of an institution's success, when grounded on practice and culture to respect these institutions, comes in handy. Establishing institutions is quite easy but making them practical, that is, with working rules, procedures and systems is an uphill task. The latter has been a challenge in South Sudan State-crafting due to a lack of rigorous political will from the political executive and the National Legislature. The institutions of Council of Ministers and the National Legislature appeared as rubber-stampers of presidency decisions that endangered the dictum of check and balance. The rule of law institutions such as police and judiciary has been compromised and could not deliver justice to the citizens. Judiciary has failed to clear the backlog cases in the courts due to corruption and incompetence. The head of judiciary, chief justice Chan Reec Madut congratulated the President on his Executive Order (EO#) 36 for dividing the country into 28 states and further into 32 states plus Abyei. His actions stifled justice as parties, such as DC, that challenged the EO# later could not get attention in the Supreme Court. On the other hand, well-articulated decentralisation system of governance in the Transitional Constitution (2011) as amended has failed to translate effective service delivery and devolution in practice. The powers have been ambiguously concentrated on one-man hands, the President, who has only given states Governors and Local Government authorities' delegatory powers. The President continued to withdraw these powers and use them against these leaders. This is a norm that has jeopardized the institutional growth and good governance and thus failing the South Sudan State. The centric power concentration on presidency is alleged by South Sudanese citizens to be one of the factors that led to the 15th December 2013 crisis that plunged the nascent state into political ignominy.

However, to leapfrog the young state out from a political fiasco, a debatable and practical rethinking of institutional design comes forth on the analysis. Given the failure of the decentralisation system of governance, a federalism system of governance is viewed as a panacea of institutional malpractice. Nonetheless, anti-federalists argue that the existence of a thin line between decentralisation and federalism systems of governance could not make the latter a suitable choice, and hence they preferred the status quo. On the other hand, the federalists argued that federalism would surrender power and resources to the states and local governments, and thus progressive states would improve their institutional and economic governance. Whatever intense the debate could be, the results of what institutional design between decentralisation and federalism South Sudan required would be seen from the rigorous analysis of empirical literature reviews. Nevertheless, Pierre Bourdieu's argument on institutions success (when based on practice and culture of adherence) remained the guide on successful state-formation.

Locating The Etymology of State and Nation Building

'State' is an ancient term for human institution dating back to some 6,000 years AD to the first agrarian societies existing in the Mesopotamia region. The origin of the modern state may be traced to the ancient Greek *polis,* or nation-state during the medieval politics.[36] Plato, Aristotle and Machiavelli eulogized the state due to its ability to meet most of the needs of the citizens, especially the ability to practice politics.[37] Other modern philosophers, such as Thomas Hobbes, John Locke and Jean-Jacques Rousseau, gave it a new dimension when they emphasised the need for the citizen's needs to enter into a social contract, whereby they would willingly surrender the power to rule themselves to a governing authority in the name of government. The legalistic Montevideo views the State as a person of international law comprising of a permanent population, defined by geographical territory with government and a capacity to enter into relations with other States.[38]

However, Max Weber does not view the state in terms of physical structures. He defines a state as 'a human community that successfully claims for itself the monopoly of the legitimate use of physical force within a given territory and with determined boundaries –the notion of territory being one of its characteristic features'.[39] Leaning on Max Weber, Joel Migdal defines the state

---

36   See Vincent, 1987

37   Joseph Kioi, 2012. International Peace Support Training Centre, Issue Brief, No 4: State and Nation Building in South Sudan after the Comprehensive Peace Agreement (Nairobi: IPSTC), 8.

38   Montevideo Convention on Rights and Duties of the States, 1933, article 1 https://www.ilsa.org/jessup/jessup15/Montevideo%20Convention.pdf (Accessed on 11th November 2019).

39   Draghics, Simone, 1989. Max Weber: The Profession of Politics (Washington DC, Plutarch), 5

ideally as 'an organisation, compose[ing] of numerous agencies led and coordinated by the state's leadership (executive authority) that has the ability or authority to make and implement the binding rules for all the people as well as the parameters of rulemaking for other social organisations in a particular territory, using force if necessary to have its way'.[40]

According to Francis Fukuyama, states have a wide variety of functions, for good and evil.[41] Fukuyama argues that the scope of a state's functions ranges from Minimal, Intermediate and Activist. The Minimal functions of state according to Ibid are based on provision of pure public goods, defence, law and order, property rights, macroeconomic management, public health, improving equity and protecting the poor.[42] The Intermediate functions of state include addressing externalities, education, environment, regulating monopoly, overcoming imperfect education, insurance, financial regulation and social insurance. Lastly, the Activist functions of State include industrial policy and wealth redistribution.[43]

Apart from Fukuyama's definition of the state, other scholars have also made similar attempts. For instance, Robert Rotberg argues that the state's prime function is to provide good political security to prevent cross-border invasions, infiltrations, and loss of territory, elaborated via the following:

- To eliminate domestic threats to, or attacks upon, the national order and social structure;

---

40   Migdal, Joel, 1998. Strong Societies and Weak States (Princeton University Press), 7

41   Francis Fukuyama, 2004. State-Building: Governance and World Order in the 21st Century (Washington: Palgrave), 1

42   Ibid, 1

43   Ibid, 6

- To prevent crime and any related dangers to domestic human security; and

- To enable citizens to resolve their differences with the state and with their fellow inhabitants without recourse to arms or other forms of physical coercion.[44]

To enable the prior functions, the state should be well-built-well built and crafted. State building therefore refers to a purposive action to develop the capacity and legitimacy, as well as the institutions, of the state in relation to an effective political process for negotiating the mutual demands between the state and societal groups.[45] Jok Madut Jok, in his special report *Diversity, Unity, and Nation Building in South Sudan* published by the United States Institute of Peace, regards State Formation as focusing on economic development, upgrading the capacity of human resources, establishing an effective security apparatus, being responsible for fiscal policy, efficient service delivery and providing general infrastructure.[46] It entails policies aimed at encouraging the growth of private sectors, including foreign investment. Francis Fukuyama further defines State formation as the creation of new government institutions and the strengthening of existing ones.[47] In other words, Fukuyama sees State formation as an institutional process that enhances institutional buildings, transitions and consolidations.

44   Robert Rotberg, 2004. When States Fail: Causes and Consequences (Princeton: Princeton University Press) 3

45   OECD, 'Concepts and Dilemmas of State-building in fragile Situations: From Fragility to Resilience'. Journal on Development 9, no. 3 (2009): 61–146

46   Jok Madut Jok, 2011. Diversity, Unity, and Nation Building in South Sudan: Special Report, United States Institute of Peace (Washington: USIP), 4

47   Francis Fukuyama, 2004. State-Building: Governance and World Order in the 21st Century (New York: Cornell University Press), ix

Nation Building, on the other hand, refers to the construction or structuring of a national identity within a framework of the state.[48] This, therefore, means developing communities, tribal groups and/ or ethnic groups to realize & consolidate shared values for State Formation. It may include the development of behavioural attributes, language, institutions and physical structures that elucidate history and culture of the people to protect the present and ensure the future identity and independence of the nation.[49] In the context of South Sudan, Nation Building is closely related to the resolution of inter-communal conflicts, reconciliation, healing and restitution of the destroyed social fabric material. When people talk generally about Nation Building on the other hand, they often refer to a national project that would produce a sense of national unity and a collective national identity with an aim to prevent discord due to ethnicity, especially as tribal violence and its ongoing destructive legacies remain part of a collective memory amongst the South Sudanese people.[50]

Though they are conceptually distinct, in practice, State Formation and Nation Building can mutually be reinforcing. Providing services, improving living standards, and strengthening security allows citizens to be proud of their country, just as pride in one's nation is the foundation for stability, producing an environment in which services can be provided.[51] So, whatever projects

---

48   Joseph Kioi, 2012. International Peace Support Training Centre, Issue Brief, No 4: State and Nation Building in South Sudan after the Comprehensive Peace Agreement (Nairobi: IPSTC), 8.
49   Nation Building: www.wikipedia.org/wiki/Nation-building, (Accessed on December 7, 2019)
50   Ibid, 5
51   Ibid, 4

a new country conceives, it has to view the nation and the state as separate but inseparable components of the same project. The government cannot focus too much on one without investing in the other. Overall State Building is fundamentally viewed as a theoretical edifice defined by its endogenous and exogenous conceptions. The endogenous paradigm suggests that State Formation is a national process driven by state-society relations.[52] On the other hand, the exogenous paradigm is characteristically interventionist and posits that the activity in one country relates to another.[53]

Given the etymology and definitions of State Formation and Nation Building as demonstrated above by various scholars, it is plausible to argue that State Formation and Nation Building are bound to occur simultaneously as they are interrelated and grounded on institutionalism. Thus, institutions cannot function without a sense of nationality and nationhood that goes beyond tribal identities and loyalties.[54] To be sure, national identities and nationhood give conceptual understanding of Nation Building and State Formation in tandem to State Consolidation.

Hence, discerning various scholars' definitions of State Formation and Nation Building as exhibited above, Francis Fukuyama's definition of State Formation and Joseph Kioi's definition of Nation Building are suitable; they stand out well and are applicable for this book. This is because Fukuyama views State

---

52   Majak D'Agoot. 'Assessing the Utility of Risk Management Theory in the Governance of New States: Lessons from South Sudan'. Journal of Risk Research: (2019), 216

53   Ibid, 18

54   Joseph Kioi, 2012. International Peace Support Training Centre, Issue Brief, No 4: State and Nation Building in South Sudan after the Comprehensive Peace Agreement (Nairobi: IPSTC), 8.

Formation structurally, looking at the processes, procedures and rules, thus it is institutional driven in nature. Kioi's views Nation Building as the building of national identities, values and norms that unite and hold communities together. Francis Deng reinforces this argument in in his seminal work *'War of Visions: Conflicting Identities in the Sudan'*, that identities are essential and should be built and recognized for peaceful coexistent of populace and state legitimacy.[55]

State Failure or Fragility of South Sudan: A Discussion

On state failure, it is important to note that nations & states fail when they are consumed by internal violence and cease delivering positive political goods to their inhabitants, as argued by Robert Rosberg in his ground breaking book *When States Fail: Causes and Consequences*. Rosberg argues that a state fails when it does not provide political goods, especially the security of its citizens from all fears and fears of threats.

South Sudan fulfils the typical characteristics of a failed state. Since it's inception, the country was born as a malformed polity because of the very fragile and dysfunctional nature of the rump state of Sudan. Since its proclamation of her independence on July 9, 2011, the legion of its doubters prophesied that the 'globe's first pre-failed state was being ushered into existence'. When political contradictions within its SPLM escalated and ballooned into skirmishes on December 15, 2013, the country was sent on a free-fall making it unable to rise up amongst peaceful nations in the world.

---

55   Francis Deng, 1995. War of Visions: Conflicting Identities in the Sudan (Washington: Brookings Institution Press), 223

The nascent state was consumed by severe corruption, inter-ethnic violent conflicts, multi-rebellions against the government, national army defections that adversely affected its ranks and files, dissident voices of civilians covertly or overtly expressed of which the government was unable to control. Broadly, however, a country's fragility is closely associated with its state capacity to manage conflict, make and implement public policy, deliver essential services and its systemic resilience in maintaining system coherence, societal cohesion, responding effectively to challenges and crises, sustaining progressive development and quality of life.

To unpack the complexities of what a fragile or failed state entailed, Brennan Kraxberger in his book *Failed States: Realities, Risks and Responses* characterises failed states into two main categories: effectiveness and legitimacy of political institutions. By "effectiveness," Kraxberger refers to the degree that governments fulfil minimal expectations for delivering public goods and services, and 'legitimacy' addresses the amount of respect that citizens of a state have for state institutions. Fulfilment of minimal expectations and legitimacy relies on physical security, which is a core problem for fragile states. Failed states are extremely violent places, though violence can come in different forms. Rebels or warlords may control large chunks of territory or engage in fighting with government forces, and on the other hand, the government security personnel may prey upon ordinary citizens, whether due to greed, organised repression or poor training.

Additionally, failed states do not have functioning social services. Kraxberger argues that failed states provide very little in the field of education; for instance, educational systems suffer from quantitative and qualitative deficiencies. Staff are not paid and are routinely absent from their posts. School buildings are in varying states of neglect or are often abandoned. School fees serve as an accessibility barrier and maybe squandered once collected and those students who do attend school often receive only a rudimentary primary education with few learning resources. South Sudan's educational system is facing institutional and infrastructural challenges with little motivation from the teachers and lecturers to address them. Teachers and lecturers often work for months without wages or salaries. Educational infrastructures are poor and pathetic.

Perturbing health outcomes is another common reality of failed states. Though data can be spotty, health indicators reveal much about the ineffectiveness of dysfunctional states; Adult life expectancy, maternal mortality, and under-five mortality rates are three indicators that can paint a grim picture. Failed states typically have far too few physicians, very limited access to clinics and hospitals in rural areas, and an uneven quality of care in cities. South Sudan's poor healthcare speaks volumes of the reality of a failed system that needs rebooting. The health access is a common phenomenon in South Sudan. Hospitals in South Sudan are just seen as buildings without physicians present. The Juba Teaching Hospital, the largest and mainly owned government hospital, has been deserted by the health workers and doctors. There is hardly any medical treatment there. Patients that visit the hospital have difficulty in meeting doctors. When questioned, health workers and doctors both state that they don't work in public hospitals because of the delayed wages/ salaries and, moreover, the salaries are abysmally low. For instance, a licensed doctor receives a salary equivalent to $20/month. This cannot meet the basic needs, especially in a hyper inflated country like South Sudan. Hence, most doctors practice private medical services to meet the basic necessities of life.

Moreover, poor transportation and road linkages characterise many failed states. The movement of people and goods into failed states is typically quite difficult, given that roads may be all but impassable for whole seasons. Only 120km^2 of road from Juba to Nimule is tarmacked thanks to generous funding from USAID. However, this tarmacked road has been eroded away by numerous seasonal rains. The rest of the interstate roads, including the capital Juba, are either non-existent or are dilapidated from gravels that are washed away during the rainy season. These roads have worn out, making South Sudan a country without interstate tarmack-cum-asphalt roads. However, the new hope is on the Juba-Rumbek and the Juba-Bor roads that are under construction by Shadong Construction & Development Co-Ltd., and Africa Resources Corporation (ARC) Co-Ltd. The Juba-Bor-Malakal road is in an advanced stage and hopes are quite high that it will be completed on time. Thanks to President Salva Kiir and his government for adopting "Oil for Roads" policy. Nile blend crude from block 1,2, & 4 of Bentiu has been allocated for construction of major inter-states roads across South Sudan. Dar blend from block 3 & 7 of Paloch and block 5A of Tharjath is the only crude left for the government revenues.

Failed States always have poor aviation and numerous fatal plane crashes. We have had 17 fatal planes crashes in South Sudan often from small fixed wings aircrafts and cargo planes. Most of these planes are old, out-dated and are banned to fly in their home countries. However, because of the corruption and weakness in our operations, these planes have been licensed and are operating in South Sudan. Indeed, the Ministry of Transport has licensed deaths to South Sudanese.

Although many residents of failed states are poorly served by publicly supported transportation, they also often lack access to effective judiciary services. When informal means of conflict resolutions are insufficient, clean and efficient courts can fairly resolve these disputes most of time and the judiciary is a linchpin in keeping criminality in check. The tradition is that South Sudan's judiciary is controlled by the executive, with the ubiquitous personal rule in place rather that a rule-of-law. A huge backlog of cases is yet to be cleared from the judiciary and all the courts of law. Judges are stuck in Arabic as a language of transacting justice. This is contrary to the Constitution of the Republic of South Sudan, 2011 as amended, which has indicated English as the official language of transacting government business in South Sudan.

In failed states, direct taxation of citizens is very minimal and disorganised because people may refuse and abscond taxes to the authorities on the ground of lack of trust to the state. They regard the state as either corrupted, wasteful, inefficient, repressive or unimportant to their lives, and thus they do not readily pay taxes. Because of this, public officials occasionally extract revenue from citizens, but this is mostly by force. Corruption flourishes at an unimaginable rate, and thus the living standard of its citizens deteriorate considerably. Human rights are subjected to arbitrary abuse by security forces. Government institutions are infested with dreadful malpractices with impunity. For example, a scam by clandestine workers of the Central Bank of South Sudan, which siphoned millions of dollars into the black market to the detriment of the state, has gone almost completely unnoticed.

Understanding State Failure and Collapse

The rise and fall of nations and states is not new, but in a modern era where national states constitute the building blocks of world order, the violent disintegration and palpable weakness of selected African, Asian, Oceanic, and Latin-American states threaten the very foundation of that system.[56] International organisations and big powers consequently find themselves sucked disconcertingly into a maelstrom of anomic internal conflict and messy humanitarian relief. Desirable international norms such as stability and predictability become difficult to achieve when so many of the globe's newer nations and states waver precariously between weakness and failure, with some truly failing and a few even collapsing.[57]

Processes of State Collapse: From Fragility to Failure

Before a state fails, the state moves from weak to fragile. A state that is unable to fulfill its social contract by providing protection and basic services for its citizens can be regarded as 'fragile'.[58] Such states are vulnerable to conflicts, humanitarian crises and environmental shocks. A useful starting point is the OECD's description of a fragile state as one that 'has [a] weak capacity to carry out [the]

---

56   Robert Rotberg, 2004. When States Fail: Causes and Consequences (Princeton: Princeton University Press), 1.
57   Ibid, 1
58   Suda Perera. 2015. State Fragility, The Concept. DLP Concept Brief No 3 (Washington, U.S.), 2

basic functions of governing a population and its territory, and [it] lacks the ability to develop mutually constructive and reinforcing relations with society'. Consequently, trust and mutual obligations between the state and its citizens become weak.[59] Often the label of 'fragile state' is used interchangeably with terms such as 'weak state', 'failed state' and 'collapsed state', with little attention paid to the subtle differences implied by each term. However, fragile states are not necessarily collapsed states. There is a great difference. While the former is weak, failed and unable to provide public goods including security for all, the latter has lost complete central authority and is engulfed in chaos, lawlessness and violent conflict.

The close link between state fragility and conflict has resulted in the concept being widely used to align development objectives with donor interests. States without the capacity or legitimacy to manage their own affairs have increasingly been framed as potential sanctuaries for global terrorism and transnational crime. Increasing the capacity of fragile states has been seen as an activity that safeguards western 'non-fragile' states from the negative effects of state fragility as much as it protects the citizens of fragile states.[60] Consequently, there is a tendency when donors talk of fragile or failed states to impose a 'bias towards western liberal statehood and market economy' and as such, 'the discourse on failed, failing and fragile states centres on State Building as the main remedy for establishing or restoring political and social order'.[61] Many OECD

---

59   See OECD Report. 2010. State Fragility (Belgium, Brussels), 21
60   Suda Perera. 2015. State Fragility, The Concept. DLP Concept Brief No 3 (Washington, U.S.), 2
61   Risse, T. (2011). Governance Without a State? Policies and Politics in Areas of Limited Statehood (New York: Columbia University Press), 1

states prioritize funding for so-called 'fragile states', which may reflect the causal link between the emergence of the fragile state's discourse and the securitisation of development.

While donors have used the concept of state fragility to justify particular patterns of development spending and programming, some actors (especially in developing countries) have rejected the term. They argue that the 'fragile' label creates a self-fulfilling prophecy, as it deters external investment that developing countries often seek when attempting to foster sustainable development.[62] State fragility has also been tied very closely to the idea of state failure, as exemplified by The Fund for Peace's decision in 2018 to change the name of its annual 'Failed States Index' to the 'Fragile States Index'. While the methodology of the index remains the same, the purpose of the name change is to move away from a discourse that shames governments towards one that supports governments to improve conditions that might lead to violent conflict. It recognizes that 'all states, to different degrees, face conditions that threaten the livelihoods of their citizens'.[63]

State fragility discourse has been used to rectify the assumption that state failure is the cause of conflict, and that state formation is the natural solution to preventing and/or overcoming such conflict. However, in many developing countries, non-state solutions promoting peace and development have been proven much more effective.[64]

---

62   OECD Report. 2012. Conceptualizing State Fragility (London, UK), 5
63   See Fragile States Index .2014. Published in Foreign Policy (New York, U.S.), 1
64   Grimm, S., Lemay-Hébert, N. and Nay, O. 'Fragile States': Introducing a Political Concept'. Third World Quarterly. 35(2) (2014): 316

Some research suggests that, rather than focusing on state fragility, it is analytically more useful to focus on the limits of statehood and to understand state power as part of a wider network of governance mechanisms. For example, statehood can be limited territorially (state weakness in certain parts of a country), sectorally (weakness in particular policy areas), socially (weakness in the eyes of parts of the population), and temporally (temporary weakness).[65] The concept of limited statehood acknowledges that, despite reduced formal state capacity, even the most fragile of states rarely remain ungoverned. The focus on state fragility obscures the myriad of ways in which societies organise themselves even in the absence of formal state structures.

Introduced by Helmen & Ratner (1993) and Zartman (1995), the concepts of state failure and state collapse have been victims of conceptual ambiguity in our times as these terms were used interchangeably.[66] Tetzlaff[67] and Rotberg[68] undertook initial attempts at conceptual clarity via distinction between the two concepts. Tetzlaff concluded that state failure is a long-term and multidimensional process whereas state collapse is the distinctive endpoint of this process.[69] He identified two aspects of state failure:

- The loss of legitimacy: the gradual attenuation of the authority of the state due to the refusal of dissatisfied citizens to obey the

---

65   Risse, T. (2011). Governance Without a State? Policies and Politics in Areas of Limited Statehood (New York: Columbia University Press), 3
66   See William Zartman, 1995. Collapsed States: The Disintegration and Restoration of Legitimate Authority (London, Lynne Rienner Publishers), 35
67   See Rainer Tetzlaff, 1999
68   Robert Rotberg, 2004. When States Fail: Causes and Consequences (Princeton: Princeton University Press), 1.
69   John Ajude, 2007. The Failure and Collapse of the African State: On the Example of Nigeria. Fride (September), 2

state, on the grounds that the state is incapable, repressive or both;

- The loss of efficiency: the increasing malfunction of the institutions of the state (which may be due to a lack of resources, or a debt burden) which makes the government irrelevant to the citizens.[70]

Rotberg's observation is similar to that of Tetzlaff's and sees state collapse as the endpoint of a process of institutional and functional decay, which commences with state vulnerability and progresses through stages of weakness, failing and failure before reaching the stage of collapse.[71] A collapsed state exhibits a vacuum of authority. It is a mere geographical expression; a black hole into which failed polity loss its central authority. William Zartman reinforces this view and considers state collapse from the perspective of the inability of the state to fulfill the functions of the state, which he summarizes as the sovereign authority, decision-making institution, and security guarantee for a populated territory.[72] Zartman came to a similar conception to Rotberg's in which he argues state collapse as 'a situation whereby the structures, authority (legitimate power), laws and political order have fallen apart and must be reconstructed in some form, new or old'.[73]

There is no self-sufficient state. There is always a degree of inter-dependency amongst states in their relations. States do have their rightful positions on the continuum to satisfy the claims their

---

70   Ibid, 2

71   John Ajude, 2007. The Failure and Collapse of the African State: On the Example of Nigeria. Fride (September), 2.

72   William Zartman, 1995. Collapsed States: The Disintegration and Restoration of Legitimate Authority (London, Lynne Rienner Publishers), 38

73   John Ajude. The Failure and Collapse of the African State: On the Example of Nigeria. Fride (September, 2007), 3.

citizens make against them.[74] A state does this within the confines of its interests and valily, a state is responsible for the provision of political goods, especially the security of its citizens from all fears and fears of threats.[75] Inability to do this makes the state a failure. Hence, nations and states fail when they are consumed by internal violence and cease delivering positive political goods to their inhabitants.[76] Their government loses credibility, and the continuing nature of the particular nation and state itself becomes questionable and illegitimate in the hearts and minds of its citizens.[77] Indeed, a failed state is one that is unable to perform its duties on vicious several levels: when violence cascades into an all-out internal war, when standards of living massively deteriorate, when the infrastructure of ordinary life decays, and when the greed of rulers overwhelms their responsibilities to better their people and their surroundings.[78]

South Sudanese State Failure

South Sudan fulfils the typical characteristics of a failed state. Since its independence, the country was born as a malformed polity because of the very fragile and dysfunctional nature of the rump state

---

74   See James Yach Garang, 2015. The Impacts of Inter-Ethnic Conflicts on National Security: A case of the South Sudan with a reference to Dinka-Nuer and Murle of Jonglei State. MSC Thesis (South Sudan, Juba), 19
75   Ibid, 19
76   Robert Rotberg, 2004. When States Fail: Causes and Consequences (Princeton: Princeton University Press) 1
77   Ibid, 1
78   Robert Rosberg in James Forest, 2007. Countering Terrorism and Insurgency in the 21st Century: International Perspectives, Combating the Sources and Facilitators (Westport, CT: Praeger Security International), 97

– Sudan.[79] Since its proclamation of her independence on July 9, 2011, the legion of its doubters prophesised that the 'globe's first pre-failed state was being ushered into existence'.[80] This prophecy would become true. When the political contradictions within its SPLM escalated and ballooned into skirmishes on December 15, 2013, the country was sent on a free-fall making it unable to rise up amongst peaceful nations in the world. The nascent state is consumed by inter-ethnic violent conflicts, multi-rebellions against the government, national army defections that adversely affected its ranks and files, dissident voices of civilians covertly or overtly expressed and of which the government is unable to control. Broadly, however, a country's fragility is closely associated with its state capacity to manage conflict, make and implement public policy, deliver essential services and its systemic resilience in maintain system coherence, societal cohesion, responding effectively to challenges and crises, sustaining progressive development and quality of life.[81]

Additionally, in failed states, direct taxation of citizens is very minimal and disorganised because people may refuse and abscond taxes to the authorities on the grounds of a lack of trust to the state's government. They regard the state as corrupt, wasteful, inefficient, repressive, unimportant to their lives; it is clear that they do not readily pay taxes.[82] Despite this (or perhaps, in response to this) public officials occasionally extract revenue from citizens, but

---

79   Majak D'Agoot. 'Assessing the Utility of Risk Management Theory in the Governance of New States: Lessons from South Sudan'. Journal of Risk Research: (2019), 21

80   See The Independent Friday, 7 January 2011 and Economist October 2010

81   See State Fragility Index and Matrix (2013), 7

82   Ibid, 17

this is mostly through force.[83] Corruption flourishes in an unimaginable rate, the living standard of its citizens deteriorating considerably and their human rights are subjected to arbitrary abuse by security forces.[84] Government institutions are infested with dreadful malpractices with impunity. A scam by clandestine workers of the central bank of South Sudan, for example, which siphoned off millions of dollars into a parallel market to the detriment of the state, has gone almost completely unnoticed.[85] Gamal Amin, professor of economics at the American University in Cairo, has dubbed this phenomenon as the 'soft state' as he argues:

'A soft state is a state that passes laws but does not enforce them. The elites can afford to ignore the law because their power protects them from it, while others pay bribes to work around it. Everything is up for sale, be it building permits for illegal construction, licenses to import illicit goods, or underhanded tax rebates and deferrals. The rules are made to be broken and to enrich those who break them, and taxes are often evaded. People clamour for positions of influence so that they may turn them into personal gain. Favours are sold or dispensed to protégés, relatives and sycophants.'[86]

For Amin, such "weaknesses of the state encourages corruption and state failure".[87] However, Augustino Ting argues that clearly, 'failure' is a relative concept derived from 'success' associated with,

---

83   Ibid, 17

84   See James Yach Garang, 2015. The Impacts of Inter-Ethnic Conflicts on National Security: A case of the South Sudan with a reference to Dinka-Nuer and Murle of Jonglei State. MSC Thesis (South Sudan, Juba), 20.

85   Daniel Akech. 2014. Features of Self-Enrichment System in South Sudan

86   Gamal Amin, 2011. Egypt in the Era of Hosni Mubarak (Cairo: American University in Cairo Press,) 8

87   Sarah Chayes, 2015. Thieves of State: Why Corruption Threatens Global Security. (USA: Norton and Company), 88

amongst others, history.[88] That means that South Sudanese state failure has a strong correlation of being a part of Sudan that has been categorized as a successful failed state. But Ting further disputes this assertion by arguing that the events that encircled the President were: the intimidation of the peoples' parliament into endorsing his speaker's nominee, the suppression of dissent within the ruling party, the dismissal of elected officials on political grounds, the expulsion of a UN human rights observer on whims, the killing of an innocent Kenyan teacher over a flag, the intimidation by some security agents of political commentators and journalists, and the murder of a formidable political analyst, Isaiah Abraham, surely distorts the country's image.[89] All of this is Sudan in practice, and maintaining such an unflattering feature ultimately sustains South Sudan's state failure in perhaps in most contexts.[90]

To be sure, after its secession, the structures as well as the maladministration practices make the state of South Sudan an imported system from Sudan. Negligence of public goods and services, intimidation, and discriminative policies still pervade the country. Contradictions amongst the ruling elites and a sizeable portion of the citizens creates a legitimacy gap in the country. In the event where the internal and international legitimacy gap is on rise, civil unrest and strife is inevitable. Furthermore, when state institutions are ill-prepared or are too weak to withstand inter-conflict, the state easily descends into a debacle such as the one South Sudan has been experiencing since December 15th 2013. Power wrangling

---

88   Augustino Ting, 'A fallacy of Failed States Index: The Case of South Sudan'.
Weekly Review: Sudd Institute (South Sudan, Juba, 18th October 2013), 2
89   Ibid, 3
90   Ibid, 3

amongst ruling elites presents an impression that the state lacks any system, which can streamline the power.[91] However, Ference David Marko argues that South Sudan is not a failed state since it makes the best passports in the region through modern biometric.[92] Others argue that South Sudan is a failed but not a collapsed state. The debate is quite endless.

Keeping South Sudan From Collapse: The Resilience of Its Citizens

The empirical literature confirmed that South Sudan is a failed state. However, it is not yet a collapsed state. Literature reviews showcased the reasons for South Sudan's state survivability. A literature review has argued that it is because of the *resilience* of the citizens that South Sudan has not collapsed. The resilience of the citizens explains the level of tolerance South Sudanese citizens have had for the running of the state's affairs despite the malfunction of the state's institutions. The nascent state failed to provide citizens with adequate public goods. The citizens' acceptance of the state, despite its total failure, is pedigreed on experiences of past wars South Sudanese citizens had gone through and thus the citizens' hopes, aspirations and synergies for positive changes continue to persevere the state of South Sudan. Moreover, the citizens' apathy in the running of state affairs in the country makes the state able to survive given that citizens appear disenchanted from the

---

91   See James Yach Garang 'The Impacts of Inter-Ethnic Conflicts on National Security: A case of the South Sudan with a reference to Dinka-Nuer and Murle of Jonglei State', MSC Thesis (South Sudan, Juba, 2015), 21.
92   Ference David Marko. 'We Are Not a Failed State, We Make The Best Passports: South Sudan Biometric Modernity'. Journal of African Studies Review, Vol (2) (2016): 113

state's roles in provision of public goods, thus avoiding demanding anything from the state. Through citizens' understanding of the challenges of the state's construction, coupled with the repressive regime policies against them, South Sudan survived the terrible collapse. Although the preceding situation is the case, South Sudanese citizens have not protested against the government but instead have developed coping mechanisms of survival, hence their resilience. This stands out as the strong reason why South Sudan could not slide into complete collapse; its people would not let it.

CHAPTER TWO
SOUTH SUDAN INDEPENDENCE

ATTAINING INDEPENDENCE on 9th July 2011, South Sudan was ushered into the world. The independence of South Sudan was one of the first independences in the 21st century and an important one in Africa, the Greater Horn and the East African region. Before the independence, Southern Sudanese people were required through a referendum to vote between the following two choices: yes, for the unity of the Sudan, or for the separation of South Sudan from the Sudan.

The requirement for the referendum vote is outlined in the CPA 2005, article 1.3:

'That the people of South Sudan have the right to self-determination, inter alia, through a referendum to determine their future status.'[93]

---

93   See https://english.dipublico.org/307/machakos-protocol-sudan/ (Accessed on 18th April 2021)

This gave both the then government of Sudan and the now act-ing government of South Sudan to organise the referendum vote. The Southern Sudanese government by then prepared itself by first passing the Referendum Act 2010 and its regulations. These laws helped in the organisation and the conduct of the referen-dum. While the government of Southern Sudan (GOSS) sensitized its citizens on the Referendum Act 2010, the citizens were already excited for the referendum vote.

Sensitization was done by the Southern Sudanese leaders in fa-vour of secession. Youth were organised into groups such as Youth for Separation (YS), Southern Sudan Youth Forum for Referendum (SSYFF), SPLM Youth League and Voice of Change, etc. Separation was the only talk in towns being preached to all Southern Sudanese. Factors that were supposed to make unity attractive; such as scaling up the developments in the Southern region and strengthening the security for the people were not implemented by the Khartoum Government. Thus, the Southern Sudanese people decided to vote for secession with 98.87% in agreement.

Registration Process and Voting

Registration for the vote started on 15th November 2010, with President Salva Kiir's appeal to registering en masse. Many of those who fled South Sudan during the civil war returned in the months and weeks leading up to the referendum, with some southern politicians trying to have them play a role in swinging the vote towards independence.[94] Almost four million citizens reg-

---

94   Jacob, Chol. When a Success Becomes a Burden: Challenges of Nation Building in Post-Liberation South Sudan (LSE, UK, 2017), 16

istered before the deadline on the 5ᵗʰ December 2010; despite the stream of returnees continuing to come unabated many still arrived too late to register for the referendum.

During the day of the vote, South Sudanese people accessed the referendum voting centres as early as 1am. I myself lined up from 2am at Dr. John Garang De' Mabior Mausoleum. It was a very exciting moment for all South Sudanese people. No one slept even with a whine. President Salva Kiir voted at 10am. I voted at 11am. The turnout was great and celebratory.

Results

Voting on the referendum began on 9ᵗʰ January 2011 as said earlier. On 12 January, after three days of voting, representatives of the SPLA/M announced that, according to their estimates, the 60% turnout threshold required for the referendum validity (corresponding to around 2.3 million voters) had been reached.[95] Official confirmation came later the same day when the referendum commission released a statement announcing that turnout would 'exceed' the required 60% threshold. Jimmy Carter expressed his belief on 13ᵗʰ January 2011 that the referendum would likely meet international standards for both the conduct of the vote and freedom of the voters. The United Nations reported that preliminary results would be expected by 2ⁿᵈ February 2011, with final results expected within the following two weeks.

According to preliminary counts reviewed by the Associated Press, consisting of 30,000 ballots in 10 polling stations, the sample had a 95% turnout with 96% in favour of secession, 3% in favour of

---

95   Ibid

unity and the rest invalid. Mohamed Ibrahim Khalil, chairman of the referendum commission, said 83% of eligible voters in the south and 53% in the north had voted. The South Sudan Referendum Commission chaired by justice Chan Rec Madut affirmed the validity of the vote; however, voting was still ongoing at the time. As voting ended, Sudan again vowed to recognise the result.

Sudan Referendum Symbols:

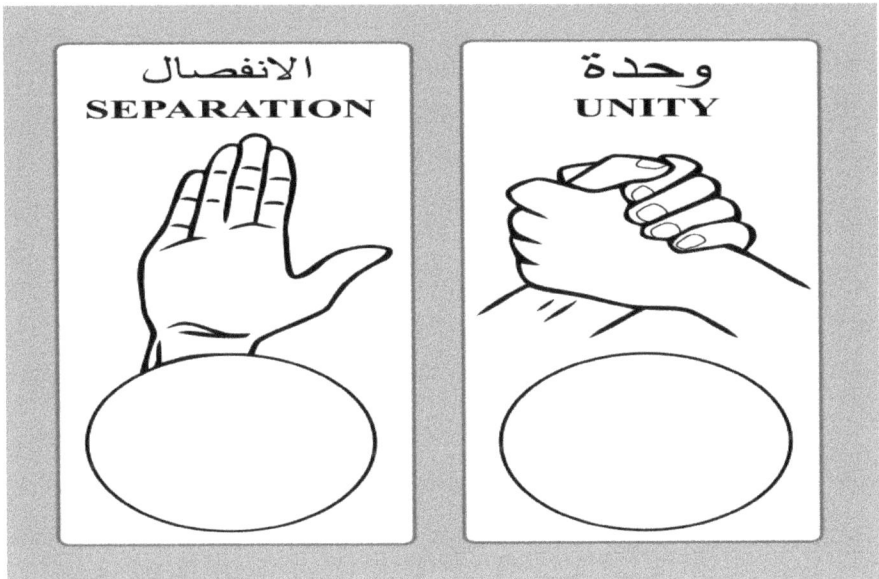

Diaspora Voting

Southerners living in Darfur were given the opportunity to vote in the referendum from special polling stations as some tribes advocated unity and others supported separation with possible ominous precedence from Darfur itself.

Polling stations were also set up in eight countries with large South Sudanese populations, namely Australia, Canada, Egypt, Ethiopia, Kenya, Uganda, the United Kingdom and the United

States. In the United States where an estimated 25,000 to 50,000 South Sudanese nationals resided there by then, polling booths were opened in eight states: Virginia, Massachusetts, Illinois, Texas, Tennessee, Nebraska, Arizona and Washington. Similar polling booths were set up in the Canadian cities of Calgary and Toronto to cater to the South Sudanese community there; an estimated 40,000 to 50,000 Sudanese live in Canada, about 2,200 of whom had registered to vote in either of the two cities.

Over 100,000 and 200,000 South Sudanese voted in a referendum in both Kenya and Uganda. 99.9% of them opted for secession. South Sudanese Students Association of Kenya (SSSAK) advocated for the secession of South Sudan from the North. T-shirts and caps were printed bearing "secession of South Sudan is the ultimate goal in the January 2011 referendum". The former association Chairlady, Ayen Tobby Maduot in collaboration with the office of President in Juba organized sensitization workshops on the referendum law. South Sudanese community in Kenya was prepared and rallied to vote for a secession, which they ultimately did.

Members of the South Sudanese in far diaspora such as Canada were split in opinions according to their support for or against separation; some of them advocated unity, while some of them supported separation. Some Canadian Sudanese people called for a boycott of the referendum, accusing the International Organisation of Migration (IOM), which was tasked with operating the vote in that country, of "being influenced by the government in Khartoum." But these claims were dismissed as 'a conspiracy theory,' noting that Southern Sudan is a very fragmented community grouped along tribal lines. Although over 99% of those in the south voted for independence, 42% of those who lived in the north at the time voted for unity.

Southern Sudanese Independence Referendum Summarized Results, 2011		
Choice	Votes	%
Yes	3,792,518	98.83
No	44,888	1.17
Valid votes	3,837,406	99.62
Invalid or blank votes	14,588	0.38
Total votes	3,851,994	100.00
Turnout required		60.00

Source: Southern Sudanese Referendum Commission, 2011

Preparation for South Sudan's Independence

The preparation of South Sudan's independence began with the Republican Order forming the High Level Committee that was chaired by former Vice President, Dr. Riek Machar, with memberships from ministries and independent commissions. Subcommittees were formed from this High Level Committee. In addition, they were sub-committees, such as sub-committee for ceremonies and parades chaired by former Minister of Cabinet Affairs, Kosti Manibe, with members drawn from the service sector, the security sector institutions and the civil society including myself who was the chairman of Youth and Students Cluster. There was also a sub-committee for venue construction and services chaired by then Minister for Presidential Affairs, Dr. Luka Biong Kuol, a sub-committee for protocol chaired by former Minister of Foreign Affairs, Deng Alor Kuol, a sub-committee of finance chaired by former Minister of Finance, David Deng Athorbei, and finally a sub-committee for the speech of the President chaired by Secretary General of the GOSS, Abdon Agaw Jok Nhial.

Those sub-committees were supposed to begin their meetings as early as February 2011. However, due to the reasons best known to Dr. Riek Machar, the sub-committees begun their meetings towards the end of June. By 5th of July the venue for the celebration of the independence was not completed. David Deng Athorbei had released 75% of 93 million SSP earmarked for independence celebrations. Realizing this procrastination, Dr. Riek ordered the arrest of the contractor, a Kenyan guy for allegedly failing to complete the task. However, this Kenyan contractor argued that he was not paid the down payment percentage of the kick-start of the work based on the contract. Having realized the gaps and the pressures of meeting the deadlines, Benjamin Bol Mel Kuol, South Sudanese businessman who is closed to the President, jumped in and commenced working on the presidential parlour and the invited distinguished dignitaries. By 8am on 9th July 2011, Benjamin Bol Mel Kuol was still working on the VVIP and VIP parlour, which he eventually completed. Nonetheless, the eastern part of the pavilion, which was meant for army generals, was not covered with any shade and thus all the generals melted in the sun. Miguna Miguna, a Kenyan lawyer and politician, who attended the independence ceremony and upset about poor organization, later concluded that the 'South Sudanese [people] were destined to slaughter each other'[96] during the eruption of 15th December's 2013 political ignominy. He argued that because of the way the independence celebrations were poorly organised, he had no doubt in his minds that 'the weather-bitten tall dark people were going to fight each other and fail [the] South Sudanese State'.[97]

The independence celebrations venue was accessible as early as 6am. The independence celebrations were well-attended. Over 30 foreign heads of states, governments and millions of South Sudanese people were at the late Dr. John Garang De' Mabior's Mausoleum (graveyard). It was the only independence celebration in the world's history where the UN General Assembly President and the UN Secretary-General attended in their physical capacities.

During the independence celebrations, a lot of activities took place. The Sudanese flag was lowered, folded and handed over to President Omar Hassan Ahmed Al-Bashir. The SPLM flag which became the South Sudanese flag was magnificently hoisted. The lowering and rising of the flags was done under the responsibility of Gen. Marial Chanuong Yol, the then commander of Tiger Division and who was the chairman of military ceremonies. Two corporals of Tiger Division trained under Gen. Chanuong lowered Sudan flag and raised South Sudan flag concurrently. Corporal Monydet Marial who hailed from Tiger Division too and a guard to Gen. Chanuong raised the jumbo flag, the tallest flag, via remote.

Several South Sudanese citizens – both ordinary citizens and dignitaries – shed tears. However, I did not shed tears during hoisting of the South Sudanese flags but I later shed tears when

96   Miguna, M 'Fighting Erupted in Juba City' Nation Media (Vol.56, 19th December 2013),
97   Ibid

President Salva Kiir Mayardit gave his speech noting the challenges laying head of governing this new republic.

No one could believe that the South Sudanese people were free from Islamic Arab's regime bondage and slavery. Kenyan specialized trained officer whom Kenya Government sent to do this assignment shot twenty-one guns salute on behalf of the military of South Sudan. The gun was a specialized gun, which South Sudan did not have but Kenyan's former President Mwai Kibaki offered it with personnel for this imperative task. The salutes ushered in the independence of South Sudan with joy and fanfare.

The South Sudanese National Anthem, which was chosen through a competitive process and adopted from the University of Juba's then College of Music and Drama now School of Music and Drama was sung for the first time. It was so beautiful, soothing and deep in meaning. The regional leaders acknowledged the lyrics and rhymes as the best in the region. A new constitution was proclaimed and President Salva Kiir Mayardit was sworn in as the first President of the Republic of South Sudan (RoSS). New national coat of arm with sharp kingfisher eagle at the centre designed by Chol Anei Ayii was adopted. Medals and awards were given to those who helped in the mid-wife and implementation of Comprehensive Peace Agreement (CPA). President Omar Hassan Ahmed Al-Bashir was awarded, Dr. John Garang De' Mabior was posthumously awarded, President Salva Kiir was too, as well as the United States of America and the People's Republic of China. The region supported the preparation of this great day. Kenya and Sudan sent military officers to train South Sudan military personnel on marching and parades formation. However, these two countries have different marching and guns handling techniques thus were unable to train South Sudanese military parades formation. Moreover, Uganda sent ground force troops to help beef-up security with then SPLA and National Security Services in Juba. On the other hand, President Mwai Kibaki sent Kenya top aviation experts to help support South Sudan aviation engineers to ensure that the VVIP and VIP planes don't get stuck due to unseen mechanical problems in Juba International Airport (JIA). South Africa sent air force security that controlled the South Sudan airspace until the departure of VVIP and VIP. Indeed, the independence was a regional and a world effort endeavour.

Many commentators argued that South Sudan was a 'destined to fail state'. The liberators now turned leaders of the new Republic, quickly brushed aside such charges. As the then speaker of Southern Sudan Legislative Assembly (SSLA), now Vice President of South Sudan for Economic Cluster, James Wani Igga read the declaration of South Sudan's independence from Sudan before an open parliamentary session (sitting number 27-2011) of the Southern Sudan Legislative Assembly at approximately 1:30pm (local time) on 9th July 2011 in front of a large assembled audience at the Dr. John Garang Mausoleum in Juba, the declaration fell short of mentioning the unity of the South Sudanese people. What the declaration focused on was the history of Southern Sudan and the establishment of a government based on democracy, justice, rule of law and respect to human rights in the new republic.

Here is the Declaration:

SOUTH SUDAN INDEPENDENCE DECLARATION
SOUTHERN SUDAN LEGISLATIVE ASSEMBLY

RECALLING the long and heroic struggle of our people for justice, freedom, equality, human dignity and political and economic emancipation;

CONSIDERING the years of conflict and the immeasurable sufferings of our people resulting from the conflict between North and Southern Sudan;

HAVING RESOLVED to overcome the past and face the future with a renewed sense of hope and in the spirit of forgiveness and reconciliation;

APPROVING that the authority of this Assembly and the Government of Southern Sudan emanates from the will of the people of Southern Sudan;

RESPONDING to the popular will of the people of Southern Sudan expressed in the historic January 2011 referendum in which they overwhelmingly voted 98.83% for the secession and the establishment of a separate independent and sovereign state in Southern Sudan in exercise of their right to self-determination guaranteed under the Comprehensive Peace Agreement (CPA) 2005, the Interim National Constitution of the Republic of Sudan 2005 and the Interim Constitution of Southern Sudan 2005;

CONFIRMING that the January 2011 referendum was conducted in a transparent manner by the national Government of Sudan in cooperation with the Government of Southern Sudan and the international community and that its outcome was confirmed by all these bodies;

RESOLVED to establish a system of governance that upholds the rule of law, justice, democracy, human rights and respect for diversity;

COMMITTED to contributing to international peace and security, regional stability and the resolution of conflicts through peaceful means in accordance with the Charter of the United Nations, the Constitutive Act of the African Union and international law; and

REMEMBERING AND HONOURING the selfless sacrifices of our martyrs, heroes and heroines who relentlessly struggled and sacrificed for the cause of justice, freedom and prosperity for our people, *HEREBY MAKES the following Declaration:*

THE DECLARATION OF INDEPENDENCE OF SOUTH SUDAN, NO. 1

We, the democratically elected representatives of the people, based on the will of the people of Southern Sudan and as confirmed by the outcome of the referendum on self determination, hereby declare Southern Sudan to be an independent and sovereign state.

What was the common uniting factor for the South Sudanese people was *Shumal* (North Sudan) and thus *Shumal* was declared gone as the Republic of Sudan forever. As *Junubins* (Southerners) commenced living alone without common unifying values, the unity of *Junubins* was going to be difficult.

As if that was not enough, the speech of the first President of South Sudan, Salva Kiir Mayardit, did not articulate a coherent vision of the new country. He failed to mention common values that could promote or deepen the unity of over 64 South Sudanese ethnic groups as they commenced living and governing themselves alone with each other for the first time. Earlier in April 2011 during the Easter Sunday celebration at Kator Cathedral, President Salva Kiir gave an interesting and deeply reflective speech. He said: 'eat what you grow and grow what you eat'. This could have been part of the independence speech so that the focus on Agriculture is emphasised, for the purpose of self-reliance and food security to the South Sudan people. As part of President Salva Kiir's independence speech, he noted that the independence and freedom of South Sudan was a good achievement. However, he elucidated that the challenge was how this newest state was going to be governed. He was later right.

South Sudan's Flimsy State Formation and its Bitter Divorce From Sudan

Copious amounts of empirical literature in state formation say that a state that hurriedly becomes independent without proper institutional structures is always faced by formation incongruencies. The proximity of the new state to the older one has thus proved to be a disturbance in neighbourly relations.[98] This is due to many unresolved issues that affect the relations of these two independent states. Southern Sudan, after it seceded from Sudan and became independent on 9th July 2011, as the Republic of South Sudan appeared as a social, economic and political loss to the government of the Sudan.

Bitterness towards the loss continues to haunt the two countries in different ways.[99] This bitterness expresses itself, for example, in

---

98   Samson S. Wassara. 'South Sudan: State Sovereignty Challenged at Infancy' London, Journal of Eastern African Studies, 2015, 13
99   Ibid, 7

the form of armed skirmishes or coercive diplomacy involving the two countries.[100] Sudan accused South Sudan of harbouring and supporting elements of SPLM-North rebel groups to destabilize and overthrow the government of Sudan. The government of South Sudan disputed this as an allegation and instead accused Sudan of arming and supporting militias' elements of South Sudan's Democratic Movement/Army (SSDM/A) and South Sudan's Liberation Movement/Army (SSLM/A) to overthrow the government of South Sudan. The Sudanese government disputed this and termed it as malicious allegation against its sovereignty. Issues of un-demarcated borders between the two countries, mistrust in transporting South Sudanese crude oil through Sudanese pipelines, and the polarization of the many ethnic communities have been outrightly traded by both countries and fuelled by each of them.

However, the relations between the two countries blossomed after the ousting of President Al-Bashir in the Sudanese revolution on 11th April 2019. The new Sudanese transitional leadership being led by Abdel Fattah-al-Burhan is cooperating with South Sudan. Because of this closed relations, Juba decided to mediate Sudanese peace talks that has brought all the Sudanese fallout parties together. All parties signed the roadmaps for peace. The next step would be the implementation of the protocols to usher in Sudan and its people to prosperity.

Other areas were cooperation is gaining momentum is on the agreement of four freedoms between these two sisterly countries: freedom of movement, freedom of trade, freedom of ownership of a property and freedom of residence. Though these are all being

---

100   Ibid, 7

implemented, the two countries are committed to see these freedoms being achieved, apart from other numerous signed bilateral agreements.

CHAPTER THREE
SOUTH SUDAN AND TASK AHEAD

SOUTH SUDAN'S INDEPENDENCE on 9th July 2011 was greeted with jubilation by millions of southerners and their supporters as discussed in Chapter Two. The hard-won, decades-long liberation struggle finally ended with the raising of the new Republic of South Sudan flag. Now, after the convoys of visiting dignitaries departed, the difficult work of building a peaceful and prosperous independent country begun. That task was going to be an enormous challenge, which would require negotiating a peaceful, mutually beneficial relationship with Sudan; democratic reforms and decentralisation; and vigorous economic development and diversification.

Despite mutual hostility and mistrust, the two states remain linked and inter-dependent. The North and the South should already have completely agreed on a host of post-separation matters, such as shared natural resource management (oil, water, grazing rights, etc.); allocation of the country's $60 billion debt (which has been agreed to be written off by IMF) and assets; the status of the contested Abyei area; citizenship for southerners who still live and work in the North and vice versa; trade as well as border demarcation and security arrangements necessary for peaceful cooperation.

On oil and gas, the Agreement on Oil and Other Related Economic Matters (AOREM) should have been made on a sliding scale and not on a fixed rate of $24.1 USD/crude barrel. This is because oil and gas is a volatile industry, particularly, on the prices. I can recall that there was a time, peculiarly, the year 2020 when the oil prices slumped between $1-$23 USD/barrel. With $24.1 USD fixed for processing, a pipeline and transportation fee, South Sudan is actually in debt to Sudan. The other fee is Transitional Financial Arrangement (TFA), worth $3 billion USD that the Republic of South Sudan should pay to the Republic of Sudan as a compensation for having seceded from Sudan. With the speed of payments of this fee to Sudan since 2011, it is going to take South Sudan a long time to clear the TFA.

To boost the domestic consumption, South Sudan has to commission quickly its 10,000 barrels crude modular topping-plant refinery in Bentiu to help reduce the prices of gasoline, diesel and heavy fuel oil. This will also serve the neighbouring East African countries of Uganda, Kenya, DR Congo, Tanzania and Rwanda.

The other important issue is unresolved status of Southern Kordofan and Nuba Mountains. The situation was further complicated by the unresolved status of some 30—40,000 former SPLA soldiers (in units recruited from Northern Sudan) in the Nuba Mountains, in Southern Kordofan, and Blue Nile. But, because many of these issues are politically charged, they were (typically for politicians) deferred (negotiations were scheduled to resume on 14th July 2011 but which they did not).

Unfortunately, with independence a reality, the incentive to negotiate had lessened even more. Some of these difficult matters could have been managed through piece-meal, or informally, but if many are delayed indefinitely and allowed to fester and create even greater resentment (as they did between Eritrea and Ethiopia) they could form the pretext for failure.

As mentioned in the previous section, the most important issue that has remained for negotiation is a new formula for allocating the South's oil revenue. Both countries are highly reliant on oil; it was reportedly oil revenues are the source of about a third of Khartoum's revenue and an astounding 88% of Juba's income. Nearly 80% of the oil is in the South, but it is entirely reliant on the North's infrastructure to export it. Conversely, many Southern border communities rely on Northern trade routes for basic commodities. When Khartoum restricted this trade several months ago, there were immediate shortages.

The two countries share a huge 2,175km long border that bisects interrelated communities and pastoralist migratory routes. Parts of the border are disputed and highly militarised. Encouragingly, the two sides had agreed to a 10km demilitarised zone and a joint monitoring mechanism, but the details still need to be resolved. The ushering of the new regime and transition in Sudan and with dependence, especially on exporting oil, the likelihood of an immediate return to war appears quite low, but renewed lower-level, tit-for-tat proxy conflict (where each side arms its neighbour's enemies) is a real concern but would be very improbable. The reasoning being that South Sudan has been helpful in mediating Sudanese conflicts as discussed earlier. So far, successes have been recorded with the signing of nine documents from nine political factions. Only two political factions - Al-Wahid and Al-Hilu - remain to join the Sudanese peace agreements with the new Sudanese political dispensation. Both Al-Wahid and Al-Hilu have agreed to sign the nine documents.

Currently, the relationships of both countries have greatly improved, especially politics and border regions. However, any move to harden the border would be economically and socially devastating to border communities, especially pastoralists who seasonally move their huge herds south in search of fresh fodder and water.

South Sudan also faces significant internal political challenges. The ruling party, the Sudanese Peoples Liberation Movement (SPLM), dominates South Sudanese politics and the government: they are virtually synonymous. It is a huge umbrella party with many strong personalities and factions, and has yet to complete its transition from an armed, military-dominated liberation movement to a traditional political party. The SPLM's authoritarian and sometimes heavy-handed leadership has triggered resentment both outside and with the party, but much of that was kept in check in the interest of obtaining independence. Now many of these grievances and fissures are likely to come to the forefront even after the signing of R-ARCSS with the determination of the general elections comes 2023. If they are not managed adroitly, there is a real possibility that losers and spoilers will launch armed rebellions to exact concession from the government. This is what Lt. Gen. George Athor did when he rebelled after he lost the April 2010 gubernatorial elections for the Jonglei state; he tried to force a new election. He since established the South Sudan Democratic

Movement and its military wing in the South Sudan Army. A number of other renegade militia leaders reportedly joined his movement, and the government claimed it received support from the North. Gatluak Deng Gai from the Unity State also rebelled against the SPLM led government, claiming that the former Unity State leader now Vice President of Infrastructure Cluster, Taban Deng Gai rigged the elections against the current Minister of Defence and Veteran Affairs, Angelina Jany Teny. Both George Athor and Gatluak Deng Gai died in mysterious deaths. David Yau Yau too disputed the 2010 geographical elections arguing that it was rigged. He later on formed the Cobra Faction/Movement, which fought against the marginalisation of the Murle people. He succeeded with the establishment of the Pibor Administrative Area for Murle and Jie people.

To peacefully manage tensions, the government will need to open up. Opposition parties, particularly those representing minority regions, claim they don't have enough of a say in the government and policy formulation. This will be particularly important for the drafting of the new constitution and laying the foundations for a robust multi-party democracy. Opening up will also require greater decentralisation of power and resources, lest Juba replicates the destructive domination of the periphery by the centre that has triggered decades of conflict with Khartoum and amongst South Sudanese ethnic groups.

The SPLM itself is also not very democratic, and that has led to many frustrations amongst grassroots members due to their ability to influence policy development by the government. Unless the party opens up its own leadership and decision-making, it risks splintering into many of its component parts. Another priority area is the security sector reform. It is still probably too early to "right-size" the army, since releasing large numbers of soldiers with few job prospects is a recipe for insecurity, but rationalising its force structure, professionalising its ranks and placing it firmly under civilian control will be important for the South's long-term stability. The country also lacks sufficient, adequately trained and effective police. At the moment, soldiers are performing tasks, such as combating banditry and cattle raiding, that are much better suited for the police.

South Sudan faces an enormous development challenge. One of the poorest countries in the world, it lacks necessary infrastructure and human capital. Most areas are very difficult to reach and are inaccessible during the rainy season. The capital was only recently linked by an all-weather road to the East African transport network centred on distant Mombasa, Kenya. The South also has a disheartening 27% literacy rate, which will make it difficult to create and staff efficient industries and government institutions. A long-term investment in education must be implemented to educate the South's future leaders and workers alike.

The one boon we have is our vast oil deposits, but that brings its own challenges. The oil industry is capital intensive and employs relatively few people. That means it creates very few jobs, those jobs often requiring significant training and expertise (something most South Sudanese people don't have), and wealth is concentrated in a very small group of companies and individuals. The price of oil is also volatile, making it difficult for governments to budget effectively. Lastly, huge amounts of oil money tends to create inflation, which makes other economic sectors less competitive in the international market. A number of mechanisms have been tried in other countries to ameliorate the "oil curse", but many have not worked well. South Sudan will have to get the technical and political aspects of its mechanism right for oil to be an engine of development. As Dr. John Garang De Mabior once said "Oil should be used to fuel agriculture". Agriculture should be the backbone of South Sudan economy as the country is naturally fertile.

The potential for economic development certainly exists. South Sudan is blessed with huge tracks of underdeveloped arable land and lots of water. It has the potential to become the bread-basket for the entire region, if the right infrastructure is put in place and if its farmers have access to modern technology and know-how to maximize its potential for agricultural production. In addition to that, there are other industries such as mining and logging that could also be very lucrative and become substantial job creating industries for South Sudan.

The tasks are daunting, but are not insurmountable. In successfully managing succession politics that brought in President Salva Kiir after the death of Dr. John Garang De Mabior, and with the signing of R-ARCSS, the Republic of South Sudan has generated a great deal of good will with its people and its international supporters. Now, the challenge will be for the government to create the right conditions for stability and development. That means it should resolve its disputes with the North, create the conditions for an inclusive and open governance, and give its people the skills and tools to create their own, better future, to promote justice and reconciliation for all South Sudanese people. The United States can help by giving generously to the government so that the government creates the right conditions to allow the South Sudanese people to help themselves. One of the areas the United States should help now is to lift sanctions on oil and gas entities as well on listed South Sudanese individuals. This will help in improving the economic growth and development as cash will flow and these will attract Foreign Direct Investments (FDI) to the country.

The Challenges of Managing the Expectations of South Sudanese People

One of the most pressing matters after the independence was the management of the expectations of the South Sudanese people. With the independence, many South Sudanese people thought that food, water, shelter, attires, and all other social services would be on their tables. Many further thought that the independence would make South Sudan the land that flows with honey and milk. Regrettably, this was not the case. The debacle has been squarely on leadership to ensure South Sudanese people enjoy the fruits of the independence.

The tragedy befallen South Sudanese's leadership begun with the sudden death of Dr. John Garang De' Mabior six months after the jamboree of the Comprehensive Peace Agreement (CPA). Dr. John Garang said severally in his speeches that if the government of the SPLM doesn't deliver to the South Sudanese people, then the South Sudanese people will drive its leaders to the sea and then they would prefer the National Islamic Front (NIF) now the National Congress Party (NCP) government, who give them salt.

With demise of Dr. Garang, Salva Kiir and Riek Machar

assumed power as president and vice president (respectively) to carry on with SPLM's vision fortified by Dr. John Garang De' Mabior. Although the implementation of CPA was a daunting task, it gave Southerners an opportunity to manage their own government and resources. From 2006 to 2020, South Sudan received approximately $25 billion USD revenues from oil. Yet, the country is still the poorest on Planet Earth, relying solely on humanitarian aid from the donor community. The development indicators are quite shocking. There is roughly an average 400km of tarmacked roads in a country the size of Kenya, Uganda and Tanzania put together. Less than 1% of 12 million people access to electricity via generators. Additionally, less than 1% of the population has access to clean water, many dozens of children and adults have no access to education and health care, and many more have been displaced from their homes.

Conflict, violence, rent seeking rebellions and insurgencies have tormented the country on all fronts, resulting from 15th December 2013's political imbroglio, fitting President Salva Kiir against Dr. Riek Machar.

It is vital to note that Salva Kiir and Riek Machar are incompatible individuals who used to never see eye-to-eye before the demised of chairman Dr. John Garang. Salva Kiir is a naturally intelligent, blameful, quiet, and humble individual that does not like confrontation and like to linger behind the scenes, with less international exposure. He is slow in decision-making and quite often relies heavily on his coterie of advisors to make decisions. On the other hand, Dr. Riek Machar is assertive, impatient, confrontational, a schemer, unpredictable with much international exposure. He is a risk-taker and independent in his actions. However, the common weakness amongst the two is that they are not good managers for a modern state given that their ethnic majorities influence their actions and inactions. Thus, the cramming of the two antithetical characters within the same party as Chairman and 1st Vice Chairman, translating into President and Vice President during CPA interim period was not only a mistake but also a historical conjecture.

With the split of the SPLM in 1991, championed by Dr. Riek Machar against Dr. John Garang, Salva Kiir has long viewed Dr. Riek as a traitor, unpredictable and someone that cannot be trusted. The reason perhaps Salva Kiir swamped on with Dr. Riek Machar during the CPA interim period towards independence was not on a trust basis but was due to a bitter marriage by historical incident of Dr. John Garang's death, coupled with the rigid leadership structure of the party. The political crisis of 15th December 2013 widened this mistrust and any slight tension between the two would always blow up into violence motivated by their ethnic commanders.

CHAPTER FOUR
15TH DECEMBER 2013 POLITICAL CRISIS AND CONSEQUENCES

THE ROOT CAUSES OF 15TH DECEMBER 2013

Background to the 15th December 2013 Political Ignominy

The political crisis that rocked the country on 15th December 2013, through a zero-sum power-struggle between President Salva Kiir and former Vice President Riek Machar was the straw that broke the camel's back. The crisis began as the internal wrangles within the SPLM party deepened through their difficulties with democracy. After the independence of South Sudan on the 9th July 2011, Salva Kiir Mayardit was sworn in as the first President of the Republic. He was given four years by the All Political Parties Conference held in October 2010 at Nyakuron-Juba as the President from July 2011 to July 2015. Before July 2015, hell broke loose in December 2013 thwarting the general elections.

As said earlier, the struggle for power within SPLM political party is the root cause of December 2013's political chaos. On 5th March 2013, Cde. Nyandeng Garang De Mabior, Cde. Pagan

Amum Okiech and Cde. Riek Machar Teny-Dhuorgon informed Cde. Salva Kiir Mayardit in the SPLM Political Bureau meeting that each of them had an interest in competing for SPLM Chairperson position comes the next party convention in May 2013. This will allow the winner of the SPLM convention to compete in the presidential elections in the SPLM ticket. On hearing such a revelation, Cde. Salva Kiir Mayardit was infuriated and disturbed. Knowing the political machinations of Dr. Riek Machar, he took back the peace building and reconciliation assignment he gave to Dr. Riek Machar and reduced his powers to that of delegatory only.

Dr. Riek Machar did not take this power strip lightly. He challenged President Kiir in June 2013 about the necessity of having a federal system of the government by drafting a parallel constitution. Having seen the visible activities of Dr. Riek, President Kiir sacked the entire executive in July 2013, including Dr. Riek Machar. He later on left the Secretary General, Hon. Abdon Agaw Jok Nhial, in charge of running of the government. In August 2013, President Kiir (who served as the Chairman of the SPLM) pronounced the SPLM party structures dissolved including the Deputy Chairmanship of Dr. Riek Machar. In September 2013, President Kiir appointed a new cabinet with James Wani Igga as the new Vice President of the Republic. Dr. Riek Machar stayed in his residence meeting various groups of persons whom they discussed the future of South Sudan. In mid-September 2013, the SPLM Political Bureau organised a meeting at the SPLM House, which Dr. Riek Machar attempted to attend but he was blocked at the entry.

Having realized that a new cabinet had been appointed, SPLM

party structures unilaterally dissolved by the chairman and himself being barred out from attending the SPLM meetings chaired by President Salva Kiir, Dr. Riek continued to challenge further the powers Cde. Salva Kiir had to dissolve the SPLM structures and leave his position intact. Thus, Dr. Riek began organising clandestine meetings with other dissatisfied SPLM members, asking them to convince chairman Salva Kiir to call for a Political Bureau meeting to deliberate on and adopt the SPLM Manifesto, Constitution, Basic Rules and the Code of Conduct. As tension increased between the two leaders, given the political profiteers shuttled between the two, Dr. Riek called for a press conference on 6th December 2013 at the SPLM House outlining the mistakes the Chairman has done in his running of the party, accusing him of having lost the vision and appealed for the conduct of political Bureau meeting. This press conference became widely known as the December 6th Press Conference. Those that attended this press conference except Nhial Deng Nhial, Michael Makuei Lueth and David Deng Athorbei became members of SPLM/A-IO and Former Political Detainees (FPDs). At the time of the press conference President Salva Kiir had travelled to Paris in France to attend the African-French Security Summit and later on to Pretoria in South Africa to attend the burial of President Nelson Mandela. Before returning to Juba in South Sudan, the Vice President (who was the 2nd Deputy Chairman of the SPLM) held a counter press conference on the 8th December 2013 at the SPLM House denouncing the December 6th press conference and calling the participants of December 6th's press conference "disgruntled members" who were impatient and corrupt. The tension between the two camps ballooned. President Kiir returned to Juba on the 9th December 2013.

Dr. Riek Machar announced that his group would hold a rally at Dr. John Garang De Mabior's Mausoleum on the 15th December 2013 to inform the masses about their next step, since the party chairman had lost the vision according to him. On hearing that, the government decided to fence-off the Mausoleum and no one was allowed in. Interestingly, the government scheduled SPLM National Liberation council meeting on the 15th December 2013 at 9am at Nyakuron Cultural Centre. On hearing that, Dr. Riek and his team postponed their rally and decided to proceed to the National Liberation Council (NLC) meeting. The NLC is the second-highest tier organ of the party after the Political Bureau.

In Nyakuron, differences were poorly managed by the two camps and they despised the counsels from Hilder F. Johnson, former Special Representative of UN Secretary General; H.G. Late Paulino Lukudu Loro, former Catholic Arch-Bishop and Metropolitan Bishop of Juba; and H.G. Daniel Deng Bul, former Arch-Bishop of Episcopal church of Sudan and South Sudan. The government camp proceeded with presentation of the basic documents, manifesto, constitution and code of conduct. Michael Makuei Lueth was the moderator of the meeting. He asked all members to pass the documents, and a majority did so through exclamations and ululations. Riek's camp felt short-changed and left the meeting. At around 9pm the same day, a sporadic gun shooting began at the main military barrack of elite presidential battalion (guards), famously known as Tiger battalion at Gyada, South-West of Juba. The fighting escalated to the SPLA barracks at Newsite and Bilpam and later to the three States of the Greater Upper Nile Region, namely Jonglei, Unity and Upper Nile, turning out as armed rebellions. Although no impeccable source could explain the real causes of the fighting, multiple sources alleged that the shooting was triggered by either an attempted disarmament of Nuer soldiers in the presidential battalion or an attempted break in into the military armoury by Nuer soldiers. However, the government has rejected these accounts. It termed the fighting as a foiled coup d'état by Dr. Riek Machar's forces and his allies. Other vital sources cited the fighting stemming from the disagreements within the SPLM members of the National Liberation Council (NLC). The African Union Commission of Inquiry in South Sudan's (AUCISS) 2015 report indicated that there was no coup attempt but there was a mutiny within the presidential elite battalion (Tiger) division fitting SPLA Dinka of President Salva Kiir and SPLA Nuer of Dr. Riek Machar. Due to his insatiable thirst for political power, Dr. Riek Machar declared a resistance movement against the people and government of South Sudan. He mobilized the Nuer white armies (Jiech Mabor) on the pretext that all the Nuer were killed in Juba by the Dinka. This led to devastating revenges on the Dinka in Bor, Malakal and Baliet by the marooned white armies.

Since inheriting the political throne from late Dr. John Garang De' Mabior, Salva Kiir and Riek Machar have never had a convergence vision and have never been at ease to see each other eyes in ferrying South Sudan to prosperity. However, with millions of civilians' blood spilled for independence, the South Sudanese people still entrusted the two leaders to guide the young state and people into stability and opulence. Yet, this had not been the case. The duo turned freedom into bondage, making independence murky and hopeless for the people of South Sudan. This begs the soul-searching question: was independence a mistake for South Sudan? Was freedom a wrong choice for South Sudanese to end up trapped by their own leaders?

The violence that turned South Sudan into a deadly battlefield was devastating, leading to the deaths of over 500,000 people. Relief came from the IGAD 2015 and 2018 Peace Agreements that led to the formation of R-TGONU in February 2020 making Dr. Riek the 1st Vice President to Salva Kiir and four other Vice Presidents for Economics, Infrastructure, Services, Gender, and Youth Clusters. The implementations of 2015 and 2018's Peace Agreements was a daunting task that will be discussed in Chapter Six in detail. However, there are roots causes (paper tigers) and failures that allowed the 2013 political crisis to take place. They are discussed as follows:

Political Parties in a Polity

Political parties are central to representing democracy and to the process of democratisation in nation and state formation. They connect society and the state, aggregate and represent its interests, and recruit political leaders.[101] They disseminate political information, socialise citizens into democratic politics and manage conflicts of interest.[102] However, in societies that have often experienced violent conflict, political parties can offer a forum for

---

101   Peter Burnell. 2004. Building Better Democracies: Why Political Parties Matter? Westminster Foundation for Democracy (London: WMFD), 5
102   Ibid, 4

social and political integration, a tool that enhances nation and state formation. Once done well, political parties become the vehicle for institutional engineering and democratisation of a polity. Nevertheless, the relations amongst the parties don't display a responsible attitude towards the practice of political competition.[103]

Viewed as state formation therapy, an institutionalised party system in a society can hold elected politicians accountable for their performance in office and their role as the people's representatives. The public standing of the political parties and of politicians themselves benefits when the parties and the party systems are in good political health. Strategies to establish and consolidate democracy that ignores the central role of parties cannot hope to be successful, no matter how much attention they pay to other vital matters such as building a civil society and the institutions of good governance.[104] In essence, the essential role of political parties in a polity cannot be underrated.

Role of Political Parties in State Formation and Failure

Political parties are institutional vehicles for capturing a state's power as well as providing strong avenue for political programmes for the polity. Political parties serve as drivers of state formation and failure. A political party built on ideological orientation rather than on an ethnic lens serves as a promoter of state formation and consolidation. However, a political party established on ethnic overtures and personified rationality tends to enhance state failure and collapse, given dearth of ideological and institutional

---

103   Ibid, 5
104   Ibid, 5

references when discharging its activities.

Although South Sudan has over twenty-four political parties with fourteen registered parties and the main parties of ruling SPLM and opposition DCP, the role of these political parties in enhancing state formation is very remote. Most of these parties are briefcase in nature and are run by family's associates, and thus are quite mute in programming and outreach. Despite such muteness, political parties have endeavoured to form the State of South Sudan through public interest. One way of doing it has been through the South Sudan Political Parties Leadership Forum that continued to challenge the decisions of the government. One such government-challenged decision was an attempted conduct of election by the government in July 2015 and the passage of the National Security Bill in 2015. However, not all political parties stuck to this task; through a constant agitation towards the perceived government draconian policies, it was then SPLM-DC and now DC, which stood as the official opposition party despite its minority leadership in the August House till the R-ARCSS brought in the SPLM-IO.

However, the South Sudanese political parties have failed the state of South Sudan on various fronts, supported by a lack of political culture and programmes. This is the reason why there is such an extreme division on the fundamental issues (such as federalism, integration and direction) of South Sudan as a functioning state. There is a rise in hypocritical culture, where political parties and their leaderships are raising conflicting elucidation of the solution to issues of the constitution, including federalism and integration

List of Registered South Sudanese Political Parties

S/no.	Name of Party	Party's Chairperson	Date of Registration	Registration Number
1	African National Congress (ANC)	Gen. George Kongor Arop	22nd February 2016	1
2	Sudan People's Liberation Movement-SPLM	H.E. Gen. Salva Kiir Mayardit	22nd February 2016	2
3	United South Sudan African Party-USSAP	Ustaz. Joseph Ukel Abango	22nd February 2016	3
4	United Democratic Salvation Front-Mainstream-UDSF-M	Hon. Francis Ben Ataba	22nd February 2016	4
5	National Liberation Party-NLP	Hon. Nkrumah W. Kelueljang	22nd February 2016	5
6	National Congress Party-NCP	Hon. Agnes Poni Lokudu	23rd February 2016	6
7	Democratic Change Party-DCP	Hon. Onyoti Adigo Nyikwec	11th April 2016	7
8	South Sudan Democratic Front (SSDF)	Hon. Dr. Martin Elia Lomuro	11th April 2016	8
9	National United Democratic Front-NUDF	Hon. Kornelio Kon Ngu	11th April 2016	9
10	United South Sudan Party-USSP	Hon. Clement Juma Mbugoniwia	11th April 2016	10
11	South Sudan Democratic Alliance-SSDA	Hon. Paskalina Philip Waden	11th April 2016	11
12	Sudan African National Union (SANU)	Hon. Theresa Cirisio Iro	13th June 2016	12
13	United Democratic Salvation Front-UDSF	Eng. Joseph Malual Dong	18th August 2016	13
14	National Democratic Party-NDP	Hon. James Aniceto	23rd September 2016	14

Source: Political Parties Council, Juba.

issues based on their political gains and advantages.[105]

Although SPLM has, so far, defined its political culture on the participation of South Sudanese spectrums in the governance, this has not been seen in practice. Instead, much is linked to the lack of internal democratic reforms that always escalate to power struggles and political violence. The SPLM's failure to act as a strong and effective ruling party that followed the transformation path it had laid out in the run-up to the 2005 transition, caused South Sudan's leadership to adopt important yet insufficient stop-gap measures towards political accommodation and governance strategies.[106] The political accommodation not only compromised accountability but it also compromised justice in the guerrilla party. This has prompted Mahmood Mamdani to caution laxity on impunity and argued a need for a bid of power that encouraged accountability and justice within the party and the state to enhance good governance and strong state formation.[107]

But gimmicks of politics in the party have overtaken the accountability programme. This has, so far, resulted in a diluted political landscape defined by profiteering and power interests instead of a defined political programme, which could have tempered the negative aspects of unaccountable alliances.[108] The result of which has been political conflicts and violence negating successful state formation.

105   Manish Thapa, 2008. Role of Civil Society & Political Party in current Nation/State Building Process in Nepal: New Dynamics of Development, Challenges and Prospects (Nepal: CETS, November), 13

106   Paula Cristina Rogue, 2014. Reforming the SPLM: A requisite for Peace and Nation Building. Policy Brief 63: Institute for Security Studies (Pretoria: August), 1

107   Mahmood Mamdani, 2014. South Sudan: The Problem and the Way Forward: New Vision (Kampala: 28th February), 3

108   Paula Cristina Rogue, 2014. Reforming the SPLM: A requisite for Peace and Nation Building. Policy Brief 63: Institute for Security Studies (Pretoria: August), 2

In the SPLM, the operational aspects of distinguishing between the state and the party and the governance sequencing of who should lead who, have been blurred. Policy has been crafted at the government level as opposed to the party level, and the driving force has been one of balancing the interests and representation of the various communities.[109] One such policy is the appointment criterion of the ministers and the state officers that the government lobbyists and rent-seekers continued to mislead the chairman of the SPLM (President Kiir), who should have at all times consulted the party's top leadership for proposals, endorsements and major decisions. The second such policy was the nomination of the party flag bearers for the elections. The 2010 general elections testified to the state of affairs whereby the deficit of party internal control and democracy was exposed; SPLM party bearers were hand-picked by the top of the party's leadership without the consultation of the National Liberation Council (NLC) and the Political Bureau (PB), leading to the various rebellions from George Athor Deng, Gatluak Deng Gai and David Yau Yau, which South Sudan has heavily paid for. Thus, a communal ethnic view of politics becomes the order of affairs in state formation and failure with centripetal interests ensued.

Conceptualizing Ethnic Parties and Ethnic Politics in South Sudan

The term ethnicity is derived from the Greek word *ethnos*, meaning race or group of people with common racial features and common cultural peculiarities. Donald Rothchild refers to ethnicity as

---

109   Ibid, 3

a subjective perception of common origins, history, memory, ties and aspirations.[110] Ethnicity is an extension of kinship based on the shared belief on common ancestry, regardless of whether or not an objective blood relationship exists.[111] Ethnicity is a presumed identity that contains the potential for group formation but does not single out the group.[112] Ethnic trust may actually find itself at odds with other forms of political identity such as class or professional affiliation. In any given society individuals have more than one identity at any given time.

Ethnicity belongs to the category of collective markers, which includes nation, class, profession, political ideology, and party amongst others.[113] African ethnic groups are understood in an external sense as the collective actors of competitive politics, in what has been termed as 'political tribalism', but also as the 'internal discursive political arena, through which ethnic identities have emerged out of multiple, selective imagining of 'tradition', culture and identity from European as well as African sources', what has been termed as 'moral ethnicity'.[114] Probably the most common political science explanation for ethnic conflict is that past discrimination and oppression lead to violence; if that discrimination took place along ethnic lines (or lines that can be perceived or

---

110   Donald Rothchild, 1997. Managing Ethnic Conflicts in Africa: Pressures and Incentives for Cooperation (Washington: Brookings Institution Press), 3-22
111   Muna Ndulo and Margaret Grieco, 2010. Failed and Failing States: The Challenges to African Reconstruction (London: Cambridge Scholars), 143
112   Roggers Brubaker, 2004. Ethnicity Without Groups (Cambridge: Cambridge University Press), 61
113   Muna Ndulo and Margaret Grieco, 2010. Failed and Failing States: The Challenges to African Reconstruction (London: Cambridge Scholars), 143
114   Bruce Berman, 2006. 'The Ordeal of Modernity in an Age of Terror', African Studies Review 49 no 1(2006): 1-14.

construed as being ethnic), the conflict will be ethnic.[115] An ethnic conflict, in the context of this book, is an incompatibility of goals in relation to the political, economic, social, cultural or territorial issues between two or more ethnic communities.[116] Such incompatibilities may arise as ethnic groups seek to serve their political, economic and social interests. Conflict arises when competition with other groups trying to achieve the same objectives disagree.[117]

South Sudan is made up of a mosaic of over 64 ethnic groups speaking different languages and with distinctive cultures. The discredited Sudan Fifth Population and Household Census of 2010 put the Dinka ethnic group at 3.2 million people, followed by Nuer at 1.6 million. The Azande ethnic group and others follow.[118] The South Sudanese government rejected the census on account that it did not adequately cover all of South Sudan's ethnic groups. Politics and state formation has been played within the manoeuvres of ethnic yardsticks. The majority the ethnic group is, the major stake in political discourse including political positions dominance and political parties causing the 2013 political catastrophe.

Reality Overlooked: Ethnicisation of Politics and Politicisation of Ethnicity in South Sudan

Ethnic-grounded political parties have harmed South Sudan's state formation; its consolidation is one of the root causes for 2013's

---

115   Ted Gurr, 1993. Minorities at Risk: A Global View of Ethno-political Conflicts (Washington: Institute of Peace Press), 34

116   Michael Brown, Ethnic and Internal Conflicts, in C.A. Crocker, F.E. Hampson and A. Crocker, eds., 2001. Turbulent Peace: The Challenges of Managing International Conflict: US Institute of Peace (U.S., Washington) 209-226

117   Aquiline Tarimo and Paulin Manwelo, 2009. Ethnic Conflict and the Future of African States (Nairobi: Paulines Publications Africa), 81

118   See Sudan Fifth Population and Household Census, 2009

political crisis. Political parties' activities have always been viewed through an ethnic lens rather than through an ideological consideration. This state-of-affairs has led to the ethnicisation of politics and the politicisation of ethnicities affecting State-Society relations.[119] This politicisation has occurred at two levels: the military and the local administration. Although the military is beyond the scope of this book, it is important to mention the extent of militarisation of ethnicities given the compatibility of SPLM and the military wing SPLA. The army is in reality a bunch of localised militia outfits, each led by an ethnic coterie of generals. Furthermore, this makes the army a coalition of ethnic militia outfits with loyalties attached to an ethnic commander. Most of these militias are drawn from communal youth groups and vigilantes who are traditional cattle and land defenders, hunters, gatherers and wartime warriors. These include the Gelweng (Cattle protectors) of Dinka, the White Army of Nuer (Jiech Mabor and wartime warriors), the Akwelek of Chollo (land defenders), the Monyimiji of Otuho (hunters), and the Maban Defence Forces (gatherers), amongst others.[120] This state-of-affairs has ballooned the SPLA, now the South Sudan Peoples Defence Forces (SSPDF), to about 240,000 persons (with ghost and fictitious names) to the extent that the army now lacks common doctrine and has become a traditional ethnic warrior company.[121] The R-ARCSS requires the unification of the forces and thus the fictitious parade of 240,000 people may increase.

119   Peter Adwok Nyaba, 2011. South Sudan: The State We Aspire To (Pretoria: CASAS), 108.
120   Jacob Chol, 2016. White Army and Spiritual Mythology in South Sudan Political Violence, APCG Newsletter (Washington DC: APSA), 4
121   See Jose, Dan. African Military Magazine, 2016, 18

Although the SSPDF is large in numbers, the personnel lack basic qualifications and modern training to pass the test of a standard national army and thus remain only as an ethnic outfit force. This has bred a military ethnicity in the post-independent South Sudan, causing South Sudan to wobble.

To be clear, the conundrum is the structure of access to the state's resources with a political aristocracy at its top, and from the set underlying norms, accountabilities and redistributions of the military.[122] This raises the question of social hierarchy; as Bruce Berman stresses, in the post-independent period, the dominant discourse of ethnicity has indeed come from 'those group[s] who gained the most from independence ... and the educated elite who interpreted traditions [only] to justify their gains and maintain control over networks of patronage that provided access for others to the resources of modernity'[123]. Mwangi Kimenyi argues that in pre-colonial Africa, tribes used to make associations on a voluntary principle; however, post-colonial African states are an association of tribes that have been forced to live together under a unitary government, producing disastrous effects. His insightful observation on that matter is worth quoting at length:

'The elimination of any form of local autonomy and its replacement by a highly centralised unitary government has created a situation where ethnic competition for resources and power dominates the political landscape. Not only is the

---

122   Muna Ndulo and Margaret Grieco, 2010. Failed and Failing States: The Challenges to African Reconstruction (London: Cambridge Scholars), 145
123   Bruce Breman, 'Ethnicity, Patronage and the African State: The Politics of Uncivil Nationalism', African Affairs 97 (1998): 305-341

decision-making process now far removed from the people, but also the leadership has the power to make inter-ethnic transfers. The fact that a lot of resources in centralised states are channelled through the public sector has shifted the scope of ethnic interaction from market exchange and cooperation to competition in political markets. As a result, political office (regardless of how it has been attained) has become extremely valuable.'[124]

Indeed, local government policy instituted by the new South Sudan ruling party SPLM made ethnic identity the basis of creating local government units, and thus access to customary land for peasants and employment for the urban population.[125] In localities where populations were ethnically mixed, ethnic identity on the basis of rights to land and employment was a sure-fire way to breed ethnic antagonism. The outcome has been severe; ethnic divisions and tensions have been mismanaged, often leading to sporadic political violence and conflicts including 2013's political crunch.

Revealing the Epicentre of Political Violence and Conflicts: Ethnic Divisions

Ethnic divisions, according to empirical democratic theory and common-sense understandings of politics, threaten the survival of democratic institutions. One of the principal mechanisms linking the politicisation of ethnic divisions with the destabilisation of

---

124   Mwangi Kimenyi, 1997. Ethnic Diversity, Liberty and the State: The African Dilemma (Massachusetts, USA: Edward Elgar Publishing), 45
125   Mahmood Mamdani, South Sudan: The Problem and the Way Forward: New Vision (Kampala: 28th February 2014), 1

democracy is the so-called outbidding effect.[126] According to the theory of ethnic outbidding, the politicisation of ethnic divisions inevitably gives rise to one or more ethnic parties.[127] The emergence of even a single ethnic party, in turn, "infects" the political system, leading to a spiral of extreme bids that destroys competitive politics altogether. This is relevant to the splits in the SPLM leading to the SPLM DC, dominated by the Chollo with 99%, SPLM in the opposition by Nuer with 85%, and SPLM in the government by the Dinka with 72%. SPLM faction led by the SPLM Former Political Detainees (FPD) has a fair representation of the ethnic diversity of South Sudan with the majority of all South Sudanese ethnic groups represented. Other parties such as United Democratic Forum (UDF), South Sudan Democratic Forum (SSDF), United Salvation African Party (USAP), African National Congress (ANC), Sudan African National Union (SANU), National Congress Party (NCP), Communist Party et cetera are run by a coterie of ethnic outfits that manifest the dominant of an ethnic group. However, this dominance cause mistrusts and suspicion in the discharges of parties' affairs. Aquiline Tarimo and Paulin Manwelo reinforce this argument:

> 'Ethnic composition within the society matters as the domination of one ethnic group over others raises mistrust that could be transferred to other dimensions of social life and institutions. Ethnic identity becomes the source of conflict when self-centred leaders use it as a means to gain political power. Unless

---

126   Kanchan Chandra 'Ethnic Parties and Democratic Stability', Perspectives in Politics, Vol 3, no 2: 2005: 235-252.
127   Ibid, 235

a political culture rooted in democratic practice is established, parties' affairs are likely to exacerbate ethnocentrism, disorder and violence.' [128]

Nonetheless, ethnicity itself does not constitute a problem. It is the implications of multiplicity/diversity for shaping and sharing of power, national wealth, public services and opportunities for economic well being that give ethnicity the potential to generate conflicts. [129] Put simply, it is the manipulation of ethnic diversity for parochial political ends, usually by the political elite, that turns ethnicity into a volatile admixture. [130]

With deeply ethnicised politics, institutions become personal and tribal fiefdoms 'run by powerful people who undermine broader social progress'. [131] This is what Kanchan Chandra argues as politics established and run on 'thin' rationality. [132] So the ethnicisation of politics and politicisation of ethnicities of South Sudan political parties, particularly SPLM, is one of the factors that led to the political violence and conflicts during 15th December 2013. This was also demonstrated against non-South Sudanese people. For instance, Fr. Christian Carlassare, bishop-elect of the Diocese of Rumbek was shot twice on the leg on the night of 26th April

---

128   Aquiline Tarimo and Paulino Manwelo, 2007. African Peacemaking and Governance (Nairobi: Acton Publishers),

129   Peter Adwok Nyaba, 2011. South Sudan: The State We Aspire To (Pretoria: CASAS),109.

130   Keneth Prah, 2006. The African Nation: The State of the Nation, Cape Town: Centre for Advanced Studies of African Society (CASAS) (SA, Pretoria,), 28

131   Daron Acemoglu and James Robinson, 2012. Why Nations Fail: The Origins of Power, Prosperity and Poverty (London: Profile Books Publishers), 364

132   Kachan Chandra. 2007. Why Ethnic Parties Succeed: Patronage and Ethnic Head Counts in India (Cambridge: Cambridge University Press), 201

2021 in the church compound in Rumbek. Although the motive of his shooting was quite shocking and scarce, a power struggle within the church with Fr. John Mathiang Machol having acted in that capacity and later on replaced is alleged to be one of the motives. While twelve suspects were arrested and would be investigated and possibly arranged in court, it was already reported in the main Juba newspapers such as *Juba Monitor* and *Dawn* that the shooting of the bishop elect was planned from Juba. At the time of writing of this edition, the outcome of the bishop-elect shooting was still being pursued by both the state and national governments.

The cacophony-competing tunes of Nuer White Armies and Dinka Gelweng of communal militias explain the gravity of the ethnic role in politics. But this conjecture is not new as Peter Adwok Nyaba argues:

'*Historically, the ethnicisation of politics in South Sudan was first undertaken as a matter of policy by the Arab-dominated northern political elite to hook its people to their model of Sudan defined by Islam and Arab culture. In this model, ethnic communities were pitted against one another to prevent unity and solidarity against their mutual oppression and exploitation. However, it could also be confidently asserted that ethnicity, a political category, became a factor of state building and political engineering in Southern Sudan during Southern Regional Government (1972-1983). The Kokora (re-division) was its anticlimax when the political elite from Equatoria turned its back against colleagues hailing from [the] Upper*

Nile and Bahr el Ghazal.'[133]

It can be argued that ethnic suspicion has contaminated South Sudan's politics to the extent that government constitutional slots and trivial jobs have been allocated to the people on ethnic relations rather than competence. Mwangi Kimenyi analyses the inter-relationships amongst ethnicity, governance and the provision of public goods.[134] He focuses on the behaviour of ethnic groups and specifically on their impacts on the provision of public goods. Kimenyi contends:

'*An explanation of why ethnicity may influence collective action, which reduces co-operative action, is that ethnic groups behave much like special interest groups. The interest group theory of government as applied to ethnic groups assumes that ethnic groups seek to maximize their welfare of their members at the expense of others. Like other interest groups such as labour unions or producer groups, ethnic groups necessarily adopt strategies that give them advantage in influencing policy decisions. The most efficient way for ethnic groups to influence policy is to capture the means of wealth transfer through the government. Unlike other interest groups, however, ethnic interest groups are more durable since entry and exit into such groups is limited. Competition amongst permanent interest groups can be expected to be more intense and continuous than is the case with other interest groups. Such competition has*

---

133   Ibid, 109
134   Mwangi Kimenyi, 'Ethnicity, Governance and the Provision of Public Goods', Journal of African Economies, 15 (Supplement 1, 2006) 68 (62-99)

implications on provision of public goods.'[135]

This characterises the current rise of ethnic and regional sentiments in South Sudan, which represent a direct response to the government's policies and attitudes toward the excluded and marginalised ethnic groups.[136] As the bulwark of survival or domination, many ethnic groups have formed ethnic lobby unions such as the Jieng Council of Elders (JCE), Nuer Council of Elders (NCE), Equatoria Council of Elders (ECE), and the Chollo Council of Elders (CCE) amongst others to champion their communities' interest in politics. While some of these elders' unions are inactive, others are more proactive and vocal than the government.

Fighting for its dominance and political hegemony, the Jieng Council of Elders has appeared as a parallel government decision-making body that influences the decisions of President Salva Kiir. Although it sounds like a social union, Jieng Council of Elders has often responded to any inflammatory speech by the non-Dinka against the President or the Jieng people. Amongst some famous responses was the call by the SPLM-IO for President Kiir to step down, a matter that would have been handled through institutional laydown of SPLM in the government. Juxtapositioning itself, the Jieng Council of Elders strongly refuted the mantra, calling President Salva Kiir their son whom they argued would not step down anytime soon. Instead, they blamed Dr. Riek Machar for murdering Dinka people and for being a power greedy fellow. As if that was not enough, the Jieng Council of Elders' pronounced

---

135   Ibid, 69
136   Amir Idris, 2015. 'Does ethnicity matter in South Sudan's conflict?' The Citizen Newspaper (Juba: Vol. 8. Issue 958, Monday, 19th January), 6

a warning to Equatorians to desist from supporting Dr. Riek Machar's rebellion. Bona Malwal, one of the Dinka elders and veteran politician reinforce this ethnic innuendo:

'Unfortunately, Equatoria, this rather unusual, indeed non-existing constitutional being in South Sudan, has now got onto the bandwagon of Riek Machar Teny, hoping to defeat and overthrow the Dinka that Equatoria has always hated. There is a clear Dinka hate-campaign now on in South Sudan. Even the elected governors of Equatoria have sent a delegation to Ethiopia to plead for the IGAD mediators to decree a new federal arrangement for South Sudan. This is Equatoria's new way of hoping to get rid of the Dinka from Juba, the land of Equatoria which happens to be also the capital of South Sudan from which no South Sudanese ethnic community can be excluded. This is now a hate campaign, which will make it very difficult, if not impossible to find a solution to the current problem, the failed attempt to overthrow the legitimate system of South Sudan.'[137]

Clarifying further the deep ethnic overtones on the muggiest power politics, Bona Malwal argues:

The Dinka have land and space from which to seek to survive and should not be expected to give away power to those who hate the Dinka! One gives away power to someone or those one does not think hate another one. The Dinka have

---

137   Bona Malwal, 2015. Sudan and South Sudan: From One to Two (Oxford: Palgrave Macmillan), 207

been described, or indeed insulted, as a foolish majority. But even a fool recognises death when they see it. Will the Dinka be so foolish to cede power to those they know hate the name Dinka? Can the Dinka be so foolish to offer their lives as a solution, in order to provide a second Rwanda of Africa?[138]

Joshua Dau Diu, the vice chairman of the JCE, lamented and incited in one of the JCE meetings that the Jieng (Dinka) is the most hated race in South Sudan because of its bravery, wisdom and accommodative leaderships. He pronounced this hatred in revolutionary style *"thaan cie maan oyee, Jieng oyee, thaan cie maan oyee, Jieng oyee"* loosely translated as *"the most hated race Oyee, Dinka Oyee, the most hated race Oyee, Dinka Oyee"*.

The inter-ethnic accusations and counter accusations could not wane away, and each individual or a member of another ethnic group was either misquoted or had sent a threat to another group. Fuelling the ethnic divisions, the then Western Equatoria State (WES) Governor Bangasi Joseph Bakosoro was alleged to have argued that Dinka leaders and their community failed the country:

'Dinka leaders and their community have failed our country, South Sudan. What's wrong with you people, wherever you go, problems and havoc follow?' The former WES governor narrated.[139] Bakosoro believed that members of the Dinka community, who were internally displaced to Western Equatoria, were the source of havoc in the former Western Equatoria State as he allegedly argued:

---

138   Ibid, 207
139   Upper Nile Times 'South Sudan's 'Dinka Leaders and Their Community Have Failed Our Country' WES Governor at the Voice of Equatoria' http//:www.upperniletimes.com (Accessed on 13th February, 2015)

"You ran from danger in your areas and only to come and cause havoc in our state [sic]. You don't like peaceful coexistence of people. Your leaders need to look themselves in the eye and find out why you are not welcomed by anyone anywhere in South Sudan"[140]

Although the above statements were viewed as wild fabrications and disputed by the Minister of Information of WES, members of the Jieng Council of Elders condemned the statement and called on President Salva Kiir to sack Governor Bakosoro from Western Equatoria's leadership. But such statements if credible could have been encouraged by ethnic animosity and suspicion as the former Governor of Central Equatoria State (CES), Clement Konga previously cautioned the Equatorians to be out of December 15th 2013's conflict, terming it as a Nuer-Dinka war. *"It is the only chance for the people of Equatoria to come together so as to bring an end to this war between Dinka and Nuer'.*[141] *'Who are you going to fight? Are you going to fight with Dinka or Riek Machar?"* the then CES Governor wondered.[142]

However, Bona Malwal in his book '*Sudan and South Sudan: From One to Two*', thinks that the wars and conflicts should squarely be blamed on the Nuer Community as he stipulates:

'It is the leadership of the ethnic Nuer Community of South Sudan who must be now [the] first [to] come out to say, clearly, that it is not right for any aspiring political leader of any

---

140   Ibid, 2
141   Ibid, 3
142   Ibid, 4

community of South Sudan to kill innocent defenceless [sic]
citizens and expect to be rewarded with political leadership of the
country. The South Sudanese [people] expect the ethnic Nuer
political leadership to tell Riek Machar Teny, even before he is
judged by South Sudanese law, whether or not he is innocent of
all the atrocities that have been committed in his name, that he
no longer qualifies to be considered as one of the future South
Sudanese political leaders to rule that country.'[143]

Despite ethnic threats by some Dinka elders, such as Bona Malwal about other ethnic groups' hatred against the Dinka, it can be discerned that most ethnic-related hatred and suspicions against the Dinka have been caused perhaps by the behaviour of some Dinka people, particularly, the grabbing of Equatorians land, random occupation, hostility to others and the trespassing of Dinka animals to Equatorian farms, especially, in Western, Central and Eastern Equatoria States. However, the mushrooming of ethnic-based unions and associations (in particular during the political violence) has thwarted inter-ethnic relations.

Apart from the internal shield for Jieng interest, JCE has assumed the protection and the defence of South Sudan's sovereignty from any external influence in search for best solution of the country's political ignominy as they argue:

'Given this situation, we would like to alert the world of the
inherent complications that will be engendered by this planned

---

143   Bona Malwal, 2015. Sudan and South Sudan: From One to Two (Oxford: Palgrave Macmillan), 207

invasion of our country. Our country is very fragile, socially, economically, and politically. The long bouts of the relentless civil wars that our people have gone through have shaken our country to the core. Any disturbance in the present setup will drastically send our country, and by extension the region, spinning dangerously into the abyss. Given the pending destruction of our country and our dignity as a people, we would like the world to know that, like any other people in the world, the South Sudanese [people] reserve the right to defend themselves against unjust aggression anywhere and at any time. Our internal contradictions notwithstanding, the world must understand that the South Sudanese will unite in their resistance against any imposed agreement.'[144]

And to the face of IGAD and African Union, JCE asserts:

'It should also be made known to IGAD and the African Union that South Sudan will not become a testing ground for crude and new governance theories and that such attempts will be resisted to the fullest. As for the proposed African Oversight Force, it should be clear to the continental body that such a force could only touch ground in South Sudan only with the government's permission. Any movement of such force illegally into South Sudan would be an act of war and will be met with a tested resistance. We want peace, but it has to be home

---

144   Press Statement by Jieng Council of Elders (JCE) rejecting imposition of peace on South Sudan: A clear message to the potential perpetrators of South Sudan destruction: http://paanluelwel.com/2015/04/01/jieng-council-of-elders-rejects-imposition-of-peace-on-south-sudan/ (Accessed on 28th March 2015)

grown, not a regional or international peace that undermines the sanctity of our sovereignty. The world should know that South Sudan's sovereignty and its independence are irrevocable and that those who will try this shall meet the rage of men and women who liberated this country.'[145]

It is worth mentioning that the JCE rhetoric warns the International Community and reveals looming ethnic resistances and insurgencies as Jieng politicians, decorated, as elders argue:

'Despite the prevailing rhetoric in the international circles that this external intervention will bring the ongoing conflict to an expeditious end, the fact of the matter is that the current situation will be worsened by this external meddling. Given the tribal nature of the current insurgencies, armed and unarmed dissidents, it is conceivable that these groups will be emboldened by their newly found power, as they will definitely attack other tribes. This will encourage an arm race amongst various tribes, as every tribe will be trying to acquire means of self-defence [sic]. What will then invariably ensue is a complicated web of tribal warfare at a scale never before witnessed in the history of South Sudan.'[146]

However, Peter Adwok Nyaba castigates the mission of JCE as he argues:

---

145   Ibid, 9
146   Ibid, 9

'The argument that it is [the] JCE, or the Jieng in general, constitutional right to form them-selves and to speak out on the national issues is reactionary and obscurant driven by a dangerous combination of ignorance and arrogance. It is meant to justify the inordinate concentration of political power and wealth in Warrap and by extension the Jieng nationality. It carries the dangers of polarising [sic] the South Sudanese and renders explosive the political engineering process of the South Sudan State. It is toxic politics and has the potential for un-making South Sudan as a sovereign country.'[147]

Hence, such ethnic lobby tone continued to portray the deepening of politicisation of ethnicity and ethnicisation of politics leading to suspicion and failing of the South Sudan State in lieu of formation. Such sectarian initiative gradually hollowed out state sovereignty, overtaking the ruling party mechanisms, deepening ethnic suspicion and soon providing channels for mobilization and organisation.[148] JCE has become a divisive, bootlicking, dirty group bent on making South Sudan a Jieng Republic![149]

It can be argued and unanimously consented that the activities of the tribal council of elders such as the Jieng Council of Elders (JCE), the Nuer Council of Elders (NCE), and the Equatoria

---

147   See Peter Adwok Nyaba comments on Development Policy Forum (DPF) on 12/04/ 2015

148   Majak D'Agoot. 'Assessing the Utility of Risk Management Theory in the Governance of New States: Lessons from South Sudan'. Journal of Risk Research: (2019), 21

149   Kuir e' Garang 'Jieeng Council of Elders, The Erosion of Jieeng's Values and 'Jieengization' of South Sudan', http://www.southsudannation.com/jieeng-council-of-elders-the-erosion-of-jieengs-values-and-the-jieengization-of-south-sudan (Accessed on 21st November 2020)

Council of Elders (ECE) have planted hatred and have polarised the South Sudanese communities in lieu of promoting unity. These councils are preaching tribalism and nepotism given that they recoil to their ethnic backyards. It is further argued that the Jieng Council of Elders (JCE) has captured the state, abused national power and offered unsolicited advice to the leaders on the helm. It has publicly issued sensitive tribal statements against anyone who oppose President Salva Kiir and has shown its prowess to protect the Jieng and the president at all cost.

Since the JCE has not been publicly rebuked, disbanded or reprimanded, it demonstrates the sense that tribalism has been legalised in South Sudan. These tribal councils should exist, but they should be confined to social issues such as local conflict resolutions and peace building to the rural areas where their communities reside rather staying and lobbying in Juba, where the seat of the Government of Republic of South Sudan is anchored. Hence, these councils should not be allowed to influence the government policies.

Given that the members of the councils, who are former and current political and military leaders were not elected or nominated by the communities they purportedly seemed to be representing, they have so far resorted to gossiping, fuelling rebellions and causing civil war as a trick to staying relevant. They have frustrated the August 2015 peace deal and they are usurping public resources for their self-interests. Thus, it is agreeable that these tribal councils of elders should be abolished.

It is apparent that some of the prominent politicians from the Dinka ethnic group realised the conundrums of South Sudan State failure and have expressed their predicaments publicly. For instance, former Minister of Defence and Senior Presidential Advisor Kuol Manyang Juuk admitted the failure of the government in rendering services to the citizens:

> *"Since July 2005, when the government of Southern Sudan was formed, what have we done? We didn't build schools, we didn't build good houses for our people, and we didn't construct roads and hospitals."*[150]

He added that them as leaders have miserably destroyed the government:

> *"We have destroyed the government by ourselves. When we fought the [sic] Sudan's government for 22 years, it was for us to become an independent country so that we can do what the government of Sudan was unable to do for us. We killed ourselves, we hate ourselves and this is a challenge that we have now made. I am not going to congratulate you [State Executives] until you prosper in providing services to the people you are serving."*[151]

Moreover, Ex-Presidential Advisor for Military Affairs Daniel Awet Akot agreed and blamed the failure of the government on President Salva Kiir:

---

150   Ex-Defence Minister Kuol Manyang Juuk Says Government Killed, Failed Citizens: https://www.sudanspost.com/ex-defence-minister-kuol-manyang-says-govt-killed-failed-citizens/ (Accessed on 23rd March 2021).
151   Ibid

"When we call for the leadership meetings, we discuss nothing about development, about the vision of the SPLM. We discuss nothing about how to move this country forward. We discuss only our own affairs. We are always quarrelling and on our necks about small issues. People look at us as the cause of their problem. Yes, we are the problem, and which is what I have always said that if we are the problem, let all of us step down, including comrade Salva and let someone with energy like Nhial Deng take over".[152]

Daniel Awet Akot further emphasised:

"I have always reiterated in our SPLM PB [Political Bureau] meetings that we are mentally incapacitated and exhausted; Let's hand over the remaining part of our vision to Nhial Deng to clean our image internationally."[153]

This later on caused Nhial Deng Nhial's job who was relieved as a Minister of Presidential Affairs-R-TGONU.

Role of Ethnic-Based Militias in South Sudan's State Formation and Failure: A Discussion

Ethnic-based militias such as the White Army of Nuer (Jiech Mabor), the Gelweng of Dinka, the Akwelek of Chollo, the Arrow Boys of Azande, the Monyimiji of Otuho and the Maban

---

152   Ex-Presidential Advisor Daniel Awet Akot Tells Kiir to Step Down: https://www.sudanspost.com/ex-presidential-advisor-daniel-awet-akot-tells-kiir-to-step-down/ (Acessed on 23rd March 2021)

153   Ibid

Grassroots Defence Forces are dangerous to the South Sudan State given that they spread violence across the country. There must be one national unified army with national character built on one military doctrine to eschew the disappearance of the state. Besides, the existence of these ethnic-based militias has led to the commercialisation of security and rebellions, and hence this is dangerous to the state and nation formation given that it compromises the rule of law. Moreover, the mushrooming of these ethnic-based militia outfits has caused tribalism, polarisation, discrimination and disrespect for the national army. The outcome has been that the ethnic-based militias are loyal to individuals rather than the state and the hungry politicians are capitalising on this ugly scenario, causing South Sudan State failure.

However, it is important to emphasise that these ethnic-based outfits have just emerged to fill the security vacuum created by the ineffectiveness of the government of the Republic South Sudan to provide security for all.

Understanding Political Elites in the State Power Struggle and Failure

Elite is a selected and small group of citizens and/or organisations that control a large amount of power.[154] Based on the social distinction regarding other groups of lower strata, most of these selected groups are constantly searching for differentiation as well as separation from the rest of society.[155] Normally, the concept of elite

---

154   Luis Garrido 'Elites, Political Elites and Social Change in Modern Societies', Revista De Sociology, no 28: 2013: 31-49
155   Jean-Pascal Daloz, The Sociology of Elites Distinction: From Theoretical to Comprehensive Perspectives (London: Palgrave Macmillan, 2010), 12

is used to analyse the groups that either control or are situated at the top of societies. The creation of elite is also the result of their evolution throughout the history of humanity. Several groups are constantly seeking different social resource bases to define their specificity.

Whereas a political elite (from looking at its activity) can be defined as a group of people, corporations, political parties and/ or any other kind of civil society organisation who manages and organises government and all the manifestations of political power. John Higley (2008) defines elites as persons who, by virtue of their strategic locations in large or otherwise pivotal organisations and movements, are able to affect political outcomes regularly and substantially.[156]

Moreover, Vilfredo Pareto (2010), a refined sociologist, defines the concept of ruling elites to consist of a small and selected political group of people with superior personal qualities that govern the *"mass of society"*, which Pareto considered as unintelligent, irrational and therefore, poorly organised.[157] Hence, Pareto argues that under these conditions, it is completely possible for the ruling elite to manipulate them through 'carefully used' political propaganda".[158]

Political elites and power struggle are often related because these groups are constantly searching to control the government. In successful state formation, political authorities must represent

---

156   John Hegley, 2008. Elite Theory in Political Sociology (Texas: University of Texas-Austin), 25
157   Vilfredo Pareto, 2010. The Rise and Full of Elites: An Application of Theoretical Sociology, 31
158   Ibid, 35

the interests of citizens based on the citizens' demands and decisions. To win elections, politicians must succeed in convincing electors and electorates, thus political life is not merely the making of arbitrary choices nor the result of bargaining between separate groups for private and individual wants. It is always a combination of bargaining and compromise where there are irresolute and conflicting commitments and common deliberations about public policy, to which facts and rational arguments are relevant.[159] Politicians frequently balance between the "mandate" of the post and the interests of people they represent. Currently, these interests are expressed by public opinion polls. Political elites must deal with power institutions and "shape" the political system. In some cases, the elites elaborate strong rules to maintain their power, avoiding political competition. In other cases, the elites must compete amongst themselves and/or with other citizens. Thus, is society always controlled by a small group of insiders? This is the paradox of political elites: it is always a mix between political representation, power struggle and the maximisation of their interests.[160]

However, since the beginning of the 1990's, several scholars studied the links amongst elites regarding political regimes and stability. This perspective has been useful for studying political transitions and, most of all, regarding the cases of the countries from Eastern Europe and Latin America. According to this theoretical viewpoint, the basic condition for having a solid and stable regime is the "unity" of the different elites, which must be expressed

---

159 Hanna Pitkin, 1967. The Concept of Political Elites Representation (Berkeley: University of California Press), 212

160 Luis Garrido 'Elites, Political Elites and Social Change in Modern Societies', Revista De Sociology, no 28: 2013: 31-49

mandatorily at an institutional level. In other words, democratic consolidation requires the achievement of elite "consensual unity", which is an agreement between all politically important elites on the meaning of existing democratic institutions as well as the respect for democratic "rules of the game", coupled with increased "structural integration" amongst those elites.[161]

Despite "consensual unity", which should exist as the backbone of political elites' drive to state formation and prosperity, South Sudanese elites have taken a U-turn, indulging themselves in divisive politics of power struggle and spirited loyalty. This state-of-affairs has instituted what has become as "secret politics" in South Sudanese society, projecting 'zolkabir' (big man) space in the powerful decision-making quarters of the government. The sacrosanct of political elites' hands in public decision-making has excluded and alienated a majority of South Sudanese people in the political life of the nascent state. The fundamental condition of class-based domination manifested in the rule of the gun-class of liberators and former counterinsurgent warlords (often in alliance with sectarian forces of regionalists and ethnic chauvinists) has remained as a new culture.[162] To be sure, the elites have drowned the young nation into wars and rent-seeking rebellions. However, South Sudanese political elites would have taken a leaf from Victor Asal argument:

'Elites have much to gain by parceling [sic] out the state and working together to maintain their hold on power. But they

---

161   Harry Vanden and Garry Provost, 2002. Politics of Latin America: The Power Game (London: Oxford University Press), 18

162   Majak D'Agoot. Dynamics of Political Risks in Fragile Environments: Lessons from South Sudan. Journal of Risks Management, (2013), 11.

also have a lot to lose if any faction defects from this bargain and conspires to usurp power. Without assurances otherwise, each side maneuvers [sic] to protect its share and safeguard against others' first-strike capabilities. Reciprocal maneuvering [sic], however, reinforces suspicion within the regime, often triggering an internal security dilemma that destroys trust and makes eliminating one's rival a vital imperative. Amidst this escalating internal conflict, rulers employ an exclusive strategy to neutralise the existential threat posed by those inside their regime and to secure their grip on power. But the cost of such a strategy, especially when carried out along ethnic lines, is that it forfeits the central government's societal control, leaving it vulnerable to civil war.'[163]

It is a common argument that post-2013's deadly political violence in South Sudan was neither cultural nor natural. It was a political one triggered by the failure of political elites who ignored reconciling their narrow-vested political and economic interests.[164] Instead of cultivating a common national belonging to the new state, the political elites began to think of themselves as ethnic beings. They forgot that leadership is about the quality of an individual vision, and have turned ethnicity into a powerful tool to secure public resources and political power.[165] Upon his ascend to leadership in July 2005, Salva Kiir pursued an unwieldy 'Big Tent Policy'

---

163   Victor Asal, 2014. Political Exclusion, Oil and Ethnic Armed Conflict (New York: Oxford University Press), 29

164   Amir Idris 'Does ethnicity matter in South Sudan's conflict?' The Citizen Newspaper (Juba: Vol. 8. Issue 958, Monday, 19th January 2015), 6

165   Ibid, 6

of courting militias through amnesties and accommodation, which relatively helped in establishing temporary peace.[166] However, this did not help in uniting the South Sudanese elites and Peter Adwok Nyaba in his book 'South Sudan The State We Aspire To' reinforced this point by arguing that political divisions amongst the southern elite have always been blamed on the dominant northern political elite but this could only be true in as far as the *ancients regimes,* whether colonial or national, were concerned.[167] Moreover, Nyaba further articulated that now that the southerners are in full command of their affairs, who should be blamed for the mess of political elites in South Sudan? He elucidates that '*we must find [an] explanation for this somewhere within the southern social and political configuration*'.[168]

In the last ten years, the dominant SPLM political and military elite was rocked to its core by embarrassing divisions almost along ethnic lines. Ethnic affiliation in the public domain is what is registered as 'tribalism' that is nothing but a petty bourgeois ideology of trans-class solidarity. Thus, the current rise of ethnic and regional sentiments in South Sudan represents a direct response to the government's policies and attitudes towards the excluded and marginalised ethnic groups.[169] The main means of ensuring fairness in distribution is the ethnic quota system, whereby different groups are guaranteed government posts, or are given additional

---

166   Majak D'Agoot. 'Assessing the Utility of Risk Management Theory in the Governance of New States: Lessons from South Sudan'. Journal of Risk Research: (2019), 219

167   Peter Adwok Nyaba, 2011. South Sudan: The State We Aspire To (Pretoria: CASAS), 109

168   Ibid, 109

169   Amir Idris 'Does ethnicity matter in South Sudan's conflict?' The Citizen Newspaper (Juba: Vol. 8. Issue 958, Monday, 19th January 2015), 6

posts in response to complaints of under-representation. However, this mechanism has been abused by ambitious people to develop ethnic backing.[170]

All this attention focuses on the causes and strategies of the manipulation of ethnicity by the elites, and too little mention of this is given to the people who perpetrated the violence or to the social structures that allowed such processes to be set in motion.[171] Acting within the increased power distance in the discharge of authority, these elites frittered away the opportunity to transform the country.[172] In effect, tenuous relationships between various elites became antagonistic and the effect of distance decay between the centre and peripheries became apparent.[173] In truth, government goals were prioritised in a topsy-turvy manner with a pernicious tendency for perversity.[174]

Presidential Palace Stained with Blood: How Elites Power and Mistrust Turned South Sudan into a State Failure.

On 8th July 2016, a day before the 5th anniversary of the independence, South Sudan descended into another deadly and chaotic violence triggered by the presidential guards of President Salva Kiir and his 1st Vice President Riek Machar. A few minutes after a security meeting began at the Presidential Palace chaired by the

---

170   Edward Thomas, 2015. South Sudan: A slow Liberation (London: Zed Books), 160

171   Peter Uvin, Aiding Violence: The Development Enterprise in Rwanda (Westford: Kumarin Press, 1998), 206

172   Majak D'Agoot. 'Assessing the Utility of Risk Management Theory in the Governance of New States: Lessons from South Sudan'. Journal of Risk Research: (2019), 22

173   Ibid, 10

174   Ibid, 10

President Kiir and attended by the 1st Vice President Riek Machar, Vice President James Wani, and ministers of the national security and interior, a lethal violence ensued in the Presidential Palace forcing all journalists to take cover in the meeting hall while the two leaders (President Salva Kiir and 1st Vice President Dr. Riek Machar) appealed for calm amidst erratic shootings and bombings. The duo admitted that they did not know what was going on and why the guards were fighting one another in the State House (J1).

This fighting later engulfed the city of Juba involving fighter jets and tanks from 8th to 12th July 2016. As a result, Riek Machar's guards were severely outnumbered and killed, leaving the remaining few running for their lives. The base of Riek was captured and pulverised, driving out the pockets of soldiers that were guarding his Jebel residence, known locally, as Pagak II or Jebel Ngundeng Bong.

The cause of the fighting is mutely argued on several accounts: One account had it that there existed a simmering tension with President Kiir's SPLA in the government (SPLA-IG) and Riek's SPLA in the opposition (SPLA-IO). As per the transitional security arrangement of ARCSS, Riek Machar was entitled to 2910 military and police personnel while Salva was entitled to 5000. Given the logistics constraint, the IGAD-Plus ferried only 1370 to Juba, leaving 1540 troops to be transported later when Riek would arrive to Juba. This was yet to be done. So, this account argues that the two troops occupying different bases melted into serious tensions. One of the tensions began from the killing of the SPLA-IO Lt. Colonel Alexander Gismala at Habalip, the southeastern part of Juba, while President Kiir's daughter's (Anok) wedding was ongoing at the Palace not far from the incident. The 1st Vice President Riek Machar attended the wedding too. SPLA-IO alleged that the death of the Lieutenant Colonel was masterminded by the SPLA in government (SPLA-IG) forces, an allegation the SPLA-IG vehemently denies.

It all began with the SPLA-IG security personnel deploying along the Gudele road, northwest of Juba. As part of their routine guns search, they decided to stop the SPLA-IO car carrying the bodyguards of Riek destined to his base at Jebel on the 7th July 2016 at 6pm. The SPLA-IO officers resisted and questioned the search of their car arguing that they were licensed to carry guns as per the peace deal, and moreover as the guards of the 1st Vice President. This feud simmered and a fight broke out, leading to massive gunfire at the Gudele road (Nguaba) between the two cantankerous forces. The result was that five SPLA-IG soldiers were killed and one SPLA-IO was wounded. The tension calmed down and Juba City remained highly alerted to the situation as the population worried that the SPLA-IG forces would retaliate the next day.

On the 8th of July the President invited the 1st Vice President to the palace for the security meeting as well as a follow-up on the other night's troops-clashing incident. The 1st Vice President drove to the palace with a huge fleet of cars for his security detail. Once arrived at the Presidential Palace's entrance, the 1st Vice President was allowed in with non-uniform security officers, leaving behind the well-armed uniformed personnel. The rest of the vehicle fleet was refused entry and was asked to remain outside the palace. A few minutes after the meeting began, sporadic and loud gunfire was heard closer to the meeting room of the duo. The President and the 1st Vice President argued that they did not really know what was going on amongst their guards.

The other account had it that while the 1st Vice President arrived for the meeting at the palace, there was an unusually large presence of the SPLA-IG soldiers around the palace and towards the University of Juba. This account had it that a pre-planned fight amongst the troops that was designed by their commanders without the knowledge of their two leaders, a situation confirmed by the duo during their press conference. Although the SPLA-IG argued that an SPLA-IO officer fired the first bullet while driving in an ambulance outside the palace along the palace-ministries road, it is certain that the first bullet was fired as a protesting gesture by the SPLA-IO uniformed protection guards who were refused entrance to the palace after their leader had gone in. On the other hand, many sources around the presidency argued that a revenge attack of five soldiers killed by SPLA-IO in the previous day was the spark for the erratic fight.

But, what is an interesting twist is how the struggle over political power between the two leaders insinuated these endless fights and destruction, staining the palace with blood. During the fight, it is argued that almost all of Riek Machar's guards (Nuer) were neutralised and the few that survived were helter-skelter dislodged, and the 1st Vice President's headquarters was captured by mostly Dinka soldiers. Yet, the 1st Vice President and the President were still sitting in the palace meeting room. Although the President protected the 1st Vice President and sent his Commander of Presidential Guards (Republican Guards), the then Maj.Gen. Marial Chanuong

Yol to ferry him home at midnight, the President argued that the 1st Vice President was carrying a pistol and was determined to kill him. He revealed this during his interview with CCTV journalist Robert Ngila on the evening of 22nd July 2016 as below:

"Riek was carrying his pistol. Inu [sic], it is not allowed to carry a gun in the meeting. I don't know if he wanted to assassinate me. He did not tell me but he had an intention. I was worried about Riek's life. My officers and men inu [sic] were not friendly to him and if I would have turned away from him [for] a minute, he would have been killed. I used to observe my officers' eyes and when I see them changing their eyes then I would point a finger to them, warning them not to do anything against Riek. I called my car to transport Riek to his home. As he was entering the car, I came close to shield him on one side and vice-president James Wani from other side otherwise he would have been shot by an angry officer. I opened the door of my car and I provided my security detail to him who took him home safely." President Kiir narrated.

Riek meanwhile had maintained his version of events that he was almost assassinated by Kiir's soldiers and ran to an unknown hideout after his base was dislodged and his military personnel killed. The fighting that commenced at the presidential palace spread to the entire city of Juba, killing over 1000 people, wounded thousands and destroyed property. This "dog fight" was a recipe of state failure. South Sudan was then again rescued from state collapse by the IGAD and the International Community through the R-ARCSS of September 2018, bringing Dr. Riek Machar back as the 1st Vice President to this date.

Political Elites, Resource Usurp and State Failure

Some states comprise of political elites whose power is based on controlling access to political and economic resources and redistributing them in support of their clientelistic base. This kind of political-economic regime is both self-perpetuating and self-destructive. On one hand, it perpetuates itself through the de-politicisation of participation and the organisation of citizens into ethnic constituencies.[175] On the other hand, it destroys itself through an imbalance of power distribution, which manifests in the form of unequal access to resources, which is bound by excluded groups in times of crisis.[176] Strengthening false relationships amongst the elites through politics and economic power, Carl Kadushin (2011) who investigated the French financial elites, found out that most of the financial elites were linked by significant ties of friendship, which certainly allow them to construct and maintain a certain level of similarity.[177] This tendency is maintained through manipulation of the country's resources.

Since independence, a small rotating set of elites - who move seamlessly between positions in government and the frontlines of the rebellion, as political situations change - has controlled South

---

175   Muna Ndulo and Margaret Grieco, 2010. Failed and Failing States: The Challenges to African Reconstruction (London: Cambridge Scholars), 145
176   Ibid, 145
177   Carl Kadushin 'Friendship Amongst the French Financial Elite', American Sociological Review, (No. 60 (2), 2011), (202-221)

Sudan.[178] The country's elites have built a kleptocratic regime that controls all sectors of the economy, and have squandered a historic chance for the development of a functional state.[179] These preda-tory economic networks play a central role on the 15th December 2013 Civil War, because much of the conflict was driven by elites attempting to re-negotiate their share of the politico-economic power balance through violence.[180]

In addition, political elites have usurped national resources for individual gains in tandem with political corruption. They have encouraged the fragmentation of communities to create a phe-nomenon of community gurus as champions, protectors and philanthropists of their communities through looted resources.

Nadir A. L. Mohammed while critiquing Mansour Khalid's book *The Government they deserve: The Role of the Elite in Sudan's Political Economy* once noted:

> 'While it is true that the colonial administration and the first national government were to blame for the civil unrest in the South, it has to be said that the southern elite must also be held responsible. Southern leaders were disunited, many of their politicians were corrupt and their loyalties were constantly and still are, continuously conflicting.'[181]

---

178   See The Nexus of Corruption and Conflict in South Sudan. Sentry Re-port, An Initiative of Enough Project, (Washington, July 2015).
179   Ibid, 2
180   Ibid, 2
181   Nadir A. L. Mohammed, 1983. On Review of Mansour Khalid's Book 'The Government They Deserve: The Role of the Elite in Sudan's Political Evolution', (Kegan Paul Publishers:: London), 3

This state of southern corruption affairs reached its apogee when the former Minister of Finance, Arthur Akuein Chol, was accused of misappropriating millions of dollars through the over-payment of contracts for first government's V8 cars from Al cardinal's foreign company in 2006. Immediately, his successor Kuol Athian Mawien was accused for the disappearance of about $1.5 billion USD through the payment of contracts for unsupplied grains to the ten states to curb catastrophic hunger, a malpractice that became famously known as 'Grains (Dura) Saga". In addition, Wikileaks made public in 2012 an alleged corruption at the John Garang Military Academy. According to the report, the government allocated $30 million USD for the construction of this academy, but only $2 million USD was accounted for and the rest of the money was allegedly spent without a trace.[182] In June 2013, another corruption practice of $7.9 million USD came to the public domain. Two former ministers, Deng Alor Kuol of Cabinet Affairs and Kosti Manibe Ngai of Finance, were relieved by the President for allegedly authorizing the transfer of $7.9 million USD to Daffy Co-Ltd in Kenya to procure anti-fire safes without adherence to procurement regulations, and above all, without endorsement of the Council of Ministers and the National Assembly.

In the height of this den of corruption, President Salva Kiir Mayardit courageously came out and accused 75 former and current government officials of stealing public funds to the tune of $4 billion USD and asked them to return the looted money through

---

182   http:/www.wikileaks.org/plusd/cables/08KHARTOUM345_a.html (Accessed on 29th August 2020)

specified bank accounts.[183] Ted Dagne, hired by the UN to advise Kiir on its anti-corruption policy and international relations, played a key role in the preparation of the May 2012 letter that was made public by President Salva Kiir to embarrass the officials who were accused of stealing $4 billion USD.[184] No empirical evidence can substantiate whether some of the undisclosed government officials have returned money or not. However, the assumption is that no funds have been returned to the public coffers by the senior officials accused by the President. Instead, President Kiir allegedly got indicted by the U.S-based Enough Project's Sentry report in September 2016 as a corrupt person altogether with his family, 1st Vice President Dr. Riek Machar, former Chief of General Staff, Gen. Paul Malong and four other senior commanders of SPLA in South Sudan.[185] Corruption was also performed at the doorstep of President Kiir by his aides, who looted over $1 billion of South Sudanese pounds and over $30 million USD from the President's office. The 16 accused, some of which got convicted and later released by the Court of Appeal, were majorly from the Dinka ethnic group; out of the 16 accused, 10 were from Dinka, making 63% of the convicts. Of the 6 acquitted in October 2017, all were from the Dinka ethnic group.

Although investigations were carried out in recovering these stolen funds, not a single dollar had been recovered. But did South

---

183   Abraham Awolic, South Sudan's Fight against Corruption: Are We Winning?' Weekly Review: The Sudd Institute (Juba: Sudd Institute, 3rd July 2013), 3

184   Sudan Tribune, 'Foreign advisor to South Sudan's President flees Juba after disclosure of corruption letter', http://www.sudantribune.com/splp.php?article43641 (Accessed on 10th April 2015)

185   Enough Project Team, 2016. 'War Crimes Shouldn't Pay: Stopping the Looting and Destruction in South Sudan', Sentry Report (Washington DC, September), 5

Sudan's political elite's palatable greed just emerge from thin air? In their study of national corruption during these years, the Sudanese economists El-Wathig Kameir and Ibrahim Kursany note:

> *'Against this background, the elite in the South wanted to en-rich themselves as quickly as possible so as to be on a level with their colleagues in the North. This is why they have resorted to corruption as the quickest way of acquiring money.'*[186]

The result of the auditing of The (then) Government of Southern Sudan accounts from 2005 to 2006, released by the Auditor General and presented to the parliament in February 2012, revealed that over $1 billion USD 'disappeared' in that period alone and could not be accounted for.[187] Also 1000 presidential tractors allegedly bought at 50,000 USD per tractor were inflated, as each tractor was later priced at 20,000 USD together with all the custom duties paid. Those who did the single sourcing of these tractors got away with a huge sum of kickbacks, and the tractors were not utilised for agricultural production in rural areas as stated by the President. Corruption in the country was permeating in every spectrum of society, causing global worries. J. Peter Pham, an analyst at the Atlantic Council and an adviser to the Defence Department's U.S. Africa Command would state that: "*Salva Kiir's*

---

186   El-Wahig Kameir and Ibrahim Kursany, Corruption as the 'fifth' factor of production in Sudan, Institute Research Report (Nordiska Afrika No. 71, Uppasala, 1995), 26

187   Sudan Tribune, 'SPLA top generals asked by anti-corruption to declare their assets', http://www.sudantribune.com/spip.php?article41727 (Accessed on 10th April 2015)

government is notoriously corrupt."[188]

The President's dictum of *"Zero Tolerance"* and terming political elite's corruption as cancer has remained in his speeches, but any action is yet to be seen thanks to a lack of institutional and political will to punish the perpetrators to set a precedence of usual business in South Sudan. Due to a reward of wrongdoings, some political elites have taken up violence in the form of what Alex de Waal terms in *Small Arms Survey* as 'rent-seeking rebellion', namely, the mutiny of army commanders or local political leaders with armed constituents, seeking a larger share of the resources dispensed by the government.[189] To think of various security institutions in South Sudan as subordinate appendages to the state today is to fundamentally misunderstand the country.[190] In essence, South Sudan is not a country with a military; rather, it is a military with a country.[191]

Members of the South Sudanese political elite, in their desire to acquire wealth as fast as possible with a determination to prevent the northern government from renting the allegiance of southern militia and thereby jeopardizing the SPLM's secessionist project, created a governing system even less regulated and no less brutal

---

188   Oren Dorell 'Corruption at root of South Sudan Violence: Analysts', USA TODAY, 27 Dec.2013, http://www.usatoday.com/story/news/world/2013/12/27/south-sudan-government-agreement/4218073 (Accessed on 10th April 2015)

189   Small Arms Survey, 2013. Pendulum Swings: The Rise and Fall of Insurgent Militias in South Sudan, Human Security Baseline Assessment, Issue Brief No. 22 (Small Arms Survey, , Geneva, 2013), 14

190   Majak D'Agoot. 'Assessing the Utility of Risk Management Theory in the Governance of New States: Lessons from South Sudan'. Journal of Risk Research: (2019), 22

191   See Astill-Brown (2014) 9.

than its northern counterpart.[192] One of the most troubling characteristics of that government is that the contending elites use of violence as a means of bargaining. A commander or a provincial leader can lay claim to a stake in state resources (rents) through mutiny or rebellion, permitting members of the elite to view it as instrument of governance and thus join the kleptocratic club.[193] The country achieved independence after a confusing security situation in which various wartime militia groups engaged in agitation as a strategy for integration into the government's machinery.[194] As a result, the security sector swelled in size and became top-heavy at the command level and was then underscored by shaky loyalties, which often stemmed from ethnic fault lines.[195] Alex De'Waal argues that President Kiir was at the top of the system but not in control of it and, as he later noted, *'once there is corruption, there is insecurity'*.[196]

The political calculus of the SPLM leaders was based on elite factors: their own resources and interests.[197] Thus they felt they were able to act in any manner without any reference to the welfare of the citizens of their country. The poor decision to close down the entire national oil production caught donors and oil

192   Alex de Waal 'When Kleptocracy Becomes Insolvent: Brute Causes of the Civil War in South Sudan', African Affairs: 113/452 (2014): 349 (347-369)
193   Ibid, 361
194   Samson S. Wassara, 2015. South Sudan: State Sovereignty Challenged at Infancy, Journal of Eastern African Studies (UK, London,), 6
195   Majak D'Agoot. 'Assessing the Utility of Risk Management Theory in the Governance of New States: Lessons from South Sudan'. Journal of Risk Research: (2019), 22
196   Salva Kiir, remarks at the Tana High Level Forum on Security in Africa, Bahir Dar, Ethiopia, 27 April 2014
197   Alex de Waal 'When Kleptocracy Becomes Insolvent: Brute Causes of the Civil War in South Sudan', African Affairs: 113/452 (2014): 364

companies entirely by surprise. A World Bank team visiting Juba one month later met with the government and later briefed international donors:

'The World Bank has never seen a situation as dramatic as the one faced by South Sudan. In (Mr. Guigale's) view, neither the president nor senior ministers present in the meeting were aware of the economic implications of the shutdown. He candidly said that the decision was shocking and that the officials present (at the previous meeting) had not internalized [sic] nor understood the consequences of the decision.'[198]

Political Elites Framework

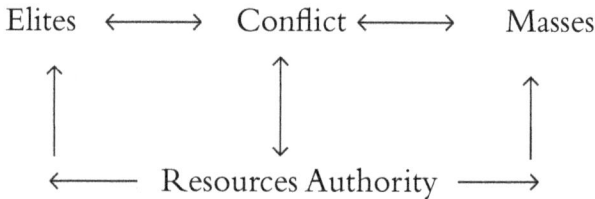

Source: Constructed by Author

As shown above, political elites are constantly controlling power and financial resources over the masses. The elites have power over the state, the civil organisation of power. Even though they could have conflicts with masses, which constantly can affect political decisions from "top down" to "bottom up", political elites

---

198   Marcelo Guigale, Director of Economic Policy and Policy Reduction Programmes for Africa, World Bank Briefing, Juba, 1 March 2012.

have authority that they use to manage these conflicts.[199] However, political elites use their authority to mobilize the masses for their ethnic gains conflicts.

To analyse the above framework, Vilfredo Pareto's *Circulation of Elites Theory* helps a great deal. Vilfredo Pareto thought that it would have been wonderful if the elites could move about freely so that the capable would rise and the incapable would sink.[200] He distinguished and identified two types of elites. Between them, there was an important difference. The "speculator" was always after wealth and new economic combination, while the "rentier" had a "fixed income" and lived within its limit.[201] The society of "speculators" was religious, militaristic, and conservative and used force as their method.[202] This makes the circulation of elites slow and economic stimulus weak. In the opposite case, economic interests supersede military ones. The costs of government is high but so is its economic stimulus; the conservative virtues decline and finally the leading class that's degenerating into humanitarianism proves unable to keep the political power.[203] Pareto is certain that "*there is a continuous change between these two forms of government*".[204] Pareto further viewed "speculators", as irresponsible and undesirable elements in a "democratic" society, who would not stop at any means or methods in order to enlarge their wealth and fortunes at the expenses of the class of "rentiers". By "rentiers", he described many

199   William Easterly 'Institutions: Top Down or Bottom Up?' American Economic Review: Papers and Proceedings: 98 (2) 2008), 262 (251-286

200   Emmanuel, Marcoglou. 1955. Pareto and His Circulation of Elites (University of Connecticut, USA), 249

201   Ibid, 249

202   Ibid

203   Franz, Borkenau. 1936. Pareto (John Wiley & Sons, Inc New York), 130

204   Ibid, 130

groups of people such as employees, small businessmen, laborers, and farmers etc. who were forced to live within the limits of a fixed income.[205] One could easily understand the hatred that this group feels for the "speculators" who by different manoeuvres and combinations (and by playing the stock market) could jeopardize the happiness and economic wellbeing of their class. The "rentier" would be the first victims in any economic crisis.[206]

This is the argument of Vilfredo Pareto in his seminal work *'The Rise and Fall of Elites"*, where he argues that it is possible for political elites to manipulate the masses through carefully used political propaganda.[207] The ultimate losers in this framework are both the elites and masses. While the masses are set to slaughter one another, the political elites pat each other's backs, hugging cheerfully in fancy hotels while unknowingly beginning to finally feel the economic challenges of the conflict.

In hatching conflicts, President Kiir through the visible hands of his political elite advisors announced the postponement of the election in May 2013, arguing that peace and reconciliation were to be prioritised amongst the South Sudanese citizens. As if this was not enough, President Salva Kiir was challenged by Dr. Riek Machar, Pag'an Amum and Rebecca Nyandeng De' Mabior to compete in the SPLM Chairperson elections, forcing him to use his executive power, with an implicit threat of coercion. In July 2013, he fired Riek Machar and the majority of his cabinet and brought in

---

205   Emmanuel, Marcoglou. 1955. Pareto and His Circulation of Elites (University of Connecticut, USA), 249
206   Ibid, 249
207   Vilfredo Pareto. 2010. The Rise and Fall of Elites: An Application of Theoretical Sociology, 35

others who were not very ambitious. Alex de Waal argues that the dissenters refused his invitation to form different political parties to compete in elections, well aware that SPLM membership was the only guaranteed ticket to being a member of the ruling club.[208] A second reason for staying in the SPLM was that they hoped to manage internal elite political competition in a non-violent way.[209]

However, each side knew that it would need to threaten the other with force, at the minimum, to maintain its leverage. But President Kiir's political management team was inept. By dismissing all his challengers at one time, he pushed them together into a single block that putatively commanded a majority in the SPLM Political Committee. He then declared his intention to suspend all SPLM organs other than the Chairman's office (his own position), but he partially reversed this by agreeing to a meeting of the National Liberation Council (NLC), the SPLM quasi-Legislature body (in which he would win a majority).[210] In NLC, differences were poorly managed; President Kiir (perhaps acting on the advice of his coterie political elite at his backyard) gave a threatening speech and assigned Mr. Michael Makuei Lueth (Minister of Information), who moderated the NLC meeting meant to pass the SPLM Constitution, the Manifesto and the Code of Conduct. The atmosphere at Nyahuron Centre Hall was charged. The former archbishops of Catholic and Episcopal churches pleaded for peace and unity. His Grace Paulino Lukudu Loro, the now late bishop, and the retired bishop His Grace Daniel Deng Bul cajoled the two

---

208   Alex de Waal 'When Kleptocracy Becomes Insolvent: Brute Causes of the Civil War in South Sudan', African Affairs: 113/452 (2014): 365
209   Ibid, 365
210   Ibid, 366

leaders and all the members of the NLC to avoid tensions and to discuss as brothers and sisters in politics. The duo implored the leaders to remember their young country and avoid violence in order for the South Sudanese to enjoy the 2013 Christmas celebrations. Former Special Representative of UN Secretary General and Head of UNMISS, Hilde F. Johnson also called for calm and reasoning to eschew bloodshed in the nascent state. Nonetheless, none heeded the advice.

Comrade Aguil De Chut Deng aka Nyan-Pagou sang very inciting revolutionary songs. As the meeting began, members of the NLC were not given time to deliberate on the documents, instead, acclamations were done by the allied political elites of the President. This strategy failed as Machar Camp left the meeting and later on around 9:00pm, 15th December 2013 fighting amongst Presidential Guards ensued leading to the rebellions. Due to insatiable greed for political power and wealth, Dr. Riek Machar seized the opportunity and declared resistance movement against the government and people of South Sudan leading to civil war and political violence across the country. The root causes of the political violence are presented through various accounts: government and opposition. However, one of the root causes was the political elites political profiteering and patronage to the SPLM Leader who the elitesy failed to tell the reality of state failure.

Mediation of political violence by IGAD was thwarted by intermittent bargaining of the political elite as argued by Alex de Waal:

'Members of the South Sudanese elite, within the government and opposition and including the larger number who identify with their own interests were attempting to subdue the peace negotiations established by IGAD immediately after the conflict exploded, and turn it into an arena for tactical bargaining. For them, the negotiating forum is entirely subordinate to both cash-based patronage bargaining and the logic of force, as well providing an opportunity for rest and recreation. The principal function of the mediation exercise is that it will be on hand when the South Sudanese leaders decide to make a deal, and legitimize the new bargain amongst kleptocrats (Greek word for ruling thieves). This point was poignantly expressed by Jok Madut Jok, head of the Sudd Institute: 'the men (Kiir and Machar) will eventually sit down, resolve their differences, laugh for the cameras, and the thousands of civilians who have died will not be accounted for.'[211]

Thus when factional elites engaged in deadlock and brinksmanship for political gain, it undermined the social contract that included pressures and measures related to power struggles, defectors, flawed elections and political competition.[212] Instead of addressing South Sudanese contradictions, the SPLM moved them into the arguments about administrative boundaries and post allocations, which are at centre of *real politik* in South Sudan. The 2010 elections was a moment when the SPLM elite could have used its potential as a mass movement to start to address the dilemmas of

---

211   Ibid, 368
212   Messner J. J. (2019) 'Fund for Peace: Fragile States Index' Washington, DC.

representation and allocation of resources in a society increasing structured around ethnicity.[213]

So, the overall thirst of resources of the SPLM political elites lies on their perceived entitlement, manifesting itself as a 'curse of liberation'.[214] The SPLM and the SPLA elites believe that all resources in South Sudan belong to them, including the oil underneath. This has deepened corruption and has tarnished the image of the nascent state. The leitmotif has remained as the 'politics of belly'.[215]

---

213   Edward Thomas, 2015. South Sudan: A Slow Liberation (London: Zed Books), 162

214   For 'Curse of Liberation' refers to Prof. Christopher Clapham http://www.gurtong.net/ECM/Editorial/tabid/124/ctl/ArticleView/mid/519/articleId/9603/The-curse-of-Liberation.aspx (Accessed on 19th January 2021)

215   Jean-Francois Bayart. 2009. The State of Politics in Africa: The Politics of Belly, 2nd Edition (Paris, Loners Publishers), 1.

CHAPTER FIVE
THE ROLE OF THE
INTERNATIONAL COMMUNITY:
THE UNITED NATIONS
AND THEIR AGENCIES

UN AGENCIES HAVE PLAYED critical roles in South Sudan's state formation and failure. South Sudan is the only country in the world's
history where UN General Assembly President and Secretary
General attended the independence celebrations in their physical capacities.[216] UN has lofty ideas of building South Sudan to
prosperity. Although it attempted to construct it, it has at the same
time contributed to its failure. This analysis should be restricted
to UNDP, UNMISS, IGAD, AU and Trioka Countries to discern
their roles in South Sudan's state formation, shocks and failure.

Participation in state failure in a region with great power, international organisations and regional organisations has similar effects
on the structures and dynamics of interaction within the units at

---

216   See Jacob, Chol 'When a Success Becomes a Burden: Challenges of
Nations Building in Post-Liberation South Sudan http://blogs.lse.ac.uk/africaat-
lse/2017/12/06/when-success-becomes-a-challenges-of-nations-building-
in-post-liberation-south-sudan/ (Accessed on 21st January 2028).

the regional level.[217] Strategic interests of outside powers may bolster the capacity of individual states to cope with threats, at the expense of their challengers. While this may increase the chances of this particular state to escape the prospect of state failure, such external intervention potentially gives rise to a phenomenon described by Martin Pugh and Nathan Cooper (2004) as conflict displacement and state failure.[218]

Most African countries that have experienced external interventions have either succeeded or failed. The interventions have been tweaked to support state formation, reconstruction and transition to democracy, but the outcome at some points has been state failure. In 2005 and 2011, the UN undertook two multilateral military interventions known respectively as the United Nations Mission in Sudan (UNMIS) and the United Nations Mission in South Sudan (UNMISS) on tandem of civilians' protection, peace building, consolidation and political stabilisation. Yet, the results have been different in comparison with each other. Hence, we have to look at the role of the UN in South Sudan state formation and failure.

The UN's Role in South Sudan's State Formation and Failure

The role of the international and developmental communities, particularly the United Nations, in South Sudan's state formation and failure have received copious amounts of empirical literature

---

217   Stefan Wolff, 2005. State Failure in Regional Context (London: University of Bath), 16
218   Martin Pugh and Nathan Cooper, 2004. War Economies in Regional Context, Challenges of Transformation (London: Boulder, Co: Lynne Rienner), 21

in scholarly arguments. Critical analyses have been paraded to discern how developing communities have either formed or failed post-conflict states.

The voyage for South Sudan's state formation and consolidation has been a multifaceted endeavour involving all stakeholders. South Sudan in September 2011 ratified the United Nations Charter and became the 193rd member, receiving applause for joining the International Government. Many UN agencies have been supporting the people of South Sudan before the signing of the Comprehensive Peace Agreement (CPA) during the interim period, towards the independence and after the post-independence of South Sudan. These supports have been spelt out in various mandates that UN agencies are executing in South Sudan. For instance, the UNDP mandate has been building strong accountable institutions of governance, rule-of-law and service delivery while UNMISS's initial mandate ranges from protection of civilians, human rights monitoring & reporting and supporting the establishment, the extension of an accountable state authority and a recent mandate for an electoral assessment and support for elections. At the time of writing this book, the UNMISS mandate had been renewed to provide the protection of civilians and monitoring and reporting human rights, as well as providing an extension to accountable state authority, humanitarian response, electoral assessment and support to general elections. So, what are the agencies up to? Have they contributed to South Sudan's state formation or failure? What has been their role in other post-conflict countries?

Anders Kompass in his ground breaking piece *The Ethical Failure: Why I Resigned From UN* argues that the organisation has always fallen short of its principles during intervention. With his twenty years' experience with UN, Kompass succinctly emphasises these UN failures as below:

> 'Cholera in Haiti, corruption in Kosovo, murder in Rwanda, cover-up of war crimes in Darfur: on too many occasions the UN is failing to uphold the principles and standards set out in its Charter, rules and regulations. Sadly, we seem to be witnessing more and more UN staff less concerned with abiding by the ethical standards of the international civil service than with doing whatever is most convenient – or least likely to cause problems – for themselves or for member states.'[219]

As a quick learning platform, DR Congo also provides historical impetus on how development partners have contributed to state failures. Severine Autesserre argues the following on DR Congo Intervention:

> 'If the international peace builders' only goal had been to set up a functioning government in the DR Congo, however, they would have withdrawn the peacekeeping troops after the 2006 general elections. If foreign interveners had wanted to maintain order in the eastern provinces, they would also have pulled out the UN troops. Yet, not MONUC stay but, as explained previously, donors even expanded and strengthened the mission. The strategy developed by UN in 2007 and 2008, and

---

219   http://www.irinnews.org/opinion/2016/06/17/exclusive-ethical-failure-%E2%80%93-why-i-resigned-un (Accessed on 20th July 2020).

later approved by the Security Council, also demonstrated that the States, mostly involved in the Congolese peace process wanted much more than a legitimate government and were pleased about the continued instability. Under this new plan, MONUC had no time to remain in DR Congo until most Congolese fighters were either integrated into the army or disarmed and demobilized, until the Congolese army and police were able to 'assume responsibility for the country's security', and until local elections were organised.'[220]

Linda Melvern who witnessed the Rwandan genocide and documented it in her thought-provoking work '*A People Betrayed: The Role of the West in Rwanda's Genocide*' argues that the failure of the UN in Rwanda's genocide was the lack of cooperation of members to apply the 1948 Genocide Convention to prevent genocide.[221] Lt. Gen. Romeo Alain Dallaire reinforces this argument by noting that the USA and UK, the traditional permanent members of UN, did not only help stop genocide but also ended up lobbying the UNSC in the withdrawal of 25,000 UNAMIR after 10 Belgians soldiers were killed.[222]

On South Sudan, one would argue that the UNDP and UNMISS have both formed and failed the South Sudan state at the same time. Two arguments are critical: institutional building and political expedient to comprehend UNDP and UNMISS state

220   Severine Autesserre, 2010. The Trouble with Congo: Local Violence and the Failure of International Peace building (New York, Cambridge University Press), 236
221   Linda Melvern, 2009. A People Betrayed: The Role of the West in Rwanda's Genocide. (Zeds Books, London), 29
222   Romeo Dallaire, 2003. Shaking Hands with the Devil: The Failure of Humanity in Rwanda, (Oxford University Press), 46

formation and failure dictum.

To begin this analysis, institutional building has been one of the core areas where UNDP and UNMISS have contributed so far in South Sudan's state formation. UNDP established its offices across the ten states of Southern Sudan as early as 2006 to build government structures and accountability systems with special support to the office of the President. In the office of the President, many advisors were contracted by the UNDP and, despite being assigned to help strengthen the accountability system and coach staff to manage decentralisation and inter-governmental linkages, they could not fix the system well. In state levels, each advisor either on governance, development, rule-of-law, peace, economy & finance, gender or health issues had been embedded at the Governor's Office, Ministry of Finance, Ministry of Local Government and Law Enforcement, Judiciary, Ministry of Physical Infrastructures, Ministry of Health, Ministry of Education, Ministry of Agriculture, Gender & Social Welfare etc to help build robust systems that could enhance accountability, transparency and service delivery. Without any denial, the UNDP did help in building and rehabilitating the state's Police Headquarters, Prison Services, Judiciary, Peace Commissions Offices and so on. These endeavours, managed by the UNDP Support for the States Project, helped in charting state formation in the desired direction. The deployment of more than 280 specialists through both the Rapid Capacity Placement Initiative (RCPI) and IGAD projects has gone a long way to provide much needed coaching and mentoring support of a durable nature and provided accountability for the UNDP's programming.[223]

However, the UNDP is viewed to have contributed to South Sudan's state failure. A compelling argument is that even with the presence of UNDP advisors to the governments in the former ten states, and even within the highest office of the President, rule-of-law and accountability systems had not helped to improve the functioning of the government. Yet, UNDP attracted billions of dollars in tandem to South Sudan's state formation and reconstruction. Much of these dollars have been allocated to policy work, service delivery and capacity building, programmes. Policy work and service delivery aside, the idea of 'capacity building' has been a 'big tent' debate and was synonymous with 'capacity sucking out' of UNDP of South Sudan. This is because 'capacity building' funds have not necessary built the capacities of South Sudan but has been reused; money was moving back to the staff of the donating countries as part of their abroad maintenance.

The Role of The United Nations in South Sudan's State Formation and Failure: A Discussion

The role of the UN in state formation and failure in South Sudan is discussed as follows. The UN has helped in the formation of the South Sudan State, particularly in development programmes, humanitarian aid services, peace building programmes, human rights and justice support. It is argued that based on its mandate the UN has done very well. One of the emphasised points is the UNDP support to states, rule-of-law, justice, health and education including the United Nations Humanitarian Air Services (UNHAS) that

---

223   UNDP South Sudan Annual Report, 2012 (Juba, UNDP Compound), 38

cover the remotest parts of South Sudan. It is imperative to argue that without this air service, remotest part of South Sudan could have been easily cut off from the rest of the state. Moreover, had there been no UN in South Sudan then there would have been a terrible genocide at the onset of 15th December 2013.

However, it is important to note that the UN had failed the South Sudan State. It is argued that the UN had taken sides with the rebels during the genesis of 15th December 2013 and had been up there for an alleged regime change. This change came from the impoundment of the UN Container Truck at Rumbek (Lakes State) with weapons and ammunitions, which was labelled as UN goods in March 2014. The truck was taking the weapons and ammunitions to the rebels in the greater Upper Nile region. However, the UN admitted the truck was wrongly labelled and argued that the weapons and ammunitions were destined to arrive at the Ghanaian Contingents in Bentiu, Unity State. Furthermore, the Chairperson of the National Bureau of Statistics (NBS), Isaiah Chol Aruai and two others boarded UNHAS plane destined to Juba but was wrongly landed in Jiech, the SPLM-IO rebels controlled area in Jonglei without their knowledge. This caused public outcry about the desired intentions of the UN in South Sudan conflicts and violence. All three passengers were Bor Dinka by ethnicity to the Nuer rebels. Though they were spared by the rebels, the incident unleashed serious psychological stress to the trio and their families. These incidents have led to mistrust between the UN and citizens, leading to widespread demonstrations against the UN, particularly the former special envoy of Secretary General and Head of UNMISS, Hilde F. Johnson. The affair remained on the citizens' minds as a potential way of undermining South Sudan's sovereignty.

Moreover, it is argued that the UN had not helped much in the protection of the civilians. Given that UNMISS was under UNSC Chapter VII with *resolution 2252* during the conflict where the peacekeepers should have defended civilians and themselves at all accounts from physical threats irrespective of the source of threats, the UN failed to prevent Akobo's attack where an angry white army youth group (Jiech Mabor) fired shots at the Protection of Civilians Site (PoCs) and killed all those who sought protection at Akobo's UNMISS base. The UNMISS Indian battalion was over-whelmed when three of their troops got killed. They were soon overrun and hence allowed the belligerent youth to massacre all 35 Dinka people in the Akobo UNMISS base. Another similar attack happened later: the Dinka-Bor youth in retaliation attacked the UNMISS Bor PoCs camp and killed more than 25 Nuer ci-vilians while the UNMISS Korean battalion merely looked on. On February 17th 2016, the Malakal's PoCs was attacked and ran-sacked by the Padang Dinka youth leading to more than 34 people dead and 51 people wounded. This attack took place before the UNMISS peacekeepers and the troops could not protect the civil-ians under their watch. Given these incidents, it is fair to argue that the UN had created differences amongst South Sudanese society by taking a backseat while watching the state of South Sudan fall-ing apart.

Furthermore, it is believed that the UN had focused on local conflicts and had left political conflicts at the national level. It is also argued that UN officials had encouraged South Sudan's state failure to prolong their stay in South Sudan. It is important to note that the UN lacks balance between the ruling and opposition parties given the comments from Ellen Margrethe Loj, the former head of UNMISS, over the need for suspension of the 32 states. Finally, it is argued that because of this role, the government responded in denying the UN free delivery of humanitarian aid to all conflicts affecting citizens in South Sudan. Given the refusal by both the UN and the government to open up and interact freely, mistrust and bad working relationships ensued.

The passing of *Resolution 2304* by UNSC on the deployment of 4000 robust Regional Protection Force (RPF) members in August 2016 to South Sudan to guard vital humanitarian premises and project installations, such as the Juba International Airport (JIA), as well as to protect civilians regardless of the source of fire validated the Government's fear on the UN's role on regime change in South Sudan. However, the outgoing head of UNMISS David Shearer firmly maintained the required balance amongst the conflicting parties in South Sudan and was viewed as a very accommodative personality that had reformed UNMISS and changed the hanging mentality that the UN was there for a regime change in South Sudan. Shearer worked extremely hard upon assuming the UNMISS head office role on 20th January 2017 by changing the narrative and he worked to improve the UN-government working relationships and the UN - South Sudanese citizens working relationships. He left South Sudan as a happy man.

Capacity Depletion in lieu of Capacity Building

To be clear, the idea of 'capacity building' is a tool that is used to solicit funds from the development community. The UNDP and other NGOs have been quite passionate about this idea. However, 'capacity building' has been a practice of 'capacity depletion'; that is 'capacity sucking out'.[224] 'Capacity sucking out" a coined term by Michael Ignatieff refers to the situation where the existing capacities in a polity are not built by the development partners; instead these capacities are attracted by the UN and NGOS, leaving the governments with an incompetent and unskilled workforce.[225] The developing community comes so richly endowed and full of capacities that it tends to crowd out rather than complement the extremely weak state capacities of the targeted countries. This means that while the governance functions are performed, indigenous capacity does not increase, and the countries in question are likely to revert to their former situations once the international developing community loses interest or moves to the next crisis area. Thus 'capacity sucking out' of UN and INGOs in South Sudan context could apply in the aforementioned argument and moreover refers to drawing out the most qualified South Sudanese from Government to work at their offices, resulting in a braindrained situation of the government of South Sudan. So far, the UN sucked the capacities of 21 professional South Sudanese civil servants into the UNDP between 2011-2013. Seven of these senior civil servants were sucked from the Ministry of Education and Instruction, four from Ministry of Health, four from Ministry of

---

224   Michael Ignatieff , 2003. 'The Burden', New York Times Magazine, (Washington: January), 14
225   Ibid, 14

Agriculture, three from Ministry of Parliamentary affairs, two from the Ministry of Public Service & Human Resource Development and one from the Ministry of Cabinet affairs.[226] This state of affairs has resulted so far in making things worse, Francis Fukuyama in his ground breaking work emphasised on this argument:

> *'There are thus grave limitations to the ability of external powers to create demand for institutions and therefore limitations on the ability to transfer existing knowledge about institutional construction and reform to developing countries. These limitations suggest that international donors and the NGO community more broadly should be cautious about raising expectations for the long-term effectiveness of its new "capacity building' mantra.'[227]*

However, not only has the hypocrisy of 'capacity building' been prevalent, but also participation of donor community in the destruction of capacity through institutional neglect has been something that many scholars overlooked. However, Francis Fukuyama provides insightful analysis:

> *'But the problem is in fact even worse: The international community is not simply limited in the amount of capacity it can build; it is actually complicit in the destruction of institutional capacity in many developing countries. This capacity destruction*

---

226   Insider view sourced from Abdon Agaw Jok Nhial, GRSS Secretary General on 17th May 2017

227   Francis Fukuyama, 2004. State-Building: Governance and World Order in the 21st Century (New York: Cornell University Press), 39

occurs despite the best intentions of the donors and is the result
of the contradictory objectives that international aid is meant
to serve. That poor or collapsing public administration is at
the heart of Africa's twenty-year development crisis is beyond
doubt; since independence, the ability of African governments
to design and implement policies has deteriorated.'[228]

This incapacitation of African countries by the developing community is long overdue. In the words of the World Bank's African Governors: *"almost every African country has witnessed a systematic regression in capacity at independence than they now possess"*.[229] This deterioration in capacity has happened precisely during a period of accelerating external aid flows to the point where the high GDP of the entire region comes from the developing community's assistance in various forms.

So in South Sudan, it is fair to argue that true emphasise on capacity building is another form of "tough love".[230] 'Tough love' a phrase borrowed from Francis Fukuyama refers to a situation where the development partner would condition or dictate the government and its citizens in offering its services.[231] These conditions may not augur well with the country's sovereignty. 'Tough love' with its conditionality could be very difficult for well-intentioned people to actually carryout. So, what we get in the meantime is lip service to the importance of capacity building and the

---

228   Ibid, 40
229   Nicolas Van de Walle, 2001. African Economies and the Politics of Permanent Crisis (England: Cambridge University Press), 37
230   Phrase borrowed from Francis Fukuyama in his seminal work: State Building, Governance and World Order in the 21st Century 2004, 8
231   Ibid, 11

continued displacement of institutional capacity by outside donors. Thus, this conundrum does not go away but in fact becomes more severe when external leverage does not come through the nation and the state building programmes but rather through arms-length conditionality. Although the developing community knows how to supply government services, it knows much less how to create self-sustaining indigenous institutions.[232]

Foreign Dominance of the UNDP Despite 'Capacity Sucking Out' in South Sudan

The United Nations Development Programme (UNDP) has been dominated by foreign staff in South Sudan despite having 'sucked capacities' from the government. One would have wished the qualified capacities 'sucked out' from the government would have been deployed to the top echelon of the developing world body. However, the UNDP cadres' development had been skewed towards the maintenance of foreign staff at the highest levels with the nationals at the middle and lowest levels. For example, the UNDP in South Sudan do have few national specialists and team leaders while international staff dominated the top management of the development agency. As a matter of capacity appreciation, the Deputy Country Director could have gone to the highly experienced South Sudanese, given the availability pool of this expertise, but this has not been the case with the UNDP South Sudan. Although this state-of-affairs has not been realised as an ingredient of UNDP's failure towards South Sudan's state formation,

---

232   Francis Fukuyama, 2004. State-Building: Governance and World Order in the 21st Century (New York: Cornell University Press), 42

the gravity of the denial of opportunities for nationals in senior management portfolios has failed the development agency in realising it goals and outcomes. This comes in the form of government institutions viewing UNDP as a foreign-managed entity that does not promote "we feeling" and thus receives apathy in the implementation of projects. Most of foreign staffs go home every month with huge chunks of money including decent house allowances and air tickets that are not given to the more experienced South Sudanese nationals. In countries such as Kenya, Uganda and Sudan, most of the salaries paid to the international staff are regulated and much of the resources are channelled to the programmes and projects within a country.

Given that the UN & NGOs tight ownership of the jobs and programmes, the Government of South Sudan attempted to threaten and expel the UN & NGOs staff that were holding senior positions so that South Sudan nationals could take over. The exceptions to this move were highly-skilled individuals holding positions where such skills are not available in South Sudan. Although a letter to over 100 international aid agencies from South Sudan's NGO forum entitled *'Increasing Trend of Harassment and Interference Targeting NGOs, Marked by Increased Hostility and Threats from Officials'*[233], the Government of South Sudan accepted the decision quickly without the analysis of pros and cons. They eventually rescinded this. Thus, the halting of an attempted expulsion of foreign workers has continued to encourage NGO forum discussions. Other UN agencies and NGOs exaggerated the government's version of laying-off

---

233   Gulf Today Article: 'South Sudan Threatens Aid Workers':http://gulftoday. ae/portal/2a4d664d-bc8f-4049-a331-5ce031d33c10.aspx (Accessed on 23rd February, 2020)

senior UN & NGOs workers to give room to some experienced South Sudan people, as a means of foreigners' surveillance and targets. Although the government may encourage the activities of the UN and NGOs, it is hard not to worry about these activities as they can compromise the national security of the country. It is because of these unfounded fears that the government enacted the NGOS Act 12th May 2015 amidst protests from the rights groups.

The Role of UNMISS in South Sudan's State Formation and Failure

Since the signing of the 'Status of Forces Agreement' (SOFA) in July 2011, UNMISS had been a technical and political wing for institutional building and citizens' protection of South Sudan. Its initial mandate ranged from the protection of civilians, human rights monitoring and reporting to the support for the establishment and extension of accounting state authority.[234] UNMISS also played an important role in keeping the UN Security Council actively abreast with the issues of peace and security in the nascent state. The recent renewed mandate includes an assessment of the elections and possible support to the conduct of general elections in South Sudan. This is the essence of political expedient.

So, on political expedient analysis, UNMISS is discerned through its roles in South Sudan's state formation and failure. From a cursory review, UNMISS has contributed to both South Sudan's reconstruction and fragility. To be exact, when the inter-ethnic raids intensified in Jonglei, especially in Pibor in 2012 and

---

234   UNSC Secretary-General Report, 20th June 2013 on South Sudan (New York:) 16

2020, UNMISS's intervention prevented possible ethnic cleansing through mass atrocity, asset stripping, wholesale displacement and starvation.[235] Moreover, it is unforgettable the applauding efforts UNMISS showcased in averting genocide during December 2013's political fiasco. Having accommodated over 400,000 civilians during the political crisis in Bentiu, Malakal, Bor and Juba PoCs, UNMISS appeared as a serious stakeholder in South Sudan's state formation and consolidation. Thousands of victims of targeted ethnic killings and revenge attacks who sought shelter with UNMISS in Juba, Malakal, Bentiu and Bor found protection.[236] But again, did the UNMISS respond on time? Why was it that the majority of civilians were lynched in Bor, Akobo, Bentiu, Malakal and Juba etc. in the presence of large numbers of UNMISS troops? Could that really be a strategic negligence on the side of UNMISS? Even though UNMISS averted genocide, it had equally allowed deaths of many poor South Sudanese people on their watch during the elite power-pursuit skirmishes. The notion that civilians have to run to the UNMISS compounds to seek protection does not really make protection protective. Yet, the responsibility to protect should be exercised for the civilians that had not run to the UNMISS precinct.[237]

Despite this, it is fair to say that the UNMISS's contribution to South Sudan's state reconstruction is applaudable. Not only did UNMISS reign its glory on the protection of civilians, it had also

235   Majak D'Agoot. Assessing the Utility of Risk Management Theory in the Governance of New States: Lessons from South Sudan. Journal of Risks Management, (2013), 22
236   Ibid, 19
237   See UN Principle of R2P: http://www.unr2p.com (Accessed on 28th March, 2021)

contributed in the strengthening of the capacities of police force, prison services and modest infrastructure development such as upgrading of unpaved roads in some parts of the country. Nonetheless, UNMISS had been viewed by some South Sudanese people to have contributed to South Sudan's state crumbling from the onset of the signing of the SOFA. The SOFA gives UNMISS's personnel exclusive rights of travelling everywhere in South Sudan without any restriction, as well as control of a special terminal at Juba International Airport (JIA) and implementation of their work programmes without governmental approval.[238] Unfortunately, the SOFA has been abused, thrown under the bus by some individuals in the UNMISS to dodge the responsibility and genuine support to South Sudan's state formation. For instance, it is alleged that some UNMISS contractors would stay after their contracts have expired to do other illicit business.[239] Moreover, some contractors would bring their partners to South Sudan on the pretext that they were also UN contractors.[240] This had not only been a pitfall on the implementation of SOFA, but also other serious posers had been associated with the trashing of SOFA. An allegation has it that many UNMISS staff had been trading dollars in the parallel market, with even some found to have sophisticated machines of faking dollars.[241]

Furthermore, given the exclusive freedom of control of its terminal in JIA, some UNMISS individuals have been alleged to have

---

238   See SOFA http://www.un.org/en/peacekeeping/missions/unmiss/resources.shtml. (Accessed on 7th April, 2021)

239   Interview with Gen. Aleu Ayieny, Former Minister of Interior-GRSS in Juba 15th May 2015

240   Interview with Gen. Augustino Maduot Parek, Former Director General of Nationality, Passports and Immigration in Juba, 18th May 2015

241   Interview with Gen. Pieng Deng Kuol, Former Inspector General of Police in Juba on 25th May 2015

smuggled in some prohibited drugs, such as cocaine, heroin and marijuana to South Sudanese soil.[242] Is this really the formation of South Sudan's state? While still connected to free traveling inside South Sudan without hindrance and together with SOFA's clause of UNMISS assets not to be inspected, UNMISS committed one of the biggest missteps in its history in the world. The impoundment of UNMISS cargos[243] by a SPLA soldier in Rumbek while transporting military hardware labelled as humanitarian goods to Bentiu, is an attestation to this claim. Although the UNMISS management, including the UN Secretary General, apologized on 2nd April 2014 for this as a grave mistake arguing that the trucks were wrongly labelled and weapons were destined to arrive at Ghanaian Battalions in Bentiu, the damage of this incident could not exonerate anything but rather pinpoint UNMISS as having an intended plan for South Sudan's state failure and not candid formation. Although the government had equally bruised UNMISS and breached the SOFA as well, the government's response had been perhaps done under deep-seated suspicion. The trading of accusations and counter accusations coupled by deep-seated political suspicion against UNMISS in person of Hilde F. Johnson made President Kiir conclude that the UN has established a parallel government in South Sudan.[244]

Moreover, the flaming of inherent suspicion made South Sudan's

---

242   Interview with Gen. Augustino Maduot Parek, Former Director General of Nationality, Passports and Immigration in Juba, 18th May 2015

243   See http://southsudantribune.org/news/states-news/128-unmiss-cargo-of-arms-destined-for-dr-riek-rebels-seized-by-security-forces-in-rumbek. (Accessed on 7th April, 2021)

244   See President Kiir comments on SSTV News Briefing on Rumbek UN Impounded Weapons, March 30, 2014

Minister of Information threaten to shut down the UN Miraya radio and the UN itself if it does not stop interviewing rebels, as he blasted out:

> *"I will shut down this so-called UN Radio, [if] it keeps on interviewing officials from the rebel groups, so that they can disseminate their ideas freely to the citizens of South Sudan (sic). Radio Miraya has been interviewing rebels and this is the last warning to the management. If it happens again we are going to shut it down. They know what they did this morning and it is unfortunate and if it continues, we will shut you down. And we will put it in writing today. We have been writing to Miraya but their leaders have refused to come. Your Muzungus (whites) are resisting coming to me because they believe they are UN. That UN we will shut down".[245]*

While the national Minister of Information threatened the UN, on a deeper note it is a revelation of the failures of the government to provide protection for its citizens. However, Michael Makuei took this to the UN, challenging sanctions on President Kiir by the UN's Independent Experts Report on South Sudan's potential for a regime change as he notes:

> *"If they are talking about sanctioning, indicting the president, indicting Riek Machar and so forth, then definitely this is a very clear plan for a regime change. We are quite aware about*

---

245   Ayuen Akuot Atem, 2015. Information Minister Threatens To Shut Down UN Radio Miraya The Citizens Newspaper, Vol. 8 Issue No. 983, Tuesday, February 17 (South Sudan, Juba,), 1 & 2

that and we will see how far it will succeed. In terms of re-
sponse, we will definitely respond to it; it is not strange for
anybody to recommend like that because their target and main
objective is the regime change; whatever is done, must be done
geared toward right direction".[246]

Other South Sudanese leaders did the same. For example, the former caretaker Governor of the Jonglei State, Gen. John Kong Nyuon slammed on the UN's intentions on propelling sanctions on South Sudanese leaders as he argues:

'*United Nations have failed Iraq, Somalia and Libya amongst*
others, so it [UN] cannot rule South Sudan. The rumor [sic] of
UNSC 10 year master plan to put South Sudan on the trust-
eeship so as the UN provide governance, civilian protection as
well as preparing elections and providing general security until
South Sudanese are ready to take off their own destiny would
tantamount to inference in the affairs of foreign State.'[247]

Even though the 10-year trusteeship has been built on the rumours, the UNSC has been serious on placing targeted sanctions on South Sudanese leaders once they fail to conclude negotiations and bring peace on time. The UN Peacekeeping Chief, Herves Ladsous provides insight:

---

246   Oyet Alphonse, 2016. UN Sanctions on President Kiir is A Regime Change, The Juba Monitor, Wednesday, January 27 (South Sudan, Juba), 2

247   Mach Samuel Peter, 2014. Governor Criticizes UN over failure in war torn countries, The Citizen Newspaper, Vol. 8. Issue No. 921, Friday, November 28 (South Sudan, Juba,), 1

'The Security Council has been threatening to impose sanctions since November 2014 but held off as the IGAD, a regional group tried to mediate the talks. As those talks continue to go nowhere, the Council has taken the first step toward imposing sanctions... The sanctions proposed resolution [which] sets out the criteria for individuals and entities that could be sanctioned, including those who contributed to the conflict, obstructed reconciliation, violated human rights or blocked humanitarian aid efforts.'[248]

Seeing the signs of sanctions and everyday socio-economic and political challenges South Sudan is dripping through, the South Sudan Government expelled the former UNOCHA Boss Mr. Toby Lanzer for his alleged statements against the government. Presidential Press Secretary Ateny Wek Ateny comprehensively articulates:

'When he talked to CNN in Geneva in May 2015, he said the leadership of South Sudan has failed and the country is on the verge of collapse. This statement is irresponsible given that it doesn't give hope to the people of South Sudan and the work of the United Nations is to support the citizens of South Sudan. This is the second time. Last time he made a statement that the country has gone bankrupt and was resorting to printing money, which will upset the balance of payment. That was not the reality. Someone like Toby Lanzer should

---

248   UN Council To Discuss Sanctions for South Sudan: Voice of Amerce (VOA), Day-Break Africa News, 7:30Am, February 25, 2015

have realized and appreciated that the fact the people of South Sudan want hope, not despair.'[249]

Although UN Secretary-General Ban Ki-Moon condemned the decision of expulsion and urged the government to immediately reverse it, his efforts were fruitless. Instead, the willy-nilly relationship between the United Nations and the government of the Republic of South Sudan continued to be precarious, full of deep-seated mistrust and wild suspicions. Given this situation, it did not come as a surprise that some commentators saw South Sudan as a *'testing ground for effective international engagement theories in fragile states'*.[250]

But a new situation evolved from fighting amongst presidential guards of President Salva Kiir and 1st Vice President Riek Machar on 8th July 2016 at the presidential palace where President Kiir and 1st Vice President Riek were in a security meeting. Although it is not empirically agreed upon which faction started the 'dog' fight, the skirmishes engulfed the entire city of Juba and its suburbs with over 1000 people killed, women raped, and property looted and destroyed. As the result of uprising political violence and chaos, IGAD-Plus met and endorsed a regional intervention force to act as a buffer between Salva Kiir and Riek Machar's troops. The African Union and the wider International Community approved the intervention. In September 2016, the UNSC passed Resolution Number 2304 authorising the urgent deployment of

---

249   Toby Lanzer expelled over CNN Statements: http://newnationsouthsudan. com/national-news/toby-lanzer-expelled-over-cnn-statements.html (accessed on July 14, 2015)
250   See Pantuliano 2009

4000 strong Regional Protection Force (RPF) members to Juba. However, President Kiir rejected the intervention as he argued:

"There are over 12,000 foreign troops here in South Sudan', he added, in reference to peacekeepers working for the UN mission. 'What do you need more forces for? What will they come and do (sic)? The UNMISS here has so many foreign troops. So we will not accept even a single soldier. We will not accept that,' Kiir emphasised.'[251]

To twist things further, the government-sponsored demonstrations in Bor, Wau and Juba initially to reject the proposed additional force in South Sudan. Thankfully, the government surprisingly rescinded and accepted the deployment of the proposed additional 4000 robust UNMISS troops in South Sudan during the UNSC members visit, led by U.S. Ambassador Samantha Power in September 2016. The Regional Protection Force's (RPF) full arrival to South Sudan awaits various logistical and operational decisions from the Government of South Sudan and the UNSC.

The impacts of government-sponsored demonstrations have not changed the decision of IGAD and the African Union in the nascent state. UNMISS said an advance party of a construction engineering company from Bangladesh arrived on 20th April, 2017 bringing essential equipment to start the preparation of accommodation and

---

251   Sudan Tribune 'South Sudan's Kiir rejects deployment of extra troops in Juba'. http://www.sudantribune.com/spip.php?article59615 (Accessed on 20th July 2016)

working areas for the RPF in Juba.[252] *"Regional troops from Rwanda would follow in June and July,"* the UN mission said, noting that the RPF headquarters have already been established in Juba under the leadership of Gen. Jean Mupenzi from Rwanda.[253]

Though the U.S backed up this intervention decision on a strong term, it argued that UNMISS was not doing enough. Samantha Power argued *"UNMISS as it is currently configured, has proven unable – and in some cases unwilling – to prevent horrors like this"*. Her stand on the resolution of UNSC is yet to be backed up by any all-powerful state members.[254] However, as the report on the investigation of UNMISS's response on 8th July 2016's political meltdown was released on 1st November 2016, the UN Secretary General Ban Ki Moon sacked the overall commander of UNMISS in South Sudan, Lt. General Johnson Mogoa Kimani Odieki, on the grounds that he failed to lead peacekeepers in protection of civilians, even at the UN precinct. The Guardian argues on the report:

> *"A UN special investigation found that a lack of leadership by the UN Mission in South Sudan (UNMISS), spearheaded by Lt Gen Johnson Mogoa Kimani Ondieki, culminated in a 'chaotic and ineffective response' during heavy fighting in the capital between 8 and 11 July'. Peacekeepers abandoned their posts and failed to respond to pleas for help from*

252   See Radio Tamazuj, 'First Batch of Regional Protection Force Starts to Arrive in Juba', https://radiotamazuj.org/en/news/article/first-batch-of-regional-protection-force-starts-to-arrive-in-juba (Accessed on 7th May 2027)
253   Ibid
254   See 'Explanation of Position at the Adoption of UN Security Council Resolution 2304 on the UN Mission in South Sudan' http://usun.state.gov/remarks/7391 (Accessed on 30th July 2016)

*aid workers under attack in Terrian, a nearby hotel compound
to UNMISS headquarters according to a summary of the
report".[255]*

The damned UN report has serious findings as emphasised
below:

*"The special investigation found that UNMISS did not re-
spond effectively to the violence due to an overall lack of leadership, preparedness and integration amongst [sic] the various
components of the mission,' said UN spokesman Stéphane
Dujarric. Chinese peacekeepers abandoned their positions at
least twice and Nepalese peacekeepers failed to stop looting
inside the UN compound, the inquiry found. Ban said he
was 'deeply distressed by these findings' and 'alarmed by the
serious shortcomings' of the UN mission. Dujarric said the
UN chief had 'asked for the immediate replacement of the force
commander', Ondieki. Other measures would follow, added
Dujarric.'[256]*

The Kenyan Government reacted negatively to the UN's
Secretary General decision arguing that its commander had been
tossed out as a sacrificial lamb for something outside of his control.
The Kenyan Government argues that Lt. Gen. Odieki assumed his

255   See Guardian 'South Sudan Peacekeeping Commander Sacked Over
'Serious Shortcoming', https://www.theguardian.com/global-development/2016/
nov/02/south-sudan-peacekeeping-chief-sacked-alarm-serious-shortcomings-ondie-
ki (Accessed on 12th November 2026)
256   Ibid

office in June 2016, a month before President Kiir's forces and Dr. Riek's dissident soldiers engaged in a bloody political showdown. Kenya vowed to disengage from peace process in South Sudan through the withdrawal of its forces and they developed a sense of apathy towards the contribution from Regional Protection Force's (RPF) members. A week later after the sacking of Lt. Gen. Odieki, 9th November 2016 to be exact, the first 100 soldiers arrived in Kenya from South Sudan on the first leg of withdrawals. The in-charge commander of the withdrawal process details below:

"We are pulling out the whole contingent in South Sudan, over 1000 soldiers. This one is dependent on the logistics that the UN is going to give us. Today we have started. We expect some tomorrow, we expect them alternatively every other day,' said Gen Bewot.'[257]

Thus, if Kenya could have completely withdrawn its peacekeeping troops in South Sudan and continued to refused to contribute troops to the robust Regional Protection Force (RPF) in tandem to the UNSC's resolution 2304, the chance of genuine peace in South Sudan would have become quite slim. It is great that the UN negotiated with the government of Kenya in the best way possible and resolved the impasse. It is appropriate that the world body negotiated and cajoled Kenya to send its troops back to South Sudan. Indeed, Kenya finally agreed and sent back its troops as part of peacekeeping UNMISS in South Sudan.

---

257   TVC News 'Kenya Withdrawals First 100 Peacekeepers from South Sudan'. http://africa.tvcnews.tv/2016/11/11/kenya-withdraws-first-100-peacekeepers-south-sudan/#.WCbjMCN97ow (Accessed on 12th November 2016)

UN Programme Duplication and Overstretching Donor Funds in South Sudan's State Formation and Failure

UN agencies have resorted to the latest deficit of programme duplication and the overstretching of donor funds. Many programmes have been tailored the same by different organisations with different donor funding. The intention could have been a strategy of chasing donor funds to support administrative functions of the organisation. For instance, the UNDP has a programme for Gender Equity and Women Empowerment that is undertaken also by UNMISS and UN-Women. Additionally, UNDP has a robust unit of support for rule-of-law and democratic governance, which UNMISS also supports rule-of- law and security institutions. Moreover, UNDP has a conflict resolution and a crisis recovery unit that supports community dialogues to resolve conflicts and bring peace amongst the communities using homegrown solutions. Similar to this is UNMISS's recovery, reintegration and peace building unit that undertakes community dialogue to resolve conflicts, build peace and dialogue amongst the communities. UNDP conflict resolution and crises recovery unit is similar to UNMISS's recovery, reintegration and peace building support and DDR programme, particularly, the security sector reform. While UNICEF supports children protection, UNMISS does entirely the same programme.

The list of these duplications goes on in a similar fashion. So, why is everyone doing all these duplications in programme design? What is the sole reason of these duplications of the programmes yet these agencies are aware of organisation competencies? As argued elsewhere in this book, most of these UN agencies (especially

146

UNDP and UNMISS) have done these duplications to attract donor funds so that they support the administrative budgets of their offices. It does not matter what paradigm to use, having the same programme design imply well thought-out intentions to milk the donor funds for development subterfuge. This has credence of a support towards state failure rather than formation.

The Role of IGAD and African Union (AU) in South Sudanese State Formation (IGAD)

The Intergovernmental Authority on Drought and Desertification (IGADD) was established in 1986 with a focus on drought and desertification, and launched in 1996 as the Intergovernmental Authority on Development (IGAD) with an expanded mandate that included conflict resolution.[258] It comprises of Ethiopia, Kenya, Uganda, Sudan, Djibouti, Somalia, South Sudan and Eritrea, although Eritrea is currently under suspension. The decision to revitalize IGAD was made by the IGAD Head-of-States and Governments at a meeting held in Addis Ababa on 18 April 1995. At the 12th ordinary summit in 2008, the Head-of-States and Governments again expanded IGAD's mandate to include regional economic integration.[259]

The expansion of the mandate was due in part to the IGAD member's state's long history of cooperation and conflict with one another. IGAD's conflict resolution attentions have historically

---

258   Korwa G. Adar, 'Conflict Resolution in a Turbulent Region: The Case of the Inter-Governmental Authority on Development (IGAD) in Sudan', African Journal on Conflict Resolution, vol. 1, no. 2, (2000), pp. 43-46, 43

259   Medhane, Tadess (2004), 'Turning Conflicts to Cooperation: Towards an Energy led Regional Integration in the Horn of Africa', (Addis Ababa, ISS), 211

focused on the north-south conflict in Sudan (and now the south-south conflict) and various conflicts in Somalia.[260] An IGAD peace process to resolve Sudan's long running second-civil war (1983-2005) was launched in the early 1990s and gained traction in the late 1990s when Kenya was IGAD's chair. IGAD's mediation, led by General Lazaro Sumbeiywo, received significant support from the "Troika" (U.S, UK and Norway), particularly at the end of the process. The Comprehensive Peace Agreement (CPA) was signed in 2005 and paved the way for South Sudan's independence in 2011.

When South Sudan descended into political violence on 15th December 2013, the IGAD Council of Ministers on 19th December 2013 flew to Juba, the capital of South Sudan for an emergency three-day visit in order to have a first-hand impression of the political crisis and violence that rocked the country from the night of 15th December 2013. The move led to the subsequent meeting of IGAD Head-of-States and Governments in Nairobi on 27th December 2013, culminating into the establishment of South Sudan's IGAD peace mediation. Amb. Seyoum Mesfin of Ethiopia, Gen. Lazaro Sumbeiywo of Kenya and Amb. Gen. Mohammed Ahmed El-Dabi of Sudan were nominated as IGAD envoys.

Given the complexity and tiring mediation process, with the missing of the 5th March 2015 deadline due to 23 months of unsuccessful negotiations, the IGAD Head-of-States and Governments agreed and expanded the IGAD to IGAD-Plus to include the African Union Commission, China, the European Union, Norway,

---

260   Healy, Sally, 'Seeking Peace and Security in the Horn of Africa: The Contribution of Inter-Governmental Authority on Development,' International Affairs, Vol 87, no 1 (2011): 132

the UK, the US, the UN and the IGAD Partners Forum (IPF).[261] With regional and international pressures, the IGAD-Plus focused on getting the warring parties to sign the Agreement of the Resolution of the Conflict in Republic of South Sudan (ARCSS) on 17th and 26th August 2015 respectively and the Revitalised Agreement on the Resolution of the Conflict in the Republic of South Sudan (R-ARCSS) on 12th September 2018. However, IGAD is viewed to have failed the South Sudanese State than formation and three cases of Uganda, Ethiopia and Sudan are discussed below:

IGAD, a Divided Mediator

As a peace broker, IGAD state members have been quite divided with various vested interests in South Sudanese conflicts and violence. From Somalia to Djibouti, Ethiopia to Sudan, Uganda to Kenya, all vested zero-sum interests have so far compromised peace efforts in South Sudan. Vested interest, as argued by Lakhdar Brahimi and Ahmed Salman, is one of the deadly sins of peacemaking in the world.[262] In understanding how IGAD contributed in South Sudanese State failure as a divider mediator, the study analyses the role-played by the Republic of Uganda, the Republic of Sudan and the Republic of Ethiopia.

---

261   Is largely comprised of IGAD's donor partners and has three-levels of membership: the ministerial, ambassadorial and technical. The IPF is currently co-chaired by the Italian government and is comprised of the following members: Austria, Belgium, Canada, Denmark, France, Greece, Germany, Ireland, Italy, Japan, the Netherlands, Norway, Sweden, Switzerland, UK, U.S., European Commission (EC), International Organisation for Migration (IOM), United Nations Development Program (UNDP) and the World Bank.

262   Lakhdar Brahimi & Ahmed Salman. 2008. Seven Deadly Sins of Peace Making (Reiner Publishers, London), 14

The Republic of Uganda

The Republic of Uganda is a founding member of IGAD. Its relationship with South Sudan is quite historical and starts from the long history of South Sudanese liberation struggles. During the onset of political violence on 15th December 2013, the Government of Republic of South Sudan (GRSS) was overwhelmed as the national army SPLA got split into two; the Dinka and the Nuer military men. The Nuer members made up of 60% of the SPLA and rebelled with Dr. Riek Machar, while the SPLA Dinka members remained with President Salva Kiir Mayardit. The South Sudanese Government swiftly invited the Ugandan People Defence Forces (UPDF) for a backup to push back the Nuer rebellions. The arrival of the UPDF and their participation in the repulsion of the rebel militias confirmed IGAD as a partisan mediator. To be clear, President Salva Kiir admitted to President Yoweri Museveni during the 3rd anniversary of independence, 9th July 2014, that *"Uganda is a friend indeed and that without your intervention [Museveni], my government would have gone forever [sic] and I sincerely thank you for this"*.[263]

Digging Out Ugandan Military's Intervention in South Sudan

As President Yoweri Museveni sent troops to support South Sudan's President Salva Kiir. Uganda has remained a staunch ally and it has often sought to benefit financially and politically from foreign military activities, and its deployment in South Sudan is a testament

---

263   President Kiir's Speech during the 3rd anniversary of Independence, 9th July 2014 at Dr. John Garang's Mausoleum.

to these sought out benefits.[264] After sealing a deal with President Kiir, President Museveni dispatched a company of UPDF soldiers on 20th December 2013 to South Sudan to secure the evacuation of Ugandan citizens from the country.[265] This view was reiterated by the Ugandan Ministry of Foreign Affairs who claimed that the UPDF intervened to secure Juba's airport and to facilitate the safe evacuation of Ugandan nationals.[266] But, it soon became evident that the UPDF had a broader mandate. This included fighting the rebels in and around Bor, the capital of Jonglei, during late December 2013 and early January 2014. Controversial methods were used, including aerial bombardment and possibly cluster bombs.[267] The UPDF fought alongside the government army, the SPLA, but the Ugandan intervention is attributed with attempted rebel advances from South Bor towards Juba city.

Since then, the UPDF has provided the GRSS with advisors and logistical support. Their main base was near Juba's airport, but soldiers were also stationed in Bor and Nisitu to guard vital installations including the main trade route to Uganda: the Juba-Nimule highway.[268] However, as the conflict escalated, Ugandan troops were increased to the estimated level of between 2,000 and

---

264   Marieke Schomerus, 'They forgot what they came for: Uganda's Army in Sudan', Journal of East African Studies, vol. 6, no. 1 (2012); 114-117, 114
265   Kasaija, Philip 'Explaining the (IL) Legal of Uganda's Intervention in the Current South Sudan Conflict', African Security Review, vol. 3, no 4 (2014): 1-26 (1)
266   Ugandan's Ministry of Foreign Affairs, Press Release 30th January 2014.
267   See UNSC Report, 2014, page 4
268   See 'UPDF Intervention in South Sudan' http://www.sudantribune.com/spip.php?article53378 (Accessed on 17th January 2027)

5,000 soldiers.[269]

Uganda participated in the initial IGAD council of ministers visit to Juba in December 2013. Following the visit, the Head-of-States and Governments appointed special envoys from Ethiopia, Kenya and Sudan. Uganda, as a belligerent party, was not included and continued to focus more on securing its interests in its country than at the Addis Ababa peace talks. Uganda is seen by many as the king maker in Juba.[270] However, political indecisiveness, displeasure with the options on the table and relative acceptance of the status quo meant that its military influence is not translating into the regional political leadership needed to end a conflict that cannot be won on the battlefield.

Uganda's posture was shaped by deep animosity towards Sudan and an often-visceral dislike of former South Sudan Vice President Riek Machar, now head of the SPLM/A-IO.[271] At the same time, officials often disparage Kiir's government. While the intervention was a military friendship endeavour, the intention carried a lot of

---

269   Kasaija, Philip 'Explaining the (IL) Legal of Uganda's Intervention in the Current South Sudan Conflict', African Security Review, vol. 3, no 4 (2014): 1-26 (13)

270   Koen Vlassenroot e tal, 'Doing business out of war. An analysis of the UPDF's presence in the Democratic Republic of Congo', Journal of East African Studies, vol. 6, no. 1 (2012); 236

271   Sudan-Uganda animosity has deep roots but reached an apex in the 1990s, when they fought a proxy war in the then southern Sudan (and northern Uganda). While the level of conflict is now much reduced, they continue to trade allegations of support for one another's armed opposition groups. Sudan alleges Kampala backs the Sudan People's Liberation Army – North (SPLA-N), Justice and Equality Movement (JEM), Sudan Liberation Army – Minni Minawai (SLA-MM) and Sudan Liberation Army – Abdul Wahid (SLA-AW). Uganda alleges Khartoum supports the Lord's Resistance Army (LRA) and the Allied Democratic Forces. The talks collapsed, they left with the supplies. Some members of that mediation (at that time led by Machar) said the support was necessary to keep the LRA in the talks; others suggest it evidences Machar's long collaboration with the LRA.

economic interests as the GRSS allegedly spent $800 million USD as part of a package to Ugandan Government's intervention to rescue the nascent state from the jaws of the rebels.

Was The Ugandan Intervention Legitimate?

Although it can be argued that the intervention was driven by friendly mutual relations of the two sisterly countries as well as the abrogation of mediation, UPDF involvement in the South Sudanese civil war raises enormous questions; specifically whether it was a legitimate undertaking or driven by other parochial interests. The Ugandan Government argues that it intervened to secure vital installations to rescue its nationals that were trapped in the conflicts. On the other hand, the same Ugandan Government argues that it was invited by the Government of South Sudan to intervene with the authorisation from IGAD. Let's analyse these two conflicting views.

Helping Nationals

I am beginning my analysis on the rescuing of the nationals. As the conflict and violence deepened in South Sudan, President Museveni in his letter to the Speaker of Parliament on the intervention, stated that '... *the deployment of UPDF to South Sudan was to ... rescue trapped Ugandans*'[272]. His statement got support from other government officials such as Kiyonga who, while addressing Parliament,

---

272   Kasaija, Philip 'Explaining the (IL) Legal of Uganda's Intervention in the Current South Sudan Conflict', African Security Review, vol. 3, no 4 (2014), 7

stated: '*we are in South Sudan to evacuate our citizens*'[273]. This followed the former Minister of State for Defence Jeje Odongo's
presentation to the Parliamentary Committee on Defence where
he stated that '*following the [UPDF] deployment, Ugandans have been
rescued and evacuated from Juba, Bor and Bentiu*'[274]. According to the
then Uganda's Chief of Defence Forces (CDF), General Katumba
Wamala, as of 14th January 2014 '*at least 30,000 Ugandans had been
rescued from South Sudan since the UPDF deployed there*'[275].

Nonetheless, there is no existing clear-cut international protocol or treaty that authorises a foreign country to just send troops to
another country to rescue its nationals. The UN Charter provides
a small leeway for military intervention to be done by members
of the UN after it has been sanctioned by the UNSC. This is done
on political ground to rescue citizens and protect them from a
genocidal regime.

In the case of South Sudan, Uganda's intervention seemed to
have gone beyond rescuing Ugandans caught up in the fighting.
The announcement that the UPDF was fighting alongside GRSS

273   Yasiin Mugerwa and Mercy Nalugo, Legislators Okay Deployment of
Ugandan troops in South Sudan, Daily Monitor, 15 January 2014, http://www.
monitor.co.ug/News/National/MPs-okay-deployment-of-UPDF-in-S–Su-
dan/-/688334/2146298/-/19nfyl/-/index.html (Accessed 17 January 2018).
274   See the Observer 2014 Report http://observer.ug/news-headlines/37531-
updf-budget-for-south-sudan-war-shoots-up-by-shs-16-2bn (Accessed on 18th
January 2021).
275   Ibid.

forces against the rebel troops supporting Machar[276] clearly violates the requirement of proportionality, which demands that the action taken must not be over excessive. The UPDF fighting on behalf of one of the factions in the conflict points to an abuse of this state's practice, which Terry Gill warned about.[277]

Invitation with IGAD Approval

The UPDF intervention is argued from the invitation of the Government of South Sudan. Legally, a democratically-elected government such as of South Sudan has legitimate authority to carry out state functions, including inviting another country's forces to come to its aid if its legitimacy is challenged.[278] Many states have attempted to justify military intervention in other states on the basis of agreement. It must be emphasised that the agreement, to produce any legal effect, must be clearly established, be really expressed (which precludes merely presumed consent), be internationally attributable to the state and be anterior to the commission of the act to which it refers.[279]

In the case of South Sudan, the GRSS claims that it was

---

276   Barbara Amongst, Museveni reveals Uganda combat role in South Sudan, The East African, 16 January 2014, http:// www.theeastafrican.co.ke/news/Museveni-reveals-Uganda-army-role-in-South-Sudan/-/2558/2148476/-/qwlots/-/ index. html (Accessed 18th January 2117); Barbara Amongst, UPDF helps South Sudan recapture Bor – says Ankunda, Daily Monitor, 20 January 2014, http://www.monitor.co.ug/News/National/UPDF-helps-South-Sudan-recapture- Bor–says-Ankunda/-/688334/2152098/-/quut86/-/index.html (Accessed on 18th January02118).
277   Gill, Rescue of nationals, 217. Gill argued that there exists no right of states to rescue their nationals caught up in conflicts mainly because '[the right] is subject to abuse'.
278   Kasaija, Philip 'Explaining the (IL) Legal of Uganda's Intervention in the Current South Sudan Conflict', African Security Review, vol. 3, no 4 (2014), 6
279   See UN, Yearbook of the International Law Commission 1999, vol. II (Part One), A/CN.4/SER.A/1999/Add.1 (Part 1), New York, NY: UN, 2008, paragraph 234.

democratically elected and the only legitimate government. This assumption is false as elections conducted in 2010 were done when GRSS was part of Sudan. It has been observed that in cases where the incumbent government controls the political apparatus of the state, it may request external assistance, or even military intervention, to assist it in maintaining control of the state.[280] Malcolm Shaw has observed: *'It would appear that in general, aid to the government authorities to repress a revolt is perfectly legitimate, provided of course it was requested by the government.'*[281] For example, France intervened in Mali in 2013 upon the invitation of the interim transition government of Mali to halt the advance of the Islamic Jihadists who were threatening to take over Bamako; they were handy.[282] Kabore and Maillart have emphasised:

> *'Considering that France had been officially invited to intervene by Malian authorities in order to defeat Jihadists in the north of the country, 'Operation Survival' can be considered as lawful under international law…as Mali gave its consent to the operation, no further legal justification was required.'*[283]

But of course, it must be observed that France's intervention in Mali has been mired in the politics of neo-colonialism.

---

280   Wippman, David. 'Military intervention, regional organisations, and host-state consent', Duke Journal of Comparative & International Law 7: (1996), 211
281   Malcolm, Shaw. 2003. International Law', 5th edition, (Cambridge University Press) 23
282   Bannelier, Karine and Christakis, Theodore. Under the UN Security Council's watchful eyes: military intervention by invitation in the Malian conflict', Leiden Journal of International Law 26: (2013) 855–874 (856)
283   Acoco, Kaboré, and J B Maillart (2013) 'The Malian Conflict and International Law', Journal of Global Studies no 5, (2013: 91-112 (91).

The only exception to the rule on aiding and abetting a government is when the recipient state (government) is forcibly suppressing the right of self-determination of a people entitled to such rights.[284] The general rule is that a government may not authorise external military intervention against a national liberation movement that opposes racist or colonial domination.[285] This scenario does not apply to the situation in South Sudan.

The UN General Assembly Declaration on Principles of International Law concerning Friendly Relations and Cooperation amongst States in accordance with the Charter of the UN states argues that '*no state has the right to intervene, directly or indirectly, for any reason whatever, in the internal or external affairs of any other state.*'[286] This would suppose that a state's intervention in a civil war in another state is prohibited. However, while there exists the suggestion that intervention in a civil war on the side of the government

---

284   Ibid, 24
285   Wippman, David. 'Military Intervention, Regional Organisations and Host-State Consent', Duke Journal of Comparative & International Law 7: (1996), 230
286   UN General Assembly, Declaration on Principles of International Law concerning Friendly Relations and Cooperation amongst States in accordance with the Charter of the United Nations (A/8082), G.A. Res. 2625 (XXV), UN GAOR, 25th Sess., 1883rd Plenary Meeting, U.N. Doc. A/8082 (24 October 1970), 123, http:// daccess-dds-ny.un.org/doc/RESOLUTION/GEN/NR0/348/90/IMG/ NR034890.pdf?OpenElement (Accessed 18th January 2018).

at its request is unlawful, there is little support for this in practice.[287] However, practice only seems to prohibit intervention on the side of those opposing the government. Since Uganda intervened on the side of the GRSS, its intervention was viewed as legal.

Nevertheless, this ground of intervention has become increasingly tenuous following revelations that the GRSS did not write a letter to Museveni requesting intervention, as had earlier been claimed by officials of the Ugandan Government.[288] This would mean that there was no consent to the intervention by South Sudan. On 14th January 2014, Crispus Kiyonga, the then Ugandan Minister of Defence, told the Ugandan Parliament that Kiir had written to Museveni, inviting the UPDF to 'help stabilize the situation',[289] but the South Sudan Parliament Speaker countered this and declared that Kiir had not written a letter requesting Uganda's

---

287   See Chatham House, The principle of non-intervention in contemporary international law: non-interference in a state's internal affairs used to be a rule of international law: is it still? London: Chatham House, 2007, http://www.chatham-house.org/ sites/default/files/public/Research/International%20Law/il280207.pdf (Accessed 18th January 2018). However, under the 1975 Wiesbaden Resolution on the Principle of Non-Intervention in Civil Wars (1975) of the Institute of International Law (IDI), which is non-binding, Uganda's intervention in South Sudan would be illegal, as the resolution in particular prohibits third-party states from giving assistance to parties to a civil war, such as 'sending armed forces ... to any party to a civil war, or allowing them to be sent or to set out'. The full text of the resolution can be found at http://www.idi iil.org/idiE/resolutionsE/1975_wies_03_en.pdf (Accessed 18th January 2018).

288   Solomon Arinaitwe, Minister fails to produce S. Sudan letter seeking UPDF intervention, Daily Monitor, 24 January 2014, http://www.monitor.co.ug/News/National/Minister-fails-to-produce-S-Sudan-letter-seeking/-/ 688334/2158046/-/ ohvflvz/-/index.html (Accessed 18th January 2028).

289   Paul Tajuba, South Sudan Speaker denies writing letter to Museveni, Daily Monitor, 27 January 2014, http://www.monitor.co.ug/News/National/South-Sudan-speaker-denies-writing-letter-to-Museveni/-/688334/2161502/-/b479 q0z/-/index.html (Accessed 18th January 2028).

intervention.[290] Although the government of South Sudan signed a military fact with Uganda, it was done after UPDF was already fighting in South Sudan alongside President Kiir.

However, the interesting twist is the invitation with IGAD approval. According to Ugandan government officials, the UPDF's presence in South Sudan was sanctioned by the states of the IGAD.[291] South Sudan's ambassador to Uganda, Samuel Lominsuk, had also stated that Uganda's intervention in South Sudan is justified under the IGAD.[292] It can be argued that IGAD commended Uganda's intervention only to help secure critical infrastructure and installations but did not authorise it to intervene in the bloody conflict. Any support contemplated by IGAD for Uganda was towards achieving this objective. The wording of the IGAD 27th December 2013's communiqué does not suggest that IGAD intended to support Uganda's intervention in South Sudan beyond what is stated.[293] It is a requirement of international law that agreements between states should be interpreted in good faith in accordance with the ordinary meaning to be given to the terms of the

---

290   Paul Tajuba, South Sudan Speaker denies writing letter to Museveni; Sekanjako, S. Sudan Speaker explains UPDF's deployment. See also Speaker: Kiir never wrote to Museveni over UPDF deployment, Red Pepper, 24 January 2014, http://www.redpepper.co.ug/speaker-kiir-never-wrote-to-m7/ (Accessed 18th January 2028).
291   Mukisa, Farahani 'Opposition blasts President over UPDF', Daily Monitor, 14th January 2014, 5
292   Musisi, Fredric 'UPDF came to prevent a genocide South Sudan', Daily Monitor, 9th January, 2014, 8
293   Kasaija, Philip 'Explaining the (IL) Legal of Uganda's Intervention in the Current South Sudan Conflict', African Security Review, vol. 3, no 4 (2014): 1-26, (10)

treaty.[294] If IGAD had intended to support Uganda's efforts beyond those stated in the communiqué, it should have stated so.[295] This is to avoid the Libyan scenario whereby the UNSC Resolution of 1973 that required 'the protection of civilians' was expanded to include the removal of Muammar Gaddafi from power.

South Sudan–IGAD Relations
IGAD as a Buddy and a Friend Indeed

After the signing of the Comprehensive Peace Agreement (CPA) in January 2005 and the referendum of the then Southern Sudan in January 2011, the South Sudan Government viewed IGAD as a friendly and caring organisation. The admission of South Sudan into the regional bloc validates the proximity of South Sudan with IGAD member states and the citizens of the IGAD countries, elucidating further cordial relations. However, with the 15th December 2013 political ignominy and the military government troops being overwhelmed by the rebels, known best as Sudan Peoples' Liberation Army in Opposition (SPLA/IO), the South Sudanese Government swiftly invited the Ugandan People Defence Forces (UPDF). The arrival of UPDF and their participation in the repulsion of the rebel militias confirmed IGAD as a true friend of South Sudan. To be sure, President Salva Kiir admitted to President Yoweri Museveni during the 3rd anniversary of independence, 9th July 2014, that "*Uganda is a friend indeed and that without your*

---

294   Vienna Convention on the Law of Treaties, concluded at Vienna on 23 May 1969 (United Nations Treaty Series vol. 1155, no. 18232), Article 31(1), https://treaties.un.org/doc/Publication/UNTS/Volume%201155/volume- 1155-I-18232-English.pdf (Accessed 18th January 2028)
295   Ibid

intervention (Museveni), my government would have gone [sic] and I sincerely thank you for this".[296]

IGAD as a Cruel Enemy

Far from being a friend indeed, IGAD has been considered as an enemy of South Sudan. While the Republic of South Sudan is the eighth member of the regional organisation, the Government of South Sudan (GRSS) views IGAD as an enemy that is working towards a regime change in the nascent state. It makes it more perturbing for the government when the IGAD mediation was expanded to include the United States, the United Kingdom and Norway known famously as "Trioka". The Government of South Sudan thinks that western countries are yearning for a regime change in its nation. This view has been held for a very long time by the GRSS. The vendetta is like hitting the silhouette of one's shade.

Suspicion, blame games and tensions between the GRSS and the U.S have continued to rise badly. In 2014, the protection guards of Vice President James Wani Igga fired two shots at the convoy of the U.S. Embassy, the then chargé d'affaires at the Buluk roundabout in Juba. Fortunately, no one was hurt given that the car was bulletproof.[297] While the government denied the intention of harm against the chargé d'affaires, the GRSS did not report on the incident until 5 months later. Nevertheless, none of the perpetrators were arrested in connection to the broad daylight incident. Despite

---

296   President Kiir's Speech during the 3rd anniversary of Independence, 9th July 2014 at Dr. John Garang's Mausoleum.
297   See https://radiotamazuj.org/en/article/us-embassy-vehicle-shot-thursday-night-juba (Accessed on 5th May, 2021)

this ugly incident, the U.S. continued supporting IGAD mediation efforts in South Sudanese political predicaments.

In that regard, the IGAD's Head-of-States and Government meeting in Kigali (the capital of Rwanda) came to the conclusion to send regional troops to South Sudan to help protect civilians and vital installations. This final resolution of IGAD Head-of-States and Governments reiterated the IGAD 56th extraordinary session of council of ministers in South Sudan held on the 11th July in Nairobi (capital of Kenya). Nonetheless, the GRSS argues that it had been let down by the IGAD and felt like an isolated member.[298]

In addition the National Minister of Information, Michael Makuei, accused the IGAD state members for supporting military intervention in South Sudan. He argued that the IGAD had been supporting Dr. Riek Machar whom they contacted daily.[299] He warned that South Sudan was also capable of supporting proxy rebellions in IGAD state members and cause havoc.[300] He above all indicated that all other IGAD state members have their problems and do have their own rebels too, not just South Sudan.[301] I hereby below analyse a few IGAD members' states on their roles in the conflict of South Sudan.

The Federal Democratic Republic of Ethiopia

Ethiopia is an important player in regional politics, as it has military power and can be stabilising thanks to its potential destabilising

---

298   Senior Presidential Advisor, Nhial Deng Nhial's press statement after Kigali's meeting.
299   See https://www.facebook.com/baak.wol/videos/10154012170209081/ Michael Makuei Lueth's interview with SSBC, evening news, 3rd August 2016
300   Ibid.
301   Ibid.

factor. The country has long historical ties with SPLM/A and links through shared border communities (the Nuer–Nuer in Gambella relationship) as well as it hosts South Sudanese refugees. Not only did Ethiopia host the negotiations on the South Sudanese political crisis, it remains a key player given its hegemonic drive including being the immediate former Chair of IGAD; a position it had held from 2006-2019. In the same vein, it chaired the IGAD Monitoring and Mechanism (MVM) and the UN Mission in Abyei (UNISFA) in the country. The late Ambassador Seyoum Mesfin, the chair of the three Special envoys was an Ethiopian and Tedros Adhanhom, the country's former foreign Minister, was on the IGAD fact-finding mission that visited Juba immediately after the breakout of violence in 2013.

The country too has security interests as well as economic and strategic interests in South Sudan that relates partly to the power generation from the Grand Ethiopian Renaissance Dam (GERD), which is 40km from the border. Moreover, the nexus between Ethiopia, Eritrea and the question of Islamic extremists infiltrating the region will remain of interest not only to Ethiopia but also to the IGAD and western countries and will be a key player in the fight against terror.[302]

The venue of the South Sudanese peace talks was Addis Ababa, and any attempt to relocate it sent the wrong signals and would lead to regional frictions, unless elites members of the Ethiopian Government stepped down voluntarily and the country's highest

---

302   Tekele Tesfaye, 2015. Ethiopia Relations with Greater Horn of Africa Countries (London, Axum Publishers), 23

authority bored no pressure to change the venue.[303] However, the country must deal with the growing perception that it supported Riek Machar and should make sure that the process is not only seen as Ethiopian-led but an IGAD-led one by encouraging a consensus amongst the parties through reassuring statements. There are numerous investments by Ethiopians in South Sudan particularly in the hospitality sector. But unless Ethiopia delinks itself from any perceived supports to SPLA-IO, its neutrality in the mediation process remained a major issue. While Ethiopia seems to have cordial relationships with the GRSS, its efforts in formation of the South Sudanese state are yet to be seen. One of the major grievances of Addis Ababa against Juba is the close relationship between Juba and Cairo, a move that Ethiopia detests given the zero-sum power game over the Grand Ethiopian Renaissance Dam (GERD) has with Egypt. This has remained a boiling and volatile subject in hydropolitics in the Horn of Africa. Thus, as a founding member and former immediate chair of IGAD, Ethiopia has never been impartial in the resolution of South Sudanese conflicts.

The Republic of Sudan

Some regard Sudan as the 'mother' of all the problems relating to the independence of South Sudan. It has been alleged that since the independence of the country, Sudan had endeavoured to ensure South Sudan is in a state of perpetual instability to demonstrate that it cannot govern itself. Since the outbreak of violence

---

303   Juba/Nairobi, March 11, 2015 (SSNA) The Government of the South Sudan has called on IGAD to move future peace negotiations out of Ethiopia, claiming that the peace process in the Ethiopian capital, Addis Ababa, have been sabotaged by countries unfriendly to Juba.

in South Sudan, President Al-Bashir has visited Juba in what some analysts have described as a ritual rather than substance. With the vast knowledge of the country, Sudan has the potential to play both a positive and a negative role as a member of the IGAD. Being the current Chair of IGAD with a new transformative revolutionary government, Sudan has a strategic influence in shaping the role of the IGAD in South Sudanese conflicts.

The country has military expertise and military resilience but also has a great economic interest related to the flow of oil, for it hosts the infrastructure and the Abyei issue amongst other outstanding post referendum issues. The country has genuine political and security interests that relate to the un-demarcated border and the proxy wars involving the various opposition-armed groups in both South Sudan and Sudan. Although Amb. Gen. Mohammed Dhabi was one of the special envoys as well as a third mediator in the IGAD led peace process, Sudan once hosted and directly supported the rebels of Riek Machar, particularly, under the former President Al-Bashir's regime. Empirical evidence showcased that the SPLA-IO militias were trained, armed and provided logistics to dislodge the government of the Republic of South Sudan by the Republic of Sudan.[304]

This is of course contingent to links between and amongst other political groupings of the National Congress Party, LRA, M23 and the Sudanese Revolutionary Opposition Force in Sudan. In a nutshell, Sudan has unfinished business with South Sudan emanating from the CPA and ironically it now hosts numerous refugees

---

304   See, Sudan a Partial Mediator www.sudantribune.comhml (Accessed on 18th January 2021)

and IDPs. On several occasions South Sudan officials have called for the expulsion of Khartoum from future peace talks claiming that the South Sudanese rebels are being trained, armed, and controlled by Khartoum.[305] Hence, Sudan, a member of the IGAD did not contribute in the formation of the South Sudanese State but rather on its failure. However, with the ushering of the new regime under the leadership of the revolutionary sovereign council led by Abdel Fattah Al-Burhan and Prime Minister Abdalla Hamdok, the relationships between Sudan and South Sudan improved greatly. South Sudan has been mediating the Sudanese peace talks in Juba, bringing all the ousted rebels groups together. The first phase of the Sudanese peace talks was signed in Juba and the second and final phase involving the missing groups have been mediated and signed.

The African Union in South Sudan's State Formation and Failure

The African Union has attempted to form the South Sudanese State as far as the resolution of political conflicts is concerned. However, this effort has been passed in a mute manner. The continental body established its mission in South Sudan in 2011 immediately after South Sudan's independence to help mirror the nascent state amongst the other 53 state members. In deepening its relations, South Sudan joined the AU on 27th September 2011, making it the 54th state member. The AU has tried to help in South

---

305   The South Sudan's Deputy Ambassador to Kenya, James P. Morgan, claimed in an interview with Kenyan-based Nation Newspaper that South Sudanese rebels are being trained, armed, and controlled by Khartoum. The diplomat also called for its expulsion from the East African regional bloc, IGAD mediation team.

Sudan's state formation, particularly, on the area of peace and security as well as mediation.[306]

The AU's Response to South Sudan's Political Crisis

On the onset of the 15th December 2013 political crisis in South Sudan, the AU dispatched members of the Peace and Security Council (PSC) to undertake fact checking and verification of the conflicting situation. The team visited Juba and met various stakeholders, both governmental and non-governmental. The fact-checking team returned to Addis Ababa with an assessment report detailing the situation of the political violence in South Sudan. It is the information from that report that made the AU Council of Ministers meet in Addis Ababa to draw out a road map on the resolution of the conflicts before the Head-of-States and Governments summit. The Head-of-States and Governments met on the 30th January 2014 and approved the AU Commission of Inquiry into South Sudan's political ignominy.

Chaired by the former President of Nigeria, Olusegun Obasanjo, the Commission of Inquiry of South Sudan (AUCISS) was established with the following mandate:[307]

a. To investigate the human rights violations and other abuses committed during the armed conflict in South Sudan;

b. To investigate the causes underlying the violations;

c. To make recommendations on the best ways and means to

306   Andrew Leki. 2016. African Union and Conflict in South Sudan (Nairobi, Panguin Publishers), 7

307   See African Union Commission of Inquiry on South Sudan Report, 2015, 2 http://www.peaceau.org/en/article/final-report-of-the-african-union-commission-of-inquiry-on-south-sudan (Accessed on 19th January 2118)

ensure accountability, reconciliation and healing amongst all South Sudanese communities with a view to deter and prevent the occurrence of the violations in the future;

d. To make recommendations on how to move the country forward in terms of unity, cooperation and sustainable development; and

e. To submit a report within a maximum period of three (3) months.

The AUCISS carried out their mandate and compiled their report with the following recommendations:[308]

a. Comprehensive reforms across all the institutions for the Government of South Sudan;

b. Justice through a hybrid court for South Sudan;

c. Reconciliations, healings and restitutions of the South Sudanese communities;

d. In view of the expressed desire to consider systems of government cited by respondents such as the United States, Canada, Nigeria and Kenya, the Commission recommends that these systems should be studied, and the best elements that suit the context of South Sudan adopted, taking into consideration the 'best practice' relating to issues considered. Political actors and drafters should resist the temptation to import 'models' deemed to have worked elsewhere without due consideration being given to context. It should however be noted that the scope and extent of the devolution of

---

308   See AUCISS Report 2015, 4 http://www.peaceau.org/uploads/auciss.final.report.pdf (Accessed on 19th January 2018).

executive, legislative and judicial function determines the nature of the federated state.

However, the conundrum is that the AU failed to enforce these recommendations. None of the reforms had been achieved, including the famous 'hybrid court' as stipulated in both AUCISS and R-ARCSS. While the R-TGONU accepted to begin the process of the 'hybrid court', the process is still very slow. The AU participated and supported the IGAD mediation with the High Representative Alpha Konera and Mission in South Sudan. However, the continental body had not helped in the full resolution of South Sudanese political debacles. It has continued with shuttle and public diplomacy and this has not formed the South Sudan State into prosperity.

The African Union Agenda 2063 and Its Critiques

The African Union Agenda 2063, famously dubbed as "*Africa We Want*", is a watershed vision of Africa's tomorrow. It is based on aspirations and hopes as follows:

1. A prosperous Africa based on inclusive growth and sustainable development;

2. An integrated continent, politically united and based on the ideals of Pan-Africanism and the vision of Africa's Renaissance;

3. An Africa of good governance, democracy, respect for human rights, justice and the rule-of-law;

4. A peaceful and secure Africa;

5. An Africa with a strong cultural identity, common heritage, shared values and ethics;

6. An Africa whose development is people-driven, relying on the potential of African people, especially its women and youth, and caring for children; and

7. Africa as a strong, united and influential global player and partner

Hence, Agenda 2063 is an endogenous plan for transformation. It harnesses the continent's comparative advantages such as its people, history and cultures; its natural resources; its position and repositioning in the world to effect equitable and people-centred social, economic and technological transformation and the eradication of poverty. It seeks to fulfil our obligation to African children as an inter-generational compact, to develop Africa's human capital; build social assets, infrastructure and public goods; empower women and youth; promote lasting peace and security; build effective developmental states and participatory and accountable institutions of governance. It is the African's vision and roadmap for sequencing our sectoral and normative, national, regional and continental plans into a coherent whole. It is a call to action to all Africans and people of African descent, to take personal responsibility for the destiny of the continent and as the primary agents of change and transformation. It is indeed a commitment from citizens, leadership, governments and institutions at national, regional and continental levels to act, coordinate, and cooperate for the realisation of this vision.

Critiques of The AU Agenda 2063

While most social scientists neglected the empirical shortcomings of the AU Agenda 2063, it is fitting that this must be unpacked to assess the realistic nature of the continental agenda. Though the AU Agenda 2063 is a very ambitious document, there is no doubt that if the African Union implement it as is, it is likely to create an economically, socially and politically advanced Africa. However, the Agenda does not adequately address some fundamental conditions that would facilitate, or impede, its realisation. These flaws are discussed below in four-fold:

The first fundamental flaw of the Agenda 2063 is that it does not place or situate African agency as the primary force or endogenous propellant of Africa's development. In this context, African agency is the absolute psycho-cultural grounding and ideological ownership of this African Agenda, devoid of compromises to any external imperatives.

African agency is grounded on the supremacy of African endocentric thought and motive forces as the propellants of development as a self-directed imperative. Without African's internalisation of this need and their assumption as a self-directed imperative, as well as lack of complete responsibility for self-actuated development, the African societies that would be produced by Agenda 2063 will remain dependent and insecure. But, in fact, the Agenda does not address or even recognise the absolute necessity for any successful African-actuated processes of transformation. The document and its producers do not seem to be aware that the major missing link in Africa's development since independence in the 1960s has been the marginalisation, diminutions and de-activation of African agency in African development. However, without the unquestioned ascendancy, centrality and directive role of African agency, African development understood as Africans self-equipment for radical transformation can never occur.

The second flaw is that the Agenda does not directly address aspects of contemporary globalisation that represents ideological and developmental constraints on Africa's participation from strength and power in this illiberal and unequal globalised system. Without question, this currently ascendant imperious Western ideology and system of globalisation, which dictates that all countries and peoples adopt capitalism and Western Liberal democracy, presents profound challenges to the possibility of Africa's autonomous self-propulsion and the promotion of its prosperity, power and participation in this new global system. If Africa is not simply going to be just a cipher, an onlooker, a cog in the wheel and a helpless and hapless disadvantaged participant in a constraining global system that disempowers and diminishes it, the current globalisation system has to be radically changed. To do this, Africa has to self-consciously create a new continental ideology and strategy of African development capacitation that equips, promotes and ensures its powerful participation in a new truly plurali-versal globalised world of autonomous but mutually interdependent national, regional and continental entities that all subscribe to and practice the principles of equitable participation.

However, in the history of human experience, freedom, respect, equity, dignity and successful development are never freely given or willingly conceded by dominators. They are won and imposed on the world by the free-peoples. Consequently, Africa can only accomplish this new world order of pluri-versal globalism through its determined ideological, political and technological self-empowerment for autonomous self-propulsion and defence against established and would-be dominators of Africa.

The third fundamental flaw of Agenda 2063 is that it does not adequately address some critical aspects of the ideological and political environment of contemporary Africa that are extremely hostile and that will make the realisation of its objectives difficult and, in fact, impossible to achieve if they are not addressed and resolved. This refers to the nature and conditions of contemporary African states. Today, it can be unequivocally affirmed that most African states are disabled states and are no longer full sovereign entities. They are neo-colonial states, or political and administrative contraptions, responsible not to their citizens but to the so-called international community through their subordination to the dictums of the multilateral imperialist agencies; the World Bank, IMF and other multinational companies. These agencies are today directly involved as dictators in African states' decision-making, policy conception and choices, programme funding, execution and above all lords of poverty.[309]

Consequently, African states today are severely constrained and are no longer full sovereignties exercising untrammelled sovereignty of nation-states. In these circumstances, as recolonised, constrained and disabled state systems tormented by deep ethnic divisions and conflict violence, they are incapable of seriously executing any transformational programmes such as Agenda 2063.

---

309   Graham Hancock. Lords of Poverty: The Power, Prestige, and Corruption of the International Aid Business. (New York Publishers, 1992), 14

As is well known, in the 1980's, the multilateral agencies undertook the systematic attack on and subversion of the Lagos Plan of Action with the Berg Report and through the imposition of the Structural Adjustment Programmes (SAPS). They destroyed African economies and disempowered African states.

Consequently, it should be expected that this new-colonial concert of imperialist globalisation would vigorously oppose and fight any efforts of their African Client states to re-assert their full sovereignty to autonomously make policies and development choices that would diminish and terminate the oppressive roles of these neo-colonial agencies. The case of Western military intervention in Libya is a case in point. Instead of sticking to the UNSC Resolution of 1973 that required 'the protection of civilians', the Resolution was expanded to include the removal of Muammar Gaddafi from power.[310] While countries such as China, Russia, Brazil, India and Germany decided to be absent from vetoing the Resolution, Gabon, Nigeria and South Africa joined the Western prepared dance floor to the downfall of Libya and its leader Muammar Gaddafi. Only a liberated African leadership and a liberated African state can achieve the objectives of Agenda 2063.

The fourth and final flaw is that the Agenda does not adequately address the nature, current structure and operations of African economies as exocentric systems that have no capacity to promote minimum development. This current neo-colonial economic system yields an Africa that is developmentally incapacitated, dependent, poverty generating and substantively disempowered.

---

310   Samuel Brockmeier, et al. The Impact of the Libya Intervention: Debates on Norms of Protections. (Taylor Francis Publication, 2016), 8

Unless this current non-developmental economic system is totally uprooted, destroyed and replaced with a new endocentric economic system that is based on African development capacitation, resource-based industrialisation and domestic prosperity, the next generation of Africa cannot achieve the objectives of Agenda 2063.

The leadership conundrums continued to affect the achievement of Agenda 2063; some of the African leaders continued to adhere to the constitutional provisions of their electoral term limits while others abrogate the constitutional term limits. The overall quality of leadership to frog-march the Agenda 2063 is still a great desire. A majority of African leaders are corrupt, nepotistic, incompetent and visionless and thus if they have not achieved their country's visions, how unrealistic is it to think that they will achieve a continental vision? While their country's visions are within their powers and control, the continental Agenda 2063 is a multilateral affair and thus would be very difficult to be achieved by already failed African leaders.

Overall, the biggest critique of the Agenda 2063 lies in what ought to be one of the pillars of the entire vision: funding. The document is pretty vague on the question of how to finance a project of this magnitude with a long list of plans and numerous continental challenges. Some of the financing mechanisms mentioned are the African infrastructural development fund, the Agenda 2063 implementation tax, the home linked solidarity fund (Diaspora) and the adaptation of public–private financing models and funds from African capital markets and financial institutions. It also rightly asserts that Africa must diversify its sources of funding and that donor funding should be tied to Africa's interest instead of donor's interest. Without adequate financing, the continental Agenda will remain as a paper forever. Africa must therefore put its house in order first and rise to the occasion. With the inherent conundrums of the African Union on its Agenda 2063, these conundrums have already been demonstrated in allowing the failing of the South Sudanese State.

Role of Trioka (US, UK And Norway) in South Sudanese State Formation and Failure

Trioka countries have played a great role in the state formation of South Sudan. This role began during the struggle for liberation of South Sudan. The US, the UK and Norway for example, supported the SPLM/A during the liberations epochs.

The United States contributions to South Sudan are enormous and speak volumes, and thus cannot be written in a few pages. Everyone including the starters believes that the independence of South Sudan was a sheer effort of the American people.

This commenced a long time ago with the US congress' enactment of the Sudan Self Determination Act in 1993, the Sudan Peace Act in 2002 and with massive support towards the Comprehensive Peace Agreement and the independence.

Realising that an independent South Sudan will be attained one day, the United States Government allowed over 3,000 South Sudanese former Red Armies to reside in America, to be later known as the "lost boys and girls', according to Peter Pan. Such a gesture was an indirect preparation of human resources development for the independent South Sudan.

Moreover, the tri-partisan coalition of the Black Caucus, the

Sudan Caucus and the Jewish Zionist movements campaigned against Khartoum atrocities. Crucially viewed as the peak of American's support for South Sudan, numerous congressmen such as Frank Wolf, Michael Capuano and the late Donald Payne advocated for South Sudan's freedom.

In 1989, Rep. Wolf travelled into the war-ravaged terrain of Southern Sudan to become the first U.S. representative to meet with the head of the Southern Sudanese rebels, the late John Garang.[311]

Payne, a black congressman, followed a few years later, and on his return to Washington pushed for the U.S. House of Representatives to pass a resolution endorsing the right of the Southern Sudanese people to exercise self-determination.[312]

Although these three played leading roles, there were others who also supported the South Sudanese people underground.

"Behind all this was and still is, a small group of people who have been working behind the scenes for almost 20 years to make this independence a success", a senior member of the U.S. government remarked during the proclamation of South Sudan's independence.[313]

Apart from advocacy, the U.S directly supported the SPLM/A through training and logistics for the success of the taxing liberation war. Equally worthy of recognition, the U.S used East African regional influence for the support of South Sudan. A report released by the Congressional Research Service in 2011 lists actions going back to the Clinton era, including the provision of

311   Rebecca, Hamilton. The Monks Who Sold Washington on South Sudan (Special Report, 2011), 7
312   Ibid, 8
313   Ibid, 9

more than $20 million of surplus U.S. military equipment to front-line states of Uganda, Eritrea and Ethiopia, which the report says *"helped reverse military gains made by the Sudanese government"* against the southern rebels.[314]

Additionally, President Barack Obama's personal commitment to South Sudan deepens this support. A few months before the vote for the referendum of South Sudan, Obama's administration sought for Sudan's lifting of sanctions and its removal from a watch list of states that harboured and sponsored terrorists, allowing the referendum of South Sudan to take place as scheduled.

Obama maintained pressure on Sudan and rallied US allies and African countries to press more on President Al-Bashir of Sudan to conduct the referendum on time. This is exhibited in letters he wrote to the nine Presidents of Kenya, Uganda, Ethiopia, Eritrea, Egypt, Libya, Zimbabwe, Malawi and South Africa cajoling them to convince Sudan to conduct the plebiscite on time.

After the independence of South Sudan, the U.S government continued its support to the nascent state in its voyage towards state formation and nation building. The U.S. has so far donated over $1 billion to South Sudan since its independence to assist with reconstruction, capacity building, development and governance programmes.

Moreover, other Trioka countries such as the UK and Norway also played a great role in South Sudan's state formation. For instance, South Sudan held its Humanitarian Conference in Oslo (the capital of Norway) on 19th May 2014, which was hailed as a great success drawing from the donors' coffers up to the tune

---

314   Ibid, 10.

of $600 million USD. The conference was attended by about 50 countries, maintaining the West as the most generous donor.

To shed a little light on this Western Society generosity, the U.S pledged $290 million USD, the EU 140 million Euros, the UK $100 million USD and Norway, the host, with $63 million USD, making the Western pledges to account for 80% of the $600 million USD pledged. Other countries from the West, the East, Asia, the Pacific and the Middle East pledged their share as well. Sudan was the only country from sub-Saharan Africa that responded to the conference by pledging 10,000 tonnes of sorghum that was freely ferried to South Sudan.

Though the humanitarian pledge's response to South Sudan's political crisis fell short by half, the conference demonstrated the global responsibility of rescuing the poor South Sudanese people from the man-made catastrophe and thus helped in state formation.

Since the December 2013 political crisis, some politicians and citizens of South Sudan have been accusing the West, particularly the United States and even the United Nations, to be behind the political fiasco that engulfed the country, which the government termed as a coup d'etat, though that government account has been highly discredited. These individuals have been accusing the Western world, particularly the US, for the regime change in South Sudan.

However, the U.S has not been bothered so much by South Sudan's accusations. It had showcased its commitment by contributing generously in the international humanitarian conference to help the South Sudanese people whom they have been supporting for a very long time. Hilde F. Johnson, despite her humiliations and insults during the onset of December 2013, took courage and sent Toby Lanzer, the UNOCHA Chief of South Sudan, and in turn lobbied her country Norway to host the donor conference and to massively pledge funds as well.

Norway is a very tiny country with a population of 5 million people, but by pledging $63 million USD, Norway has demonstrated a continued special friendship with South Sudan. This special friendship goes back to the dark days where the Norwegian People Aid (NPA), the Norwegian Labour Party (NLP) and Hilde F. Johnson supported the SPLM/A until the signing of the Comprehensive Peace Agreement and consequently the independence of South Sudan.

Even today, the NPA, the NLP, the Norwegian Refugee Council (NRC) and other NGOs from Norway are still helping the people of South Sudan in tandem with state making, nation building and state consolidation.

The UK has continued with its support towards South Sudan's state formation through various aid packages. For instance, the UK is the sole country that supports the young girl's education programme across South Sudan. Moreover, the UK is a great donor that contributes massively to the health pool funds supporting the treatment of malaria, tuberculosis and HIV/AIDS.

On the flipside, the Western World has played a negative role in the shocks and failures of the nascent state. This has been done through the sanctions of the governmental top officials and the oil and gas sector. Sanction of the oil and gas entities has negatively impacted the economy of South Sudan as the technology and cash flows transferred around the world have been halted. Currently, companies in the oil and gas sector cannot make international and regional transfers via USD in their accounts. This has impacted negatively in the growth of this sector. Technology from the U.S, which is a very key ingredient in the success of this sector, cannot be transferred to these companies.

To confound this precarious situation, the U.S through the support of the UK and the UN championed a resolution for an arms embargo on South Sudan. This decision has affected South Sudan in terms of acquiring new arms for its security and its defence of its sovereignty. Thus, the propelling of sanctions and an arms embargo on South Sudan's government has contributed to shocks and failures of the South Sudanese State.

CHAPTER SIX
2015 AND 2018 PEACE AGREEMENTS AND THEIR IMPLEMENTATIONS

The 2015 ARCSS and the Challenges of its Implementations

Signed in August 2015, the Agreement on the Resolution of the Conflict in the Republic of South Sudan (ARCSS) helped in the temporary halting of conflicts. Outlined into eight chapters, the Agreement faltered on the 8th July 2016 due to lapses in chapter two: Permanent Ceasefire and Transitional Security Arrangements. This chapter contained the following topics:

- The Permanent Ceasefire
- The Pre-Transitional Period
- The Transitional Period
- Mechanisms for Security Arrangements
- Strategic Defence and Security Review Board (SDSRB)

ARCSS culminated in the formation of a Transitional Government of National Unity (TGoNU) on the 26th April 2016 with the return of Riek Machar, who had fled Juba following the outbreak of the civil war. However, events on the night of 7th July 2016, less than 48 hours before the celebration of the country's fifth anniversary of independence, were characterised by violent confrontations in Juba between the SPLM/A-IG and SPLM/A-IO and spread to many parts of the city, resulting in the deaths of many soldiers and civilians, the destruction of property and the displacement of people as discussed in chapter four. This quick returned to violence provoked rethinking and reflection on the processes leading to the signing of the ARCSS.

Contextualising the 2015 ARCSS

The civil war that broke out in December 2013 came after South Sudan attained its independence in July 2011 because of an affirmative secession vote in January 2011. The build-up to the civil war can be traced back to the difficult, strained and uneasy political relationship between Kiir and Machar, both in government and within the Sudan People's Liberation Movement (SPLM). During the Comprehensive Peace Agreement (CPA) interim period from 2005 to 2011, the two political leaders were seen working together and supporting the SPLM in April 2010's polls.

Furthermore, factional political struggles within the SPLM became rife in 2013 as South Sudan approached its first general elections after independence, which were scheduled for 2015. Machar, together with Pagan Amum Okiech (the SPLM Secretary-General) and Rebecca Nyandeng de Mabior (a fellow member of the SPLM Political Bureau and widow of the late SPLM leader, Dr. John Garang de Mabior), openly criticised the SPLM chairman and announced that they would contest the presidency against Salva Kiir. The non-cooperative relations between the Office of the President and that of the Vice President, and contestations over skewed constitution and irregular army recruitments in 2013, were also factors in the civil war, which was triggered by disagreements within the presidential guard over alleged orders to disarm Machar-aligned Nuer members from an alleged coup.

The conflict was mediated by the Inter-Governmental Authority on Development (IGAD), an East African regional integration-inspired organisation premised on Chapter VII of the United Nations (UN) Charter, which provides regional initiatives in conflict mediation and resolution. The peace talks commenced on 4th January 2015 in Addis Ababa. They were fraught with missed deadlines, although they eventually delivered the ARCSS in August 2015, and this subsequently resulted in the formation of a TGoNU in April 2016. The TGoNU also included James Wani Igga as the second Vice President of South Sudan, although he is not a signatory to the ARCSS.

Just prior to the signing of ARCSS, the continued fighting in South Sudan had resulted in a deteriorating humanitarian situation in the country. For example, the United Nations (UN) reported that "*South Sudan faced the worst levels of food insecurity in its history*" with "*4.6 million people projected to face severe food insecurity during the months of May-July 2015 and more than 4.1 million people were in critical need of water sanitation and hygiene services*".[315] It is against this background that the ARCSS had been negotiated and signed.

It should not be ignored, however, that President Kiir reluctantly signed the ARCSS with reservations, amidst apparent pressure from the UN Security Council Resolution 2206 (2015) that had

---

315   UNOCHA 'Report on Humanitarian Situation in South Sudan', May 2015, 6

"created a system to impose sanctions" on those engaging in, inter alia, *"actions or policies that have the purpose or effect of expanding or extending the conflict in South Sudan or obstructing reconciliation or peace talks or processes, including breaches of Hostilities Agreement"*.[316]

This is exhibited by the President's statement after signing the deal pointing to the existence of 22 reservations on the text that were to be attached to the agreement as an addendum. However, the U.S out rightly rejected these reservations after signing. Susan Rice, the National Security Advisor argues:

> *"However, we do not recognize [sic] any reservations or addendums to that agreement' ' ... We will work with our international partners to sideline those who stand in the way of peace, drawing upon the full range of our multilateral and bilateral tools."*[317]

With the rejection of reservations to the peace agreement by the U.S, the Government of South Sudan singled out the U.S. as the champion for regime change. This allegation has led to the worsening of relations between the two countries as many ugly incidents dawned on the U.S. Embassy. In May 2016, "unknown gunmen" attacked the U.S. Embassy's residence killing the longest serving security guard. On the 7th of July 2016, a group of SPLA soldiers' shot the U.S. diplomatic car carrying seven diplomats in the capital of Juba, but luckily the diplomats survived given that

---

316   James Werner 'UN Sanctioned South Sudanese Leaders' (Crisis Group, 2015), 8

317   See https://www.theguardian.com/world/2015/aug/27/south-sudan-president-salva-kiir-signs-peace-deal-despite-serious-reservations (Accessed on 5th July 2020)

the car was armoured and bulletproof.[318]

To be sure, the relations between 'Trioka' countries and GRSS got more strained during the genesis of the 2013 conflicts. As argued earlier, the GRSS viewed the western nations, particularly, U.S as an advocate of regime change in South Sudan. President Kiir seemed to be referring to this allegation as he argues:

"This peace was designed in a way that we cannot sign it. It is difficult to implement and I said this from the day I signed it … 'I blamed the international community for pressurizing me to form interim [sic] with a promise of funding it, only to backtrack. Riek Machar returned to Juba on April 26 2016 and took [an] oath of office on the same day. How many days have passed to May 06 [Friday] today? Has anyone heard over media any country pledging to support the peace implementation? No, he said without naming donors that pledged to fund the transitional government'."[319]

He went on to further accuse unnamed countries of holding onto a strategy to oust him from power.

"The regime change policy has not got [sic]. It is still there. There are people who want us out from here and bring in new faces. So, we have to work hard to implement the peace agreement by following the implementation matrices. I think

---

318   See https://radiotamazuj.org/en/article/us-embassy-vehicle-shot-thursday-night-juba (Access on 6th July 2020)
319   See http://www.sudantribune.com/spip.php?article58888 (Accessed on 5th July 2020)

it is possible."[320]

Moreover, the Minister of Information, Michael Makuei, reiterated the regime change phobia as he argues below:

"If they [the UN & the U.S] are talking about sanctioning, indicting the President, indicting Riek Machar and so forth, then definitely this is a very clear plan for a regime change. We are quite aware about that and we will see how far it will succeed. In term of response, we will definitely respond to it; it is not strange for anybody to recommend like that because their target and main objective is the regime change; whatever is done, must be done and geared toward right direction'."[321]

However, with the deadly battle between the bodyguards of President Salva Kiir and 1st Vice President Riek Machar at South Sudan's capital Juba on the 8th, 10th and 11th July 2016 that killed more than 1000 people (the majority being Dr. Riek Machar's guards). The IGAD council of ministers met in Nairobi on 11th July for the 56th extraordinary session on South Sudan. The session demanded, amongst other things, the re-opening of the Juba International Airport to be protected by regional forces and urgent revision of the UNMISS mandate to establish an intervention brigade and increase numbers of troops from the region to, inter

---

320   Ibid.
321   Oyet Alphonse, UN Sanctions on President Kiir is A Regime Change (Juba: The Juba Monitor, Wednesday, January 27, 2016), 2

alia, secure Juba.[322] This resolution sent a wave of trusteeship to the Government of South Sudan making President Kiir's sacked Deputy Minister of Foreign Affairs, Dr. Cirino Hiteng, arguing that he failed to reject the IGAD demands. Dr. Hiteng got nominated as the Deputy Minister on the ticket of the SPLM Former Political Detainees (FPD) in accordance with the ARCSS power sharing formula. His sacking by President Kiir contradicted the peace deal. But it is imperative to note that President Kiir's swift action was influenced by the cowardice thinking that the IGAD was slowly taking over South Sudan to manage it as a trustee. President Kiir revealed this to the Aljazeera reporter Peter Dobbie on 12th July 2016 by saying "*I am just like a child being ordered by everybody*".[323] This statement was referring to the IGAD's strongly worded communiqué.

Furthermore, President Kiir expressed fears and frustrations on the survivability of the peace agreement after the July 2016 skirmishes:

> "*The problem, that we are not moving smoothly on the implementation of the agreement are the issues with the way the agreement was designed. And when I signed this agreement in August last year, I said this in front of the President [sic] of Uganda. I told him that this agreement was not made to be implementable [sic]. It was wrong. It was wrong because even then — to sign it was the problem. They said that if there is a*

---

322   http://igad.int/attachments/1388_Final%20Communique%20of%2056th%20 IGAD%20Extra%20Ordinary%20Council%20(1).pdf (Accessed on 12th July 2020).
323   See http://www.chimpreports.com/gen-kiir-im-just-like-a-child-being-ordered-by-everybody/ (Accessed on 12th July 2020).

*wrong sentence in English, don't correct it. Don't put a comma
or a full stop'.*[324]

Amongst others, President Kiir's reservations are related to the following subjects:

1. The scope of the permanent ceasefire and transitional security arrangements;
2. The functions of the Joint Monitoring and Evaluation Commission (JMEC);
3. The amendment procedures for the ARCSS;
4. The transitional justice, accountability, reconciliation and healing mechanisms;
5. The powers and status of the vice presidents in the TGoNU;
6. The structures and composition of state governorships;
7. The power-sharing in the executive;
8. The control of the humanitarian and reconstruction initiatives;
9. The management of resources, the economy and finance; and
10. The timelines for the reconstitution of the Constituent Assembly within the parameters of drafting the permanent constitution.

President Kiir's statement upon the signing of the ARCSS should have sent warning signals to the mediators in Addis Ababa and stakeholders in the South Sudanese peace process about the level of commitment in the future implementation of the agreement. Kiir stated:

---

324   Ibid

"With all those reservations that we have, we will sign this [ARCSS] document … some features of the document are not in the interest of just and lasting peace. We had only one of the two options, the option of an imposed peace or the option of a continued war'.'

Further, whilst assuring the South Sudanese people that he had *"fully committed the government to the faithful implementation"* of the ARCSS, Kiir declared in his public statement to the nation regarding the ARCSS on 15ᵗʰ September 2015:

'This IGAD prescribed peace document on the [Agreed] Resolution of the Conflict in the Republic of South Sudan, is the most divisive and unprecedented peace deal ever seen in the history of our country and the African continent at large … this agreement has also attacked the sovereignty of our country … there were many messages of intimidations and threats for me in the last few weeks, to just sign the Agreement silently without any changes or reservations … there is no doubt in my mind that the implementation of some of the provisions of the Agreement will be confronted by practical difficulties that will make it inevitable to review or amend such provisions.'

This statement, when scrutinised thoroughly, would lead one to the inescapable conclusion that the events leading to the conclusion of the ARCSS may have largely undermined the ownership, buy-in and commitment of the SPLM/A-IG and other aligned stakeholders to the South Sudanese peace process. His assurances of "full commitment" may be read as political rhetoric in front of an expectant nation and hopeful regional peace brokers.

What further complicate the peace equation are the perceptions and positions in Riek Machar's political camp. It is instructive to note that even Machar's SPLM/A-IO had its own reservations about the ARCSS:

'We dropped our reservations in favour of peace and [Kiir] should also drop his reservations in favour of peace. If [Kiir] has reservations he should keep them to himself like we kept ours to ourselves.'[325]

In reality, Machar's proposition to Kiir is easier said than done. Whilst the reservations appear to have more to do with competition for power, influence and control by both SPLM/A-IG and SPLM/A-IO, and less to do with how sustainable peace can be secured and how the welfare of the South Sudanese people will be transformed. It would be a disservice to the peace process to ignore the respective positions of these key players in the conflict, especially given their influence on the conflict's dynamics.

Kiir's Reservations: Power Politics, or State Formation?

The 16 reservations held by President Kiir have largely been swept aside by many analysts and those involved in the South Sudanese conflict. The danger is that they quickly forget how this erodes the SPLM/A-IG's political will and ownership of the ARCSS. Even

---

325   See Sudan Tribune: President Kiir and Riek have Reservations on the ARCSS (Accessed on 19th December 2020)

in the ARCSS's preamble, the parties to the agreement were expected to acknowledge *"the need to promote inclusivity and popular ownership of this Agreement"*,[326] to ensure effective implementation.

Two of Kiir's substantive reservations was the scope of the permanent ceasefire and the transitional security arrangements. Article 5.5 of ARCSS provides for the redeployment of military forces in Juba and within a 25km radius from the capital city. Kiir interpreted this as the de facto demilitarisation of Juba, yet according to him, *"the army has the responsibility to protect the nation, its people and leadership,"* which is a *"matter of sovereignty"*; hence, it should remain stationed in the capital. He added that the army *"protected the capital during a failed coup"*. His reservations appeared unreasonable, especially given that the ARCSS Article 5 (5.1) has exceptions on presidential guards; guard forces to protect military barracks, bases and warehouses; and the Joint Integrated Police, which are enough to defend the sovereignty of South Sudan. Kiir's insistence that the army protected the capital during a failed coup in December 2013 was against the spirit of reconciliation. This follows revelations in the African Union's (AU) Final Report of the AU Commission of Inquiry on South Sudan that there was not any available evidence to suggest an attempted coup in South Sudan. Kiir's referenced to the "failed coup" is a signal that mistrust and suspicion would still characterise his working relationship with Machar in the TGoNU.

The SPLM/A-IG also objected to the transition of the monitoring and verification mechanism (MVM), which is responsible for reporting implementation progress of the permanent ceasefire and transitional security arrangements (PCTSA) to the ceasefire

---

326   ARCSS, August 2015, 1

and transitional security arrangement monitoring mechanism (CTSAMM). Kiir objected to the MVM role, arguing that its current performance was unsatisfactory as its reports were based on unofficial information, further suggesting that the MVM transition to CTSAMM should only be based on government approval.

Whilst the over-reliance on unofficial information or statistics in security reporting can be detrimental to peace efforts as such information is often over-exaggerated and manipulated in pursuit of narrow sectional interests, there is no justification to eliminate whatever can be useful and positive. Apparently, the work of CTSAMM would be overseen by a more independent and representative Joint Monitoring and Evaluation Commission (JMEC), as provided under Chapter VII (2.7) of the ARCSS. Hence, any progressive and constructive discussions could have been centred on strengthening the JMEC's capacity to execute its oversight role, instead of contemplating government interference into the transition of MVM. This was potentially destructive, considering the extent of political polarisation occurring in South Sudan.

Kiir also had reservations on the roles and functions of the JMEC, which, according to Chapter VII (3) of the ARCSS, is responsible for the "*monitoring and overseeing [of] the implementation of the Agreement, the mandate and [the] tasks of the TGoNU, including the adherence of the parties to the agreed timelines and implementation schedule*". He objected to the "overseeing" function; according to him, this would make the JMEC "*the governing authority of the Republic of South Sudan*", leaving the government and the national legislature uninvolved. Furthermore, the SPLM–IG commented that the provisions under Chapter VII (5) of the ARCSS, which mandates the

JMEC to report regularly in writing to the TGoNU Council of Ministers, the Transitional National Assembly as well as the IGAD, the AU Commission, the AU Peace and Security Council (PSC) and the UN Security Council (UNSC) on the status of implementation of the Agreement, makes the JMEC *"the actual ruling body in South Sudan"*.

Whilst Kiir's reservations on the JMEC were reasonable, it must be noted that all political parties in South Sudan represented in the JMEC were part of the deliberations. Moreover, Chapter VII (9) clearly provides that the JMEC quorum *"be 18, of which at least 10 of the members shall be from South Sudan and the other 8 from regional and international groups"*. This makes the JMEC's agenda, proceedings and outcomes national and/or regional in outlook, dispelling sovereignty threats and fears. If the government were made to oversee the functions of the JMEC, an institution that the mediators attempted to make independent and impartial with minimum interference from the implementers of the ARCSS, it would be tantamount to have the government (SPLM/A-IG and SPLM/A-IO) monitor and evaluate itself. This would make the JMEC vulnerable and pliant to elite manipulation.

The amendment procedure for the ARCSS, as stipulated under Chapter VIII (Article 4), provides that the agreement can only be amended with at least two-thirds majority from the Council of Ministers and at least two-thirds majority votes from the JMEC. The SPLM-IG strongly objected to this, considering this arrangement as *"effectively neo-colonialism"* and confirming *"the supremacy of the JMEC over the TGoNU and national legislature"*. Here, the SPLM/A-IG's objections might have been motivated by the reality

that unilaterally amending the ARCSS might have been techni-
cally impossible, given that the SPLM/A-IG, just as the SPLM/A-
IO, only had 2 out of the 18 members who made up the JMEC
quorum. The SPLM/A-IG had 16 ministers out of the total of 30
ministers prescribed by Chapter 1 (Article 10) of the ARCSS to
make up the Council of Ministers. The amendment procedure,
involving two well-balanced institutions (in terms of composition
and structure) in the form of the Council of Ministers and the
JMEC, appeared to be appropriate as a check-and-balance mechanism against politically motivated unilateral amendments to the
ARCSS. If there are well thought-out and progressive amendments, there is no doubt that the provided procedures would not
be a stumbling block.

The SPLM-IG also had reservations on the Compensation and
Reparation Authority (CRA) provided under Chapter 5 (4), whose
role was to manage the Compensation and Reparation Fund for
the compensation and reparation of crime victims. He argued that
this would be prone to abuse and that instead, the funds should
be channelled to "*the reconstruction of the infrastructure and rebuilding
of livelihoods of communities in the states most affected by the conflict*".
The SPLM-IG cited impracticalities of the same model in Sierra
Leone, South Africa, Liberia and Rwanda. SPLM-IG fears were
understandably justified, given the sensitivities and complexities
that are associated with any national healing and transitional justice
mechanism. It requires much caution. However, the mere fact that
a policy initiative failed elsewhere is not sufficient to justify policy
dismissal. Circumstances and contexts differ. In fact, the cited cases
of Sierra Leone, South Africa, Liberia and Rwanda should present

a golden opportunity for South Sudan to draw lessons and develop a unique model that can be successful. The success of such initiatives is largely dependent upon the political will of the leadership.

Moreover, the idea to compensate victims of war atrocities appeared progressive in light of international law obligations derived from declarations, such as the Declaration of Basic Principles of Justice for Victims of Crime and Abuse of Power (1985); the Convention against Torture and other Cruel, Inhuman or Degrading Treatment or Punishment (1984); and the Convention on the Prevention and Punishment of the Crime of Genocide (1948). This would assist in building the legitimacy of the newest state within the international community. Nevertheless, SPLM-IG's prioritisation of infrastructure reconstruction and rebuilding the livelihoods of the South Sudanese people should have been welcomed, unless it was being used as a diversionary tactic to underplay and discount the merits of the compensation and reparation scheme. Generally, compensation and reparation would have been seriously considered as essential elements of transitional justice, national healing and reconciliation, and key aspects in any post-conflict situation.

There was also a reserved voice about having two vice presidents with different statuses. Kiir preferred having two vice presidents with equal status, arguing that having a first vice president and a second vice president would be *"a reward for rebellion"* and *"a humiliation to the second vice president and his constituency and has the potential to cause more problems in the entire South Sudan.'*[327] Other

---

327   See Sudan Tribune: President Kiir and Riek have Reservations on the ARCSS (Accessed on 19th December 2020)

opposition factions objected to the power-sharing ratios proposed for the State Council of Ministers in Unity, such as the Jonglei and Upper Nile states, as well as the nomination of governors from Kiir's Government of the Republic of South Sudan (GRSS). These factions include Machar's South Sudan Armed Opposition (SSAO), Amum's Former Detainees (FDs) and other political parties, which were collectively referred to as "rebels" by Kiir in his reservations. Kiir's continued use of the term "rebels" in reference to individuals who would be his partners in government may be interpreted as being against the spirit of accommodation and reconciliation, and this attitude may create sour relations within the TGoNU.

Whether Kiir's/SPLM-IG's reservations were reasonable and valid, only mediation dialogue and further engagement could have established them. Such a dialogue would assist to discern reservations motivated by the desire to gain and retain power, from substantive and genuine reservations driven by nationalist desires to protect the "sovereignty and territorial integrity" of South Sudan, as claimed by President Kiir.

The Status of The Implementation of the ARCSS

Since the signing of the ARCSS, there have been calls from both the regional and international community questioning the slow pace at which the peace deal was being implemented. There was lack of implementation progress and a violation of prior agreements, notably the Cessation of Hostilities (CoH) Agreement, signed on the 23rd January 2014; the Agreement to Resolve the Crisis in South Sudan on the 9th May 2014; and the Areas of Agreement on the Establishment of the Transitional Government of National Unity in the Republic of South Sudan, signed on the 1st February 2015.

In terms of the implementation progress, the leaders in South Sudan did not move as fast as expected when their progress was measured against the milestones stipulated in the ARCSS. The leaders in Juba should be credited for managing to form the TGoNU, as well as constituting the Council of Ministers in April 2016, as provided in the ARCSS. They started establishing the necessary institutions of governance provided in the ARCSS. However, the implementation of other provisions of the ARCSS has been very slow.

There was lack of progress on the formation of the Transitional National Legislative Assembly (TNLA) through the expansion of the existing 300-member National Legislative Assembly by an additional 68 members, 50 members were from the SSAO, one member from the FDs and 17 members from other political parties, as provided for under Chapter 1 (11) of the ARCSS. The JMEC also reported that there were disagreements in the selection of the speaker of the TNLA, a lack of a consensus over the appointment of any presidential advisors and a lack of movement with regard to reviewing the 28th and 32nd states. The 28th and 32nd states were unilaterally created by President Kiir after he dissolved the 10 regional states in South Sudan through the issuance of Order 6/2015 on the 2nd October 2015, with the aim of *"devolving power and bringing resources closer to the people, reducing government expenditure and promoting development"*. However, the decision to create more states was criticised as a veiled attempt by the SPLM/A-IG *"to grab other communities' land in Upper Nile and Bahr el Ghazal and annex them to the Dinka lands".[328]*

The CTSAMM, with the mandate provided for under Chapter II (4) of the ARCSS of monitoring compliance and reporting to the JMEC on the implementation progress of the PCTSA, is reported to be facing restrictions in doing its work while humanitarian deliveries were reportedly being obstructed in Western Equatoria and Northern Bahr el Ghazal. In addition, there were reports that the CTSAMM monitoring and verification teams in areas such as Yambio, Torit and Juba were being intimidated and restricted in terms of carrying out their operations, with some local authorities demanding to see presidential authority before any access was granted.

The government departments and offices within the TGoNU appeared to be disjointed and lacked collaboration. Of course, this is one of the serious challenges any government of national unity faces as interparty trust, consultation, communication, cooperation, dialogue and consensus are difficult to forge. For example, Machar and Igga issued a joint press statement on the 1st June 2016 saying to the effect that the South Sudan presidency, comprising Kiir, Machar and Igga, had agreed to review the 28 states of South Sudan through a 15-member committee, constituted by 10 South Sudanese and 5 representatives from international partners. However, on the 3rd June 2016, Tor Deng Mawien, a senior presidential advisor to Kiir on decentralisation and intergovernmental linkages, dismissed the press statement whilst denying that the consensus had been reached to review the 28 states. Such actions

---

328   Richard Modi '28 States in South Sudan and Dinka Domination' (Blackstone Publishers, Kampala, 2018), 9.

affected the continued effective implementation of the ARCSS.

The slow implementation of the ARCSS was also evidenced by the delays in the formation and reconstitution of transitional institutions and mechanisms, as provided under Chapter 1 (14.1) of the agreement and including, inter alia, the Peace Commission (PC); Relief and Rehabilitation Commission (RRC); Refugees Commission (RC) and other institutions such as the Commission for Truth, Reconciliation and Healing (CTRH); the Hybrid Court for South Sudan (HCSS); the CRA; and the Board of the Special Reconstruction Fund (BSRF). All these were not established, yet most were supposed to be in place within the first month of the TGoNU as provided in the ARCSS.

With respect to the National Architecture and Joint Military Ceasefire Commission (JMCC), the JMEC has also reported that the JMCC, whose mandate under Chapter 1 (3.3) was to oversee and coordinate forces in cantonments and barracks, was not fully operational as its chair was distracted by other commitments. In addition, the Strategic Defence and Security Review Board (SDSRB) was not carrying out its work, as it was failing to reach a quorum with other security institutions such as the Joint Integrated Police (JIP), the Joint Operations Centre (JOC) and the Joint Military Ceasefire Team (JMCT). The SDSRB was also failing to perform its functions due to a shortage of working space, lack of transport and communication essentials. However, Festus Mogae, the then chair of the JMEC, dismissed the explanation that these institutions were failing to operate due to funding shortages, arguing that there was no political will.

Mogae also noted that the JMCC's failure to meet and work

as a team *"impeded the integration of forces"*, resulting in widespread violence committed by members of the Shilluk and Dinka communities in Malakal, which culminated in 18 deaths and 50 injured people, as reported in February 2016. Again, in March 2016, there was reported violence in Western Equatoria, Central Equatoria, Western Bahr el Ghazal, Malakal and the Upper Nile states. The UN Secretary-General Ban Ki-moon expressed his concern over the fighting between the SPLM/A-IG and SPLM/A-IO in Juba, Wau and Bentiu, as well as reported attacks on the UN and humanitarian operations.

Due to the reported violence and hostilities in most parts of South Sudan, in March 2016 Ban Ki-moon urged the warring parties to *"rebuild mutual trust and confidence from the people and the international community to set the country on a path to stability"*. He further implored the South Sudanese leaders to *"put peace above politics"* through compromise to bring stability.

More importantly, Ban Ki-moon made remarks at the IGAD Extra-Ordinary Summit in Kigali, Rwanda on the 16th July 2016, after reports of renewed fighting in Juba, attacks at the UN compounds and the pillaging of the UN humanitarian food stocks:

> *'We are all appalled by the magnitude of the violence, the indiscriminate attacks on civilians and peacekeepers, and the immense loss of lives and suffering this crisis has inflicted on the people of South Sudan. The renewed fighting is horrendous and totally unacceptable'.*[329]

329   James Kariere 'Renewed Catastrophic Violence in South Sudan' (East African Newspaper, 2016, Vol.54), 2

At the AU Summit in Kigali on the 13th July 2016, the AU's outgoing chairperson, Nkosazana Dlamini-Zuma, also condemned the fighting in Juba:

> *'During the implementation of the ARCSS, we saw the resurgence of the conflict in South Sudan, after more than two years of talks. Hardly two months after the formation of the Government of National Unity, the belligerents seem to be back in the trenches, and the people of South Sudan, instead of celebrating five years of independence, once again are barricaded in their homes or must flee like sheep before the wolves.'*[330]

The slow progress recorded in implementing the ARCSS is one of the main causes of this return to violence of 8th July 2016. Political will has also been singled out by the JMEC as one of the key factors behind this limited implementation progress. The fact that key signatories to the peace deal, specifically Kiir, signed the peace pact with many reservations obviously has a bearing on his will and commitment to the agreement. This, however, does not in any way downplay the other factors contributing to the limited progress in implementing the ARCSS, notably the struggle for power and control between SPLM/A-IG and SPLM/A-IO leaders Kiir and Machar; the exclusion of other stakeholders to the conflict in the ARCSS negotiation process; and nation-building complexities that naturally face the South Sudanese, as the state is still in its formative stages with very little institutional infrastructure to anchor governance and other systems. With the failure of the

---

330   Ibid, 3

2015 ARCSS, the Revitalised Agreement on the Resolution of the Conflict in the Republic of South Sudan (R-ARCSS) was signed on the 12th September 2018, signalling hope for South Sudan.

The 2018 R-ARCSS and the Conundrums of its Implementation

On September 12th 2018, The South Sudanese President Salva Kiir and Vice President turned rebel leader Riek Machar signed a renewed peace agreement to end the 5-year-long civil war in South Sudan. The agreement, dubbed as the Revitalised Agreement on the Resolution of the Conflict in the Republic of South Sudan (R-ARCSS), borrowed heavily from a previous agreement signed by both leaders gives hope for South Sudan. The Agreement has eight chapters as follows:

- Chapter I: Revitalised Transitional Government of National Unity (R-TGoNU)
- Chapter II: Permanent Ceasefire and Transitional Security Arrangements
- Chapter III: Humanitarian Assistance and Reconstruction
- Chapter IV: Resource, Economic and Financial Management
- Chapter V: Transitional Justice, Accountability, Reconciliation and Healing
- Chapter VI: Parameters of Permanent Constitution
- Chapter VII: Joint Monitoring and Evaluation Commission (JMEC)
- Chapter VIII: Supremacy of this Agreement and Procedures for Amendment of the Agreement.

Chapter I outlines clearly the pre-transitional and transitional periods. It envisioned an eight month "Pre-Transitional Period," which focused largely on stabilising the security situation in the country. After eight months, the agreement stipulates the beginning of another eight month "Transitional Period," where the country would be led by a united government with Kiir as President and Machar as Vice President. The proposed united government structure was largely similar to the ARCSS signed on August 17th, 2015. Under that agreement, Machar was also to be appointed Vice President. However, the formation of the government was delayed until April 2016 as Machar refused to travel to the capital, Juba, out of fear for his security. Fighting between the two sides broke out in Juba in the summer of 2016. Machar fled the capital, and eventually the country, and widespread violence resumed.

The R-ARCSS Implementation and Associated Hurdles

Under the R-ARCSS timeline, the transitional period began in mid-May 2019 with the appointment of the Revitalised Transitional Government of National Unity (R-TGoNU). The current government, nominally referred to as the Transitional Government of National Unity (TGoNU), was established under ARCSS and does not include SPLM/A-IO leader Riek Machar, who fled the country in 2016. Under the R-ARCSS, the R-TGoNU was appointed in February 2020. The delays of the formation of the R-TGoNU has been attributed to the Covid-19 pandemic and other hurdles, such as a lack of funds to pay salaries, transportation and accommodation for the members of R-TGoNU.

Under this Agreement, Riek Machar was appointed as the

country's 1st Vice President, a position he once held for three months when he was appointed in April 2016 under the ARCSS. The difference between the R-ARCSS and the ARCSS is the appointment of five Vice Presidents: the 1st Vice President Riek Machar from SPLM-IO and in charge of the Governance Cluster, the 2nd Vice President James Wani from SPLM-IG (Incumbent) and in charge of he Economic Cluster, the 3rd Vice President Taban Deng from the SPLM-IO Taban Faction (Incumbent) in charge of the Infrastructure Cluster, the 4th Vice President Hussien Abdelbagi from SSOA in charge of the Service Cluster and the 5th Vice President Rebecca Nyandeng from FDs in charge of the Gender, Humanitarian and Youth Cluster.

After the appointment and swearing-in of the Vice Presidents, 35 Ministers were also appointed based on the equities stipulated in the R-ARCSS. For instance;

- Incumbent TGoNu: 20 Ministries
- SPLM/A-IO: 9 Ministries
- SSOA: 3 Ministries
- FDs: 2 Ministries
- OPP: 1 Ministry

Additionally, 10 Deputy Ministers were allocated and appointed as follows:

- Incumbent TGoNU: 5
- SPLM/A-IO: 3
- SSOA: 1
- OPP: 1

After the formation of the executive branch of the national

government, state governments were also formed based on the ratios in the agreement. However, what has just been done in Chapter I is the formation of the Revitalised Transitional National Legislature, which has both the Transitional National Legislative Assembly and the Council of States. The expanded Transitional National Legislative Assembly has 550 members and shared by the parties as follows:

- Incumbent TGoNU: 332
- SPLM/A-IO: 128
- SSOA: 50
- OPP: 30
- FDs: 10

The Council of States has 100 members, totalling to 650 members in the National Legislature. All members of parliaments including the 10 sates have been appointed.

The first challenge, which is associated with the late formation of the Transitional Legislative Assembly and the Council of States, has been the lack of funds to remunerate the 650 members. However, on the 10th May 2021, President Kiir issued a decree reconstituting the 650 members of parliament. 550 members of the National Legislative and 100 members of the Council of States will constitute the National Legislature. This is the highest number compared to the population of 12 million people. In comparison, the U.S, which has a population of 332 million people, has 535 Members of Congress (100 Senators and 435 Representatives). India, which has a population of 1.35 billion people, has 250 members of parliament (238 members representing states and union territories and 12 members nominated by the President).

The second challenge has been a lack of political will from the parties for the agreement. Other chapters such as Chapter II and so on are being implemented slowly. For instance, Chapter II on Permanent Ceasefire and Transitional Security Arrangement is going at a sluggish speed. The Joint Security Forces (The Police, The Army and Intelligence Services) have not been fully cantoned, trained and passed out. A majority of the members of the armed forces have deserted the cantoned sites, citing a lack of food, medicine and uniforms. The R-GoNU, particularly, and President Kiir told Trioka state members that they could not train and graduate the unified forces due to a lack of weapons, blaming those Trioka countries for supporting an arms embargo against South Sudan.

The parties agreed on the location of the cantonment sites for DDR in February 2019, but it is unlikely that the DDR process will be completed by the deadline due to lack of funds and strategy.

The original DDR implementation timetable, truth be told, was entirely unrealistic. The DDR and the creation of a unified armed force was slated to be fully completed within 30 days, which was never feasible. In peace implementation data, CPAs do not reach full implementation on disarmament, demobilisation, and reintegration provisions until 4-5 years on average. Only one CPA, Bangladesh's 1997 Chittagong Hill Tracts Accord reached full implementation on all three provisions within a year due to the extremely small size of the rebel force. Under the R-ARCSS, two committees were assigned to solve issues involving the number and border demarcation of states in the federal system. The Technical Boundary Committee (TBC) was made up of experts nominated from the Intergovernmental Authority on Development (IGAD), an East African intergovernmental association that mediated the agreement, as well as the UK, the U.S and Norway. The TBC was scheduled to produce a report within 60 days. Based on this completed report, the second committee called the Independent Boundaries Committee (IBC), would make recommendations on state boundaries within 90 days of receiving the report. The TBC issued its report on the 27th of March 2019. However, it was unlikely that the IBC will be able to propose a solution to the boundary issue before May 2019. R-ARCSS has stopgap language stipulating that, if the IBC cannot fulfil its mandate, the number of states will be determined by a referendum. However, the opposition members of the NPTC have already suggested that they would see such a referendum as illegitimate, given that it would be supervised by the incumbent TGoNU.

Therefore, how the signatories deal with the complications of moving to the Transitional Period will determine the long-term trajectory of the R-ARCSS. Under the ARCSS, the transitional government was put in place in April 2016 without any significant progress on the security sector reform and under heightened tensions resulting from President Kiir's unilateral decision on how to divide South Sudan's existing states. This situation proved unsustainable and the peace collapsed by July 2016. The fact that this has happened before certainly highlights the risks associated with another unilateral move to define state boundaries before the unity government is established.

The alternative that delayed the formation of the RTGoNU, as SPLM/A-IO officials suggested, posed its own risks. The

R-ARCSS provides no framework for such a delay, meaning the signatories would have always delayed in the implementation of all the eight chapters. A delay would also leave the current government under Kiir in place without an agreed upon transition, particularly, on the elections, come 2023.

Other chapters have not moved an inch in their implementation. It is Chapter V on Transitional Justice, Accountability, Reconciliation and Healing and Chapter VII on JMEC that have a basic semblance of the implementation. Formation of the Hybrid Court has been accepted in principle by the R-TGoNU and the R-JMEC has been formed. However, the R-ARCSS has been a very ambitious and compacted document. It is the only peace agreement document where the name of God has not been mentioned.

Chapter VI on Parameters of Permanent Constitution begun its implementation by the parties to the R-TGoNu on the 25th May 2021 with the Constitutional Making Process workshop, which was convened by the Reconstituted Joint Monitoring and Evaluation Commission (R-JMEC). President Salva Kiir opened the workshop and the outcome of the workshop based on article 6.9 of the R-ARCSS shall form the basis for drafting the legislation to be enacted to govern the constitution making-process. The outcomes/resolutions of the workshop signed by all parties on the 28th of May 2021 at the Freedom Hall are as follows:

Mechanisms of The Permanent Constitution-Making Process: The Constitutional Drafting Committee (CDC)

1.1. A Constitutional Drafting Committee shall be established as a technical, independent non-political and neutral body to draft the constitutional text under the direction of the key mandated institutions/mechanisms of the permanent constitution-making process, namely the Revitalised National Constitutional Review Commission (R-NCRC) and the National Constitutional Conference (NCC). The CDC shall not have the final decision-making powers over the draft constitutional text and shall not be institutionally attached to any of the institutions/mechanisms of the permanent constitution-making process. It shall act as a body of experts who shall accompany each stage of the constitution-making process, receiving input from mandated institutions/mechanisms and they shall be .

1.2. The CDC shall formulate its rules of procedure and appoint a Senior Legal Drafter and Deputy from amongst the 12 South Sudanese members.

1.3. The CDC may request logistical and administrative assistance from the mandated institutions/mechanisms at each phase of the permanent constitution-making process.

The Composition of The CDC

1.4. The CDC shall be composed of 15 members comprising:

1.4.1 Twelve South Sudanese nationals, consisting of 8 practicing lawyers and 4 non-lawyers (2 political scientists and 2 economists) with relevant academic qualifications and practical experience.

1.4.2 A South Sudanese lawyer who seeks to be appointed as a member to the CDC must possess a law degree from a recognised university and at least 5 years' proven experience in legislative drafting, and constitutional law and/or constitution-making. Of the 4 non-lawyers, 2 shall be qualified political scientists and 2 shall be qualified economists, all of whom shall have at least five years' proven experience in their respective fields.

1.4.3. Three non-South Sudanese legal experts shall be qualified lawyers with the relevant qualifications and at least 1 years' proven experience in legislative drafting, with and constitutional law and/or constitution-making.

1.4.4 At least 35% of the members of the CDC shall be comprised of women who satisfy the relevant professional qualifications and experience for appointment as members of the CDC.

1.4.5 A person shall not be eligible for appointment as a member of the CDC if such a person occupies any of the following positions:

- They are a member of the R-NCRC;
- They are a member of the NCC;
- They are a member of the Legislature; and
- They are a political or constitutional office holder

The Nomination and Recruitment of the CDC Members

1.6 The R-NCRC shall conduct a competitive recruitment process for members of the CDC based on the criteria set out in paragraph 4 above. The R-NCRC shall select the 15 most qualified national candidates and rank them after verifying their academic and professional credentials.

1.7 The R-NCRC shall submit the list of 12 candidates to the

RTGoNU for appointment. The remaining 3 candidates shall be placed on a reserve list to be drawn upon at the first instance, should a vacancy arise during the term of the CDC.

1.8 The three non-South Sudanese legal experts shall be recruited and appointed through the same process.

2. The Reconstituted National Constitutional Review Commission (R-NCRC)

2.1 The Executive of the RTGoNU shall reconstitute the NCRC on the basis of nominations submitted by the parties to the agreement and other stakeholders to the R-ARCSS to the Taskforce of the Ministry of Justice and Constitutional Affairs (Taskforce of the MoJCA).

2.2 The R-NCRC shall facilitate and promote civic education and conduct public consultations in collaboration with non-state actors.

2.3 The R-NCRC shall formulate its rules of procedure.

The Nomination, Appointment and Composition of the R-NCRC

2.4 Nominations for appointment to the R-NCRC shall be submitted by the following groups: RTGoNU, political parties, faith-based groups, women groups, youth, ethnic minorities, representatives of the private sector, CS0 groups, academics, people with special needs and other professions. At least 35% representation of women shall be ensured.

2.5 In nominating candidates for appointment as members of the R-NCRC, the nominating groups shall ensure diversity of relevant qualifications and backgrounds, giving due regard to ethnic and regional diversity, amongst other considerations.

2.6 The nominating groups shall ensure that their nominees possess proven knowledge of and experience in relevant fields, including but not limited to: comparative constitutional law; systems and structures of government; human rights; women and gender issues; land and land law; governance and ethics; electoral systems; South Sudanese customary law and practice; and anthropology.

2.7 The Taskforce of the MoJCA shall consult with the nominating groups on the qualifications of the candidates on their respective lists. Upon the conclusion of the consultations, the Minister of Justice and Constitutional Affairs shall transmit the names of the proposed nominees to the Executive of the RTGoNU for appointment as members of the R-NCRC.

2.8 The composition of the R-NCRC shall reflect, amongst others, the gender, political, social, ethnic, religious and regional diversity of South Sudan in recognition of the need for inclusivity, transparency and equitable participation. Due regard shall be given to the equitable representation of groups mentioned in Article 6.14 of the R- ARCSS, amongst others.

The Size of The R-NCRC

2.9 The R-NCRC shall comprise of 57 members, inclusive of the Chairperson and Deputy Chairperson, who shall be of opposite genders, appointed by the Executive of the R- TGoNU. 45% of the members shall be representatives of the stakeholder groups and 55% shall represent the RTGoNU and political parties.

3. The Preparatory Sub-Committee

3.1 The Executive of the RTGoNU shall appoint the Preparatory Sub-Committee for convening the National Constitutional Conference on the basis of nominations submitted by the parties to the Agreement and other stakeholders to the R-ARCSS to the Taskforce of the Ministry of Justice and Constitutional Affairs (Taskforce of the MoJCA).

3.2 The PSC shall be responsible for convening the NCC and shall stand dissolved after the last sitting of the NCC.

3.3 The PSC shall formulate its rules of procedure.

The Nomination, Appointment and Composition the PSC

3.4 Nominations for appointment to the PSC shall be submitted by the following groups: political parties, faith-based groups, women groups, youth, ethnic minorities, representatives of the private sector, CSO groups, academics, people with special needs and other professions. At least 35% representation of women shall be ensured.

3.5 In nominating candidates for appointment as members of the PSC, the nominating groups shall ensure diversity of relevant qualifications and backgrounds, giving due regard to ethnic and regional diversity, amongst other considerations.

3.6 The composition of the PSC shall reflect, amongst others, the gender, political, social, ethnic, religious and regional diversity of South Sudan in recognition of the need for inclusivity, transparency and equitable participation. Due regard shall be given to the equitable representation of groups mentioned in Article 6.14 of the R-ARCSS, amongst others.

The Size of The Preparatory Sub-Committee

3.7 The PSC shall comprise a maximum of 25 members inclusive of the Chairperson and Deputy Chairperson, who shall be of opposite genders, appointed by the Executive of the R-TGoNU. 45% of the members shall be representatives of the stakeholder groups and 55% shall represent the RTGoNU and political parties.

4. The National Constitutional Conference (NCC)

4.1 The NCC shall be an inclusive deliberative body with representation from all sectors of South Sudanese society. The NCC shall examine, deliberate upon and adopt the draft constitutional text.

4.2 Cognizant of Article 6.6 R-ARCSS, the Preparatory Sub-Committee (PSC) shall convene the NCC, including delegates representing the following categories:

a) Political parties;

b) Civil society organisations;

c) Women organisations;

d) Youth organisations;

e) Faith-based organisations;

f) People with special needs;

g) IDP representatives;

h) Refugees and diaspora representatives;

i) Traditional leaders;

j) War widows, veterans and the war wounded;

k) Business leaders;

l) Trade unions;

m) Professional associations;

n) Academia; and

o) Other categories to be determined

4.3 Following its appointment, the PSC shall commence consultations with all of the above mentioned categories for the purpose of convening the NCC. In the event that a delegate to the NCC is unable or unwilling to fulfil their functions, he/she shall be replaced in consultation with the nominating category.

4.4 The Secretariat of the R-NCRC shall equally function as the Secretariat of the NCC.

4.5 The NCC shall be comprised of a minimum of 1,000 delegates.

4.6 In its deliberations, the NCC shall seek to achieve consensus. The quorum for adoption of the final constitutional text shall be two-thirds majority of all members of the NCC. The final draft constitutional text shall be adopted by consensus. If consensus is not achieved, the NCC shall adopt the final draft constitutional text by two-thirds majority of members present and voting.

The Civic Education and Public Participation in The Permanent Constitution-Making Process

5. The institutions/mechanisms involved in the permanent constitution-making process shall give due regard to inputs received through public participation/consultation. The Civic education and public participation within the permanent constitution-making process shall be multi-phased and multi-faceted. The R-NCRC shall consider public submissions throughout the permanent constitution-making process.

6. In facilitating and promoting civic education and conducting public participation/consultation, the R-NCRC shall ensure that

appropriate means and methods are used, as the context requires. The chosen forms of civic education and public participation/ consultation should not exclude any parts of the public for reasons of physical ability, level of education, language, geographic location, religious beliefs, ethnicity, political affiliation, or any other reasons.

7. Civic education shall cover all constitutional issues of relevance to the Republic of South Sudan.

8. The R-NCRC shall guarantee the accessibility of civic education materials to all sectors of the public.

9. The state media shall offer their platforms to support civic education.

The Phases of The Permanent Constitution Making-Process: Phase 1

10. The enactment of the legislation to govern the permanent constitution-making process shall mark the beginning of the first phase of the process. Upon enactment of the legislation, the Executive of the RTGoNU shall reconstitute the NCRC and appoint the PSC for convening the NCC.

11. The R-NCRC shall become operational upon formulating its rules of procedure. Thereafter, it shall develop its action/work plan and subsequently launch the first civic education campaign and public consultations to raise awareness on constitutional issues and promote public debate.

12. The CDC shall be established after the reconstitution of the NCRC. Members of the CDC shall attend R-NCRC deliberations throughout the first phase of the process. The R-NCRC shall collect, collate, consider and analyse the outcomes of the first

phase of public consultations and continuously transmit them to the CDC.

13. The R-NCRC shall formally present to the NCC and the CDC a report containing the outcomes of the first phase of public consultations. The CDC shall develop the first draft of the constitutional text based on the results of the first phase of public consultations and R-NCRC deliberations.

14. The CDC shall submit the first draft of the constitutional text to the R-NCRC for validation, after which the R-NCRC shall make the draft public. The publication of the first draft of the constitutional text by the R-NCRC shall mark the end of the first phase of the permanent constitution-making process.

Phase 2

15. The convening of the NCC by the PSC shall mark the beginning of the second phase of the permanent Constitution-making process. Seven days after convening, the NCC shall adopt its rules of procedure and develop working modalities to guide the fulfillment of its mandate.

16. Upon the convening of the NCC, the R-NCRC shall submit the report outlining the results of the first phase of public participation as well as the first draft of the constitutional text to the NCC. This shall also mark the start of the second civic education and public participation campaign, which shall be conducted based on the first draft constitutional text. The public shall thus have the opportunity to express its views on the first draft constitutional text.

17. Throughout the second phase of the process, members of the CDC shall attend NCC deliberations and continuously incorporate the results of the deliberations into the draft constitutional text. The members of the CDC shall also attend R-NCRC deliberations throughout the second phase of the process. The CDC shall produce a second draft constitutional text for final deliberation and adoption by the NCC. The publication of the constitutional text as adopted by the NCC and its submission to the Minister of Justice and Constitutional Affairs shall mark the end of the second phase of the permanent constitution-making process.

Phase 3

18. On the first day after the 27th month has passed of the transitional Period of the R-ARCSS, the Transitional National Legislature shall transform into a Constituent Assembly for deliberation and adoption of the final constitution. The CDC may assist the Constituent Assembly upon request regarding clerical corrections that might be required.

19. Following the adoption of the permanent constitution by the Constituent Assembly, the third phase of civic education shall be conducted to disseminate the contents of the permanent constitution amongst the people of South Sudan.

For the above 18 detailed resolutions of the national constitution-making process, it is important to note that the R-ARCSS lacks dispute resolution mechanisms as found in other peace agreements, which would be critical in resolving disagreements that arise in planning for a transition and for all the chapters including the national constitution-making process. Previous research has shown that dispute resolution bodies are needed to advance implementation. These provisions feature concrete procedures for resolving disagreements over implementation between the signatories, sometimes empowering a body with membership drawn from both sides to make recommendations on how to break the impasse.

At worst, the delay would freeze the current status quo, with government and opposition military forces controlling different parts of the country. A similar situation emerged during Ivory Coast's civil war after the Linas-Marcoussis Agreement was signed in 2003. Under the agreement, the country was temporarily divided between the rebels in the north and the government in the south pending the establishment of a united government. However, the inability of the parties to agree on the composition and powers of the united government, coupled with delays in the implementation of the DDR, led to the collapse of the agreement and renewed war.

CHAPTER SEVEN
CIVIL SOCIETY: THE PURPOSED VOICE
OF THE VOICELESS

THERE HAS BEEN NO AGREED definition of a civil society by the scholars and pundits of political science because the concept emerged from western-centric notions, miscued and taken in diverse trajectories. Since this is a very important subject matter, two scholars' etymologies shape this debate.

Bernard Lewis (1994) discusses the origin of the concept: "*the term first appears in Western Europe in the thirteenth century, in the translation of Aristotle's politics, a translation that had a momentous effect on the development of political thought in the European Middle Ages.*"[331] The idea was taken up by others, notably by St. Thomas Aquinas in his *Summa Theologica;* finding the term "*civitas*" used in the Latin translation to render the Greek polis or *politeia* inadequate; he preferred to use "*communitas civilis,*" which was later translated into English, French, and other languages as "civil society".

However, for the purpose of this book, civil society refers to the non-partisan, non-profit legal associations that work to articulate

---

331   Bernard Lewis. Historical Origin of Civil Society (Princeton Publication, 1994), 30

the interests of citizens and defend their rights. They include trade unions, students' unions, women's movements, youth groups, professional associations, business associations and so on.

Civil Society in South Sudan State Formation

Civil society has played a critical role in South Sudanese state formation. I equate the important of civil society to its functions in state formation and illustrate my arguments on *the 'new broom that sweeps the house'*. Metaphorically speaking, the new broom (civil society) sweeps the room (South Sudan) very well but does not knows all the corners of the room since it is new. My argument towards the important of *new broom* (civil society) in South Sudan's state formation is justified as follows:

The emergence of new broom can be argued to have contributed to the improvement of the quality of governance, particularly in the public accountability and transparency sector in South Sudan. However, it is obvious to reinforce in this claim by saying that most of our politicians and political leaders are not morally upright in the management of public funds and execution of public programmes. The parliaments or legislatures that are empowered by the constitutions or by-laws to act as the watchdogs to the public affairs in their narrow tinge "checks and balances" have continued to fail to supervise the governments because of their corrupted practices. Then, who else is left to sweep away dirt in the governments? It's the civil society organisations. Burnell and Calvert (2004) reaffirmed this claim by saying *"civil society can play a disciplinary role in relation to the state by enforcing standards of public morality and performance and improving the accountability of both politicians and administration'.*[332]

In a very crystal-clear judgment, civil society activists have been in the forefront in making the governments of the day responsible for its public actions through what Jan Andrea (2004) called *Policy Monitoring and Review*. However, can this argument be valid to an autocratic country and the newly aspiring democratic South Sudan? Larry Diamond (2003) tilted the claim as "*new democracies, following long periods of arbitrary and statist rule, lack the legal and bureaucratic means to contain corruption at the outset. Without a free, robust, and inquisitive press and civic groups to press for institutional reform, corruption is likely to flourish.*"[333] Hence, civil society endeavours to press for public accountability in the process of democratisation and has been quite successful in the developing countries of South Africa, India, Kenya, Uganda, Spain, Brazil, Argentina, etc. The *new broom* (civil society) could sweep away the malpractices of the dictatorial leaders through lobbying, advocacy, demonstrations and in many instances this could lead to a breakdown of authoritarian regimes. Though this has not been successful in the case of South Sudan, a few achievements have been noted. The work of the Community Empowerment for Progress Organisation (CEPO), the Organisation for Responsive Governance, the Gender Empowerment for South Sudan Organisation, the South Sudan Civil Society Alliance, the Women's Bloc, the Human Rights Society for Advocacy, the Anataban Youth groups and academia amongst others have endeavoured to voice the concerns of or-

---

332   William Burnell and John Calvert. Role of Civil Society and State (Millimines, 2004), 57
333   Larry Diamond. Necessary Conditions for Democratization. (Standford, 2003), 6

dinary South Sudanese people to hold leaders accountable. They have done this through advocacy to support the formation of the South Sudan State.

Besides, the CSOs can be argued to have built a bridge by limiting state power through altering the balance of power between state and society thus forming a kind of opposition. Larry Diamond (1993) reinforces this argument: *"the basis for the limitation of state power results into the control of the state by society, and hence for democratic political institutions as the most effective means of exercising that control."*[334]

This puts the pro-dictatorial regimes in a very awkward position where they have to either succumb to the change or be toppled, hence the collapse of the state's totalitarians. The limitation of state power by civil society is not an easy task and quite risky given the magnitude of mobilisation the members have to do and the best strategies they have to deploy to see the action through. Failure of the demonstrations or street protests to influence the government reforms or alter the power can be focused on the leaders of the protests, and it is likely that a ban of the activities of the civil society in totalitarian regimes will occur. It's debatable but civil society has endeavoured in this process. The mighty demonstrations in Arabic countries for the change of the totalitarian leaders serve as an indomitable example. Indeed, the impact of civil society has been felt through the reforms and Jean Grugel (2002) reaffirms this by saying *"civil society organisations and associations try to influence or reform the state, at times they also take on issues of corporate power and have pressed states to redress the power imbalance generated by*

---

334   Larry Diamond. Democracy and the State (Princeton, 1993), 18

capitalism."[335]In South Sudan, civil society members are limited by a lack of resources and deepening ethnicity in discharging their roles.

On the other hand, civil society has been as a transmission belt between the state and society. By "transmission belt", I refer to the communication conduit that makes citizens understand how the government functions. This has been noticed in various national events such as national celebrations, debates of new constitutions, poverty, and economic crisis and so forth in South Sudan. It's cardinal to argue that civil society organisations keep the citizens abreast of what is going on in power corridors through the use of media and their networks. However, civil society in this case doesn't sweep away any dirt but identifies areas in the state to be swept through, giving out information to the citizens about the functionality of the governments or regimes. By disseminating information, the concept of civil society becomes inalienably necessary to citizens and the society in turns builds trust on it. When the trust has been built on it then the information received from it becomes quite plausible and useful for public consumption.

But one may pose, is all the information disseminated by civil society credible? No. Some of the information shared by civil society are flawed and lack credence. To be clear, civil society organisations should also contradict their official information if they lack authenticity.

Further still, civil society organisations enhance government legitimacy through provision of essential services such as carrying out civic education trainings to the political leaders and politicians

---

335   Jean Grugel. The Orgin of Civil Society (Washington, 2002), 5

as well. They go beyond this by deploying observational programmes in case of referenda or elections. Larry Diamond (1993) expounds this view further by saying *"Non-partisan election monitoring efforts have been critical in deterring fraud, enhancing voter confidence, affirming the legitimacy of the result, or in some cases (as in the Philippines in 1986 and Panama in 1989) demonstrating an opposition victory despite government fraud."*[336] This function is particularly crucial in founding elections like those, which initiated democracy in Chile, Nicaragua, Bulgaria, Zambia, and South Africa. Civil society sweeps away the 'dirt' of stealing of elections and referenda by the totalitarian regimes' leaders. The effort has been reinforced by international governments like the United Nations and regional bodies such as the African Union, the European Union etc.

In developing countries as alluded above, the elections and referenda have been marred with high-level frauds, rigging of results and further intimidation of the voters. The phenomenon has created a deep mistrust between the leaders and citizens, and filling up this gap by civil society has been bleak. Indeed, it is plausible to argue that in South Sudanese context, the civil society members don't 'sweep the dirt' well as most of them are compromised by the state. In African elections, for instance, there is so much perceived democracy that the elites often confuse the masses. One can argue and analyse these democracies are as follows: *democracy at elections* and democracy *in elections*. The former means voting by the electorates and the latter means rigging by the greedy leaders! I have called them democracies because the only chorus song you hear is that elections were free and fair, and the process was

---

336   Larry Diamond. Democracy and the State (Princeton, 1993), 18

quite democratic. Where? Quite ridiculous! Therefore, civil society organisations become irrelevant in most of the totalitarian regimes because their efforts of giving civic education trainings and monitoring elections go unrecognised including their reports. Notwithstanding, the only way to give legitimacy to the governments in such circumstances is through international pressure by transnational civil society and international organisations. Indeed, this is where the 'new broom' may sweep very well.

Further still and most importantly, civil society encourages citizens' active participation; a state with a vibrant civil society encourages participatory political culture of the citizens which in turn increases their awareness and skills in state formation. Larry Diamond (1993) backs up this argument by saying "*a rich associational life supplements the role of political parties in stimulating political participation, increasing the political efficacy and skill of state formation by the citizens, and promoting appreciation.*"[337] The more active the citizens participate in a polis without restriction, the more democratic the state is.

Civil Society Organisations in South Sudan has tried to enhance citizens' voices and participation in governance and peace-building. In the negotiations of ARCSS and R-ARCSS, civil society members represented the citizens in the High-Level Revitalisation Forum (HLRF) where both the August 2015 and the September 2018 peace agreements were inked. Of these peace agreements signed, members of the civil society acted as guarantors.

Apart from signing as guarantors, members of civil society formed a coalition called the South Sudan Civil Society Forum

---

337   Ibid

(SSCSF) to track the implementation of the R-ARCSS. SSCSF is a coalition of more than 200 independent civic groups, including civil society organisations, women and youth groups, academia, community-based organisations, and faith-based organisations from across South Sudan. The coalition was established in December 2017 to provide unified contributions from civil society to the HLRF and to act as a bridge between the HLRF and the South Sudanese population. SSCSF members work in government and opposition-controlled areas, internally displaced persons (IDPs) camps, and South Sudanese refugee camps in neighbouring countries. Members are united by a common interest in peace, freedom and respect for human dignity. The SSCSF derives its mandate from both its members and the thousands of ordinary citizens it consults with regarding the peace process.

The Voluntary Civil Society Taskforce on Implementation of the Peace Agreement is a coalition of diverse, independent and impartial CSOs, organisation academia, women's organisations, youth organisations, and faith-based groups. It was formed in February 2016 to facilitate and coordinate technical and strategic contributions of civil society towards inclusive and peaceful political processes in South Sudan through research, objective analysis and gauging of citizens' opinions. The taskforce has undertaken the Peace Implementation Monitoring Initiative as a joint project with the Institute of Peace, Development and Security Studies (IPDSS) of the University of Juba. The objective of this initiative was to provide analytical support to CSOs in their monitoring and evaluation of the status of implementation of the peace agreement.

The taskforce produces evidence-based periodic reports through contributions from 50 trained peace monitors located in the ten states of South Sudan and shares these reports with stakeholders of the agreement and the wider public. The taskforce is interested in ensuring that there is genuine commitment to the implementation of the peace agreement and a durable solution to the suffering that has been inflicted on innocent citizens of South Sudan due to the crisis of the war in the country. From holding leaders accountable to the participation in the peace building and conflict resolutions, CSOs have laboured to support South Sudanese state formation in lieu of failure and shocks.

Civil Society in State Formation of South Sudan

Civil society as a concept and a practical actor in the state formation mission has challenges that hinder its fight for a democratic world. Some hiccups can be argued as a lack of resources, as well as physical, financial and human hiccups. CSOs have been associated with weak internal controls, thus some members are easily bought off to shelf a particular matter by the governments' elites. The other challenge is a lack of cooperation or networking of the members or acting as a block, thus inhibiting most desired reforms, and finally a lack of objectivity in political actions.

In the case of South Sudan, CSOs have failed to represent the voices of the citizens. This has been demonstrated by the division amongst the members of civil society. For instance, there are civil societies that are viewed to support the government and these groups are called civil societies of the government. However, there are those who are viewed to be leaning towards oppositions and they are called civil societies of the oppositions. While the members of civil society downplay these divisions, the impacts of these divisions have disabled the so-called independent civil societies. The division in some cases is driven by deep ethnicity affiliations. For instance, members of the Dinka ethnic group would form and champion a CSO and proceed with their ethnic agenda. This also applies to Nuer ethnicity and other ethnic groups in South Sudan. By focusing on ethnicity and leaving out ideology, CSOs will remain as a divided house in South Sudan. The division has been deepening, leading to the state failure and shocks in the nascent state.

Besides, most CSOs lack resources to implement their work. Hence, they rely heavily on donor community. While donors would help these CSOs to perform, the donor would wish the CSO to 'dance to its tune'. This has massively affected the neutrality of the CSO. This rings true to the words: "he who pays the piper causes the tune". Thus, he who pays dictates the agenda and controls the narrative. A majority of the CSOs are being driven by foreign organisations and thus they have become agents of foreign governments. Hence, they have failed the South Sudan State physically and institutionally.

CHAPTER EIGHT
THE WOMEN OF SOUTH SUDAN: THE ROCK IN THE MUD

THE WOMEN OF SOUTH SUDAN have played both a role in state formation and a role in the failure of South Sudan. Regarding state formation, women have continued to support the institutional development and governance of South Sudan. For instance, most of the South Sudanese women working at the public sector have continued to keep integrity and advanced good governance as far as corruption is concerned. Out of the corrupt officials named and shamed in South Sudan, none has been identified as a woman.[338] It is plausible, and it has been agreed by many, that women are very trustworthy and dependable and exhibit a high level of honesty and integrity. They are dedicated, reliable and committed to family and national aspirations and goals.

Additionally, women have aided in peace-building and conflict resolutions across the world, and particularly, in South Sudan in tandem with state formation. This has justified the existence of women as peace-loving and conflict resolution advocates.

---

338   Jacob Chol. Role of Women in Governance Process of South Sudan. Journal of Eastern Africa Studies (Vol 5: 2019), 116-134.

The belief that women should be at the centre of peace-building and resolution processes is not based on essentialist definitions of gender.[339] The field of sociology makes a distinction between sex and gender. Human beings are not born 'men' or 'women'; masculinity and femininity is learned, rehearsed, and performed daily.[340]

It would be naïve to assert that all women respond in a similar manner in a given situation or that women are 'natural peace builders.'[341] Gender identity is performed differently in different cultural contexts. Gender identity must always be viewed in relationship with an individual's other identities such as his or her ethnicity, class, age, nation, region, education, and religion. It is important to note that there are different expectations for men and women in various sectors of the society and gender roles shift with social upheaval. In a conflict situation, men and women face new roles and changing gender expectations. Their biological and sociological differences affect conflicts and peace-building. To be certain, most societies value men and masculinity more than women and femininity.[342]

Despite the existence of 'sexism' and 'patriarchy', there are some widely accepted reasons why women are important to all peace-building processes. Women are important because they constitute half of every community, and the task of peace-building, a

---

339   Lisa Williams & Manjrika Peters. Essentials of Gender in the Society (Brookhouse-London, 2020), 5

340   Andrea Butler. The History of Masculinity and Femininity in African Societies (Cuea Press- Nairobi, 1999), 16

341   Lisa Wiiliams & Manjrika Peters. Women in Peace Building in Post-Colonial African States (Pretoria, University Press, 2005), 7

342   Ibid, 9

task that is so great, must be done in partnership with both women and men. Secondly, women are the central caretakers of families in most cultures, and everyone is affected when women are oppressed and excluded from peace-building. Therefore, it is essential that women be included in the peace-building and conflict resolution processes.

In addition, women play in the process of peace-building; firstly, as activists and advocates for peace, women wage conflict non-violently by pursuing democracy and human rights. Secondly, as peacekeepers and relief aid workers, women contribute to reducing direct violence. Thirdly, as mediators, trauma healing counsellors, and policymakers, women work to 'transform relationships' and address the root of violence. Lastly, as educators and participants in the development process, women contribute to building the capacity of their communities and nations to prevent violent conflict. This is made possible because of socialisation processes and the historical experience of unequal relations and values that women bring to the process of peace-building.[343]

Without Women There is No Peace

Women are the backbone of our social system and culture and this is clearly exhibited in South Sudan. Without women there is no peace. They possess the capacity to transform the society into a desirable direction. Women are significant players in the process of change and development. In their quiet existence lie the will and the making of a better tomorrow. Women, who constitute half the world's population, are the true strength of a nation. There is no other revolutionary moment in a woman's life than when she is

---

343   Ibid, 10

privileged to bring forth into the world the miracle of a new life. Instantly, she becomes inseparably linked to the human chain of life. There, she becomes an active participant in the peace process for a better world. Education, employment and empowerment are the three vital weapons in ensuring the progress of women who, in turn, will play their role to free the world from violence and war. Mervat Tallaway, 2016, emphasises that women must be recognised as key actors in conflict resolution and must be fully included in all strategies and effort for peace-making and peacekeeping in state building.[344] Kofi Annan stresses that women understand the root causes of tension and are more likely to know which group within communities and countries are likely to support peace initiatives.[345]

A girl, who is being born today around the world, will grow up as a beautiful woman to contribute her might to a peaceful world order tomorrow. But conflicts continue to threaten the Great Horn of Africa. In such calamitous situations, women and girls are often exposed to acts of violence, which seriously undermine their human rights and deny them opportunities arising from gender inequality.[346] Studies have shown that women are the worst hit in situations of violent conflict and are also affected differently from men during these crises. It is becoming increasingly obvious that women have unique opportunities for conflict resolution and peace-building due to the unique role they play in society and in the state.

---

344   Mervat Tallaway. The Role of Women in Conflict Prevention and Resolutions (Waterloo-London, 2016), 26
345   Kofi Annan. Women in Peace Building and Conflict Resolution (Stockholm, 1994), 7
346   John Agbalajobi. Women and Girls in Violence Africa (Lagos-Nigeria, 2009), 9

Women as Natural Peace Makers

The newest approach in the process of conflict resolution and peace building process must emphasise on gender uniqueness.[347] The majority of women are displaced by war so it is now understood that they could play an important role in efforts to resolve conflicts. Women are 'beautiful souls' loving peace. The feminist theory also argues that women are inherently peaceful, capable of preaching, teaching and preserving peace. There is an innate ability in women that makes them prefer non-violent actions.[348] Conflict resolution with just women will come out with more constructive discussions than groups with mixed gender. It is important to re-iterate that women are very trustworthy, dependable, and exhibit a high level of honesty and integrity. They are dedicated, reliable and committed to family and national aspirations and goals. Women, the life givers of the world, therefore have a stake in the world pursuit of peace since they exhibit a high level of perseverance, patience and tolerance in achieving set objectives. Women have been proactive in the resolution of conflicts, but their roles have previously not been given deserved prominence and recognition.[349]

The Bejing Conference of 1995 emphasised on women's capacity for leadership that must be utilised to the full and to the benefit of all in order to progress towards a culture of peace. Their historically-limited participation in governance has led to the distortion of concepts and a narrowing of processes in such areas such as

---

347   Joseph Mbagwu. Gender Uniqueness and Conflict Resolutions. Journal of Peace Studies (Vol 7: No: 3, 2019) 112-131

348   James Ferris. Women Internal Absorption of Violence (Cambridge University Press, 2010), 11

349   Simon Bukky. Women Unappreciated Role of Conflict Resolution in China (Peking University Press, 2005), 19

conflict prevention, the promotion of cross-cultural dialogue and the re-dressing of socio-economic injustice, women can be the source of innovation and much needed approaches to peace building. Therefore, it is important to deeply understand the dynamics of women's peaceful engagements. Indeed, conventional wisdom has tended to undervalue women's contributions, assuming that they are non-political citizens, and that their preoccupation is primarily with domestic issues. It is noted that women agitate against externally-imposed big development projects as it leads to ecological degradation, affects subsistence activities like farming and fishing, and reduces employment opportunities for the local people as such projects prefer non-natives in their recruitment. They also address the lack of basic social infrastructure and economic development opportunities at the grassroots, non-compensation for land use, corporate insensitivity on the part of the multinational, divide and rule tactics, sexual harassment of local women, as well as epidemics. It is worth mentioning that these women-led protests remain mostly non-violent but effective and point to how the intellect and energy of women can be harnessed for peace.[350]

The Role of The International Community in Women's Peace Building Efforts

The road to peace should be out of concerted effort and concern of all. Third parties serve as mediators with various strategies towards maintenance of peace. Statesmen have been engaged in initiating peace settlements and establishing international systems for

---

350   Daniel Ukeje. Harnessing Women Intellect and Energy in Peace Building (Oxford University Press, 2004), 606

the maintenance of peace and security since the World War I. The Treaty of Versailles, the establishment of the League of Nations and now the United Nations' Organisation are the outcome of these endeavours. The UN reaffirms its faith in fundamental human rights, in the dignity and worth of the human person, in the equal rights of men and women and of nations large and small. It strives to establish conditions under which justice and respecting the obligations arising from treaties and other sources of international law can be maintained; to promote social progress and better standards of life in larger freedom; for these ends to practice tolerance and live together in peace with one another as good neighbours; and to unite our strength to maintain international peace and security.

The year 1975 was declared as the Year of the Women by the General Assembly of the United Nations with a threefold objective: equality, development and peace. The Beijing conference on women in 1995 was also the demonstration of mobilisation for the struggle for equality, development and peace. The conference handed over the flame of peace, symbolising the daily struggles of women to promote the settlement of conflicts, appeasement, peace-building and a sustainable existence. Similarly, the United Nations declared the year 2000 as the international year of the culture of peace and 2001 to 2010 as the international decade for a culture of peace and non-violence for the children of the world. Governments, local organisations and individuals all over the world are using these years to probe deeply into the nature and practice of a peace culture. September 21st annually is also declared as the

International Day of Peace.[351]

It would not be out of place if I quote Kofi Annan, the then U.N. Secretary General, *"the future of the world belongs to women."* At the United Nations talk in Geneva, women gathered for 5 days in October 2002 for the first time in history to talk about new initiatives aimed at promoting world peace, and eliminating the causes that lead to conflict.[352] Despite the efforts made by the UN to successfully deal with the many serious issues confronting it, international conflicts have nevertheless persisted and many remained unresolved and a plethora of more complex conflicts keep occurring globally. With the provision of Article 52 of the United Nations Charter allowing regional organisations to make arrangements for settlements of their disputes, many of such regional and sub-regional bodies have not relented in their endeavours on peacekeeping and peacemaking. Organisations like the African Union (AU), the Organisation of American States (OAS), the League of Arab States, the Economic Community of West African States (ECOWAS), the East African Community (EAC), the Southern African Development Corporation (SADC) and the European Union, amongst others have demonstrated their efforts towards peace.

Individual member states have made efforts to complement the global efforts towards peace making and peace building. It must be pointed out that whilst national interests and other factors militate against the success of the United Nations in its attempts to maintain international peace and security through peacekeeping, it has made tremendous success in many ways. This fact explains

---

351   Simon Bukky. Women Unappreciated Role of Conflict Resolution in China (Peking University Press, 2005), 22
352   Ibid, 23

why during its 40th anniversary, the Norwegian Nobel Committee awarded the Nobel Peace Prize to the peacekeeping forces of the United Nations. In realising their work, the military wing is usually assisted by negotiators and other civilians who employ diplomatic options in form of peace-talks, meetings, conferences, negotiations, third parties, NGOs, regional and other groupings to break the deadlocks.

The Women's Role at a Grassroots Level for State Formation

Women often organise things at the grassroots level in order to promote peace and state formation but their access to formal peacemaking and peace-building processes continues to be limited. Very few women are included in peace negotiations and politics of governance in general in countries affected by conflict and war. Very few peace agreements have taken a gender and human rights perspective into account. Women's voices and concerns have often been excluded in decisions that affect the economic and power structures of post-conflict reconstruction, from land and property rights to legislation issues. Women continue to be excluded from negotiations, treaty-making, interim and transition-appointed governments, planning and implementing humanitarian aid, post-conflict reconstruction planning and policy making. Overall, peace processes remain a male-exclusive endeavour where men negotiate power, and largely set the post-conflict agenda. It is vital that both women and men have equal opportunities to participate in the ongoing processes for the principles of democracy and good governance to take root in countries coming out of conflict.[353]

353   UNMISS Report in the Conflict Situation in South Sudan (Juba, 2008), 3

The Roots of South Sudanese Women's Peace Building Efforts: Katiba Ban'at

Katiba Ban'at in Arabic refers to the battalion of women in South Sudan. It was a military movement that was founded together with the SPLM/SPLA in 1983 to allow women to participate in the liberation struggle. The number of women in Katiba Ban'at was roughly between 1000 to 2000 women.[354] The movement was the entry point for South Sudanese women's participation in war, peace and state formation. The South Sudanese women helped in the provision of food, intelligence gathering and actual field combat in war theatres. Although many women performed satisfactorily in the *Katiba Ban'at,* women deserted the movement out of fear and due to family commitments.

The Participation of The South Sudanese Women in Peace Processes and State Formation:
The Wunlit Peace Accord, 1999

South Sudanese women have been steadfast in peace processes as a way of support to state and nation building in South Sudan. The etymology of this effort is the Wunlit Peace Process between the Dinka and the Nuer in 1999. Hailed as a successful people-to-people peace, Wunlit peace accord halted the deepest conflicts and animosities between the grassroots Dinka and the Nuer in the triangle states of Warrap, Unity and Lakes. The then Sudan Council of Churches played a critical and great role of facilitation, and indeed of impartial mediation. However, women from the Dinka and the Nuer took traditional roles to mobilise their men and

---

354   John Aden. The History of Katiba Ban'at in Sudan (Khartoum, 1999), 8

ensured that the peace event was successful.[355] The slaughtering of a white ox (Mior Mabior/Mabor) was done amidst ululations of the women for peace and reconciliations of the two long time bitter enemies-turned-friends. The women ensured that the white ox was well-cooked and evenly divided amongst the two communities who ate it and enjoyed the peace ritual. Without women, the Wunlit Peace Accord would have not been possible.

The Comprehensive Peace Agreement (CPA) of Sudan

The CPA was a peace deal negotiated between the National Congress Party (NCP) of Sudan and the Sudan Peoples' Liberation Movement/Army (SPLM/A) of the South. The agreement was inked on the 9th January 2005 at the Kenyan Capital, Nairobi, at the Nyayo National Stadium. The success of this peace deal though viewed as the effort of chairman, Dr. John Garang De Mabior and Ustaz. Mohammed Ahmed Taha, was made successful by the women of Sudan and particularly, from Southern Sudan. The organisation groups of the women, namely the Sudan Women Action Network (SWAN) and the Women in the Churches formed in the early 2000's and championed for the peaceful resolution of conflicts in Sudan. During the signing of the CPA at the Nyayo National Stadium, in Nairobi on the 9th January 2005, women, particularly, from Bor Dinka performed and danced majestically with a song. "*Ba-ngu-loi-de thany-ye, xen diarr ayaliya, cha ben-kony ni-xon bany thok*" loosely translated to "*what can I do when peace is signed, I have to dance and stand at the door of the chairman*'.'

---

355   Ibid, 10

The Role of Women in the Signing and Implementation of The ARCSS and The R-ARCSS

The ARCSS was signed in August 2015 in Juba to end the conflict amongst the South Sudanese pivoted between President Salva Kiir and Dr. Riek Machar during the eruption of the political crunch on 15th December 2013. During the negotiations of this deal, women were critically involved. Groups such as the Women Bloc and the Women Coalition and Gender Empowerment for South Sudan Organisation amongst others were involved in successful negotiations of the deal. Eminent personalities such as Madam Rebecca Nyandeng De Mabior, Madam Angelina Teny and Madam Awut Deng Acuil were all in the forward negotiating ARCSS representing their parties in the voyage of state and nation formation.

The Revitalised Agreement on the Resolution of the Conflict in the Republic of South Sudan (R-ARCSS) was also supported by women. The Women's Civil Society Groups such as the Women Bloc, the Women Coalition and other women's civil society organisations gave pressure to ensure this agreement was inked. The eminent personalities mentioned above played essential roles in convincing the leaders to finally sign the deal on the 12th September 2018. This has demonstrated the South Sudanese women roles in state formation and prosperity.

Apart from peace-building and conflict resolution efforts, women also played intellectual roles in strengthening South Sudanese state formation. This has been done through the South Sudanese Women Intellectuals Forum (SSWIF). The SSWIF has continued to organise both physical and virtual debates and panels addressing the issues of gender inequality, Sexual Gender Based Violence (SGBV) and women empowerment opportunities. These efforts have been done to mirror and highlight women's strengths and opportunities in promoting the nation and state formation of South Sudan.

Although women have helped form states, particularly in the context of South Sudan, they have also caused South Sudanese state failure in taking their judicial rights as follows:

The Rigidness of R-TGONU to Implement a 35% Women Quota for Political Representation

The Transitional Constitution of South Sudan 2011 after it's amendment provided a threshold for women's political participation. It stipulates a 35% women quota in political representations across all governmental departments. However, the application of this provision has been problematic. Currently, women's political representation stands at 14% in the national cabinet. This is far below the threshold. In the Transitional National Legislative Assembly, 20% of 550 MPs are women. This is also below the threshold. Failure in the acquisition of the women's quota, though can partially be blamed on men's control, is a failure of women to unite and demand their legal rights. In neglecting their rights, women have thus contributed to state failure.

Hyper-Masculinity Dominance

The dominance of hyper-masculinity remained a great conundrum to women's progress in South Sudan. This is due to cultural influences. For instance, women are not allowed to sit with men in meetings as well as when making decisions. Women are not allowed to sit in traditional bench courts, as well as not allowed to take the inheritance after the death of their husbands. However, the continued existence of hyper masculinity can be apportioned on the women who have naturally accepted that hyper masculinity dominant can never be altered. This is an unfortunate acceptance of status quo hence leading to the state failure. Men are entirely blamed and responsible for this control. However, women should unite, organize themselves and stand free from this hyper masculinity society. Without organizing themselves as women, men will not organize them.

Retrogressive Cultural Barriers

Retrogressive cultural barriers have prevented women from participating in peace-building, conflict resolutions and state formation. Heavy shouldered home chores such as preparing for family meals, uncontrolled children bearing and keeping female children out of school remained a critical challenge for women emancipation in peace-building and conflict resolutions, and thus a biggest contributor to state failure. Early child marriage and Sexual Gender Based Violence (SGBV) have continued to undermine women participation in peace-building, conflict resolutions and state formation. It is indicated that 60% of female children dropout of school every year due to early child marriages.[356] This has negatively affected the emancipation of women and hence a recipe of state failure. Men are responsible for these retrogressive cultural barriers. However, women have continued to relax in rallying their efforts together to stem out these cultures that retinue to demean their progress.

---

356   Philips Homes. Retrogressive Cultures of Women Impediment (Mamilian, 2019, 7)

Perpetual Envy and Mutual Suspicion Amongst Women

This has been a challenge to women's empowerment, as well as their progress in political participation, nation and state formation. Most women possess perpetual envy and suspicion amongst themselves and thus don't support themselves, hence failing the state's formation. Studies have indicated that 55% of women envy and don't support politically their fellow women across the world.[357]. In South Sudan, this perpetual envy and mutual suspicion has continued to cause women political downgrading and state failure. During the 2010 elections, 90% of women decided to vote for men instead of their women candidates in geographical constituencies.[358] Thus, this perpetual envy and mutual suspicion has continued to edge out women in meaningful peace-building and conflict resolution programmes and given that majority of women would not do things together. This has contributed negatively to state formation.

---

357   David Dame. Women and Electoral Envy. Journal of World Quarterly (Vol 3. No.9: 2017), 285-305

358   Jacob Chol. Electoral Voting Analysis of the Sudan. Journal of African Review (Vol 2. No.4, 2010), 140-161

CHAPTER NINE
THE YOUTH OF SOUTH SUDAN:
THE YOUNG LIONS

The Role of Youth in South Sudanese State Formation and Failure

The youth, which are referred to as the young lions, make up 72% of the South Sudanese population. The youth is distinguished between the ages 18-35 years according to South Sudanese laws. It is different in other areas; a person is considered a youth if they are between 15-35 years according to the African Union and 15-24 according to the United Nations.

Although one can argue that the South Sudanese youth contributed to South Sudanese state formation, this argument is not sufficient and widely lacks evidence. It is prudent to argue that the South Sudanese youth contributed to South Sudan's state and nation failure. This is demonstrated in the hoodwinking and recruitment of the youth to political elite's base-conflicts for the primitive accumulation of power and wealth.

In December 2013's political ignominy, a majority of the youth were fragmented and recruited into ethnic-based outfit militias. These militias were drawn from the Nuer, the Dinka, the Azande, the Lutuho, the Mabanese and the Chollo ethnicities. For the Nuer, the White Army, a communal Nuer ethnic-based militia known locally as Jiech Mabor, emerged in the early 1990's with empirical links to the spiritual mythology prevalent in South Sudanese politics. A major aspect of this spiritual mythology was the notion that Dr. Riek Machar, South Sudan's erstwhile vice president, was a messiah who could bring spiritual and political liberation to the Nuer. Although empirical evidence demonstrated it to be false, this belief has animated the Nuer's youth participation in South Sudan's recent civil conflict. Unfortunately, outsiders have largely ignored this element of the conflict that has led to state failure.

The literature on youth communal militias argues that the existence of the White Army dates to as early as the late 1980's. The White Army is a predominantly Nuer youth outfit. This traditional militia is drawn from four sub-groups of Nuer ethnic people, namely the Lou in the south, the Jikany and Gawaar in the east, and the Bul in the north. These four Nuer sub-groups reside in the northern part of the Unity State, the Upper Nile State, and the eastern parts of the Jonglei State in South Sudan.

Like other non-state armed actors in South Sudan, the White Army's primary purpose is to protect the community against external threats and to defend property and livestock. In fact, the White Army first emerged as the protectors of cattle. Cattle played an extremely important role in the life of the agro-pastoralist Nuer. Cattle ownership is a source of status, fertility, health, and general prosperity. Cattle are also the principal medium through which social ties are created and conduits through which new alliances with outsiders are forged.

Groups akin to the White Army have long been common in many African pastoralist societies. For example, amongst the Dinka Bahr el Ghazal youth, the traditional militia group is called Gelweng; amongst the Otuho in Eastern Equatoria, the defence youth group is called the Monyimiji; and amongst the Chollo, the youth vigilante group is known as Akwele Grassroots Defence Force. In response to the South Sudan state's inability to provide security, however, new youth groups have emerged. For instance, Azande militants created the Arrow Boys in response to the activities of the Ugandan Lord's Resistance Army in the Western Equatoria State in 2014. Amongst the Bor Dinka, an armed group called the Bor Panda Youth emerged and was implicated in the killing of the Nuer internally displaced persons (IDPs) under the United Nations protection site in Bor in April 2014. Moreover, a notorious group called the Maaban Defence Force became known to the world in August 2014 when it killed six Nuer aid workers, forcing aid organisations to halt activities in the Maaban County of the Upper Nile State. Amongst the Padang youth, their groups are called Abushok and Mutholom.

These youth groups are typically transitory in nature, tribal-based, defensive in orientation, and lacking any ideology or long-term objectives. The White Army is an exception, however, having played an active part in Sudan's second civil war in 1983-2005. While similar armed groups remained under community control, the White Army became an independent entity that was sometimes destructive to the community from which it originated.[359]

---

359   John Young. The Nuer White Army in South Sudan Civil War (Palgrave, 2007), 3

Smearing their faces with white ash to protect themselves from bugs, members of the group presented a fearsome aspect to both their enemies and their fellow Nuer.

The 1991 split of Machar from the Sudanese People's Liberation Movement (SPLM), led by Dr. John Garang, saw an estimated 30,000 Nuer youth mobilised and ordered to attack the Dinka of Bor, the area from which Garang hailed. The aim of the attack may have been to expose Garang as a "weak leader," one who could not protect his own backyard. The attack on Bor was devastating in scope and ferocity: villages were razed; male captives were disemboweled; and women were raped, shot, or burned alive. Human rights organisations estimated that 5,000 people were massacred.

This fratricide cost Machar his credibility amongst the South Sudanese people, in addition to cementing the reputation of the White Army as merciless killers.[360] Machar's White Army attack was met with fierce vengeance, as Garang's Dinka soldiers executed many Nuer of Gajaak clans. Garang's faction retaliated with force and summarily executed all Nuer that they captured.[361] Near Bor, one group of 19 Nuer men were tied up in a cattle shed and speared to death.[362]

Yet the interesting question is what motivated a large number of young Nuer militants, originally defenders of cattle, to fight for a political cause on behalf of leading politicians? Long before the current civil war, studies demonstrated that the White Army relied on the interpretation of prophets and medicine men in their sojourns of both bravery and looting. These Nuer prophets were revered for their role in blessing barren women, healing, and settling disputes. While preaching peace, however, the "main social function of the leading [Nuer] prophets in the past was to direct cattle raids on the Dinka and fighting against various foreigners who troubled the Nuer". Evans-Pritchard (1956) described the prophets as individuals possessed by spirits and having charismatic powers. When these prophets spoke, they spoke in the name of the divinities that possessed them. As such, 'what the prophet says and what the spirit says are all mixed up together, the two being interspersed together in such a manner that they cannot be separated'.[363]

---

360   Sharon E. Hutchinson. The history of Nuer White Army (Routledge, 2012), 6

361   Scott Peterson. Me Against My Brother: In War in Sudan, Somalia and Rwanda (Routledge, 2001), 26

362   Amnesty International Report, 2000, 2

363   Evans Pritchard. Nuer Religion (JSOR, 1956), 45

Sharon Hutchinson (1996) argues that the White Army united under the powerful prophet, Wuornyang Gatakek, who drew heavily on the legacy of an earlier prophet, Ngundeng Bong.[364] Bong lived between 1830 and 1906, and prophesised a fierce battle between the Nuer and the Dinka, in which the latter would be conquered. According to the prophecy, drums would sound, spears would be sharpened, and the Nuer would be mobilised for the battle by a messiah from the village of Nasir. Other accounts of the prophecy describe the messiah as being left-handed, unmarked by tribal scars, and gap-teethed; the prophecy also indicated that he would marry a white woman.

With his headquarters in Nasir, Machar perfectly fit the profile of the messiah-to-be: he was left-handed, unmarked, gap-toothed, and married to a white British aid worker, Emma McCune. Although Machar eschewed the messiah label, he did nothing to dispel the ancient fable. Machar's calls for President Salva Kiir to step down confirmed his answer to the prophetic calls. Machar received the prophetic Dang from Juba International Airport, the magical stick once carried and, with disputations, used positively by the prophet Ngundeng Bong against the British from the British government in 2009. The same British later took the Dang away when the prophet's son commandeered powers after the death of his father. Taking over Ngundeng's role, Wuornyang prepared and blessed Jiech Mabor, or the White Army, for the battle, buttressed by the use of Nuer religious symbolism.

Guided by a new prophet, Dak Kueth, in the political conflicts of

---

364   Sharon Hutchinson. The Origin of Nuer Prophets (Oxford University Press, 1996), 8

December 2013, the White Army of approximately 25,000 young people marched from their base in Lou Nuer and captured Bor en route to Juba. Their motivation for attacking Bor was linked to the alleged target killing of Nuer in Juba during December 16-17, 2013. Although the vengeance of the White Army hit hard at Bor and Akobo, targeting members of the Dinka ethnic group, the belligerent group also attacked Dinka members in Malakal and Bentiu. Dinka Padang Abushok and Mutholom vigilante avenged on these white armies attacks in the Upper Nile state.

The new conflict in greater Jonglei fought by Nuer Lou and Gawar-Nuer with Dinka Bor Alliance against the Murle has been very devastating. The Nuer and Dinka Bor have been taking revenge for their cattle and children taken by the Murle. All the parties have inflicted casualties in the fighting. The interesting part is the emergence of the young and latest prophet of Gawar-Nuer, known as Makuach, who has been commanding the entire Nuer White Armies against the Murle. Prophet Makuach before going to the battle would always perform rituals of fire-licking to berate his fighters. He has been quite successful in his prophecy of the Nuer defeating the Murle with huge casualties on the Murle's community. He is still at the bushes of the Murle commanding both Lou and Gawar Nuer at the time of writing of this book. Regarding empirical analysis, the youth have played a role of state failure in lieu of strong state formation of the nascent state as far as insecurity and civil wars are concerned.

What is more, the youth have proven to be more corrupted than the elders. The Office of the President's thieves who looted money that were convicted by the high court in Juba were mostly youth by age. The youth have lost the mantra that "*they are the future leaders"* of South Sudan. Hence, they have gone on a spree of looting and robbery of government resources.

It is plausible to argue that the main root cause of South Sudan's conflict is the lack of literacy in the youth that are recruitable and armable. Put all the young people into high schools/polytechnic/ colleges, and give them quality education. They will be running around all over the country looking for money to feed themselves and their families, buy comfort, and make friends, not war. They will reject guns and spears. Anything else written in here is just elements of instability which they fuel.

The hope for Africa and South Sudan, in particular, is the youth in areas of entrepreneurship and innovation. We have seen how the youth in Rwanda have made successful careers in the ICT field. Applications such as Tap and Go, Ekonnect, Smart Cities, drones technologies etc. have placed Rwanda as an ICT-revolutionary country. In Kenya, we have seen how massively innovative the youth there can be. We saw the birth of M-Pesa mobile money, Ushahidi Conflict Early Warning Data Centre and numerous ICT outbursts. In Uganda, we have seen various youth innovations from entrepreneurship, ICT and above all the building of cities. We have the Ikere City built by Ojok Okello, a city built in the deep rural sections of Eastern Uganda. We also saw this innovation in West Africa with international singer Akon working towards building the Akon City in Senegal. In South Sudan, we are seeing youth innovations; for instance, Nile Pay and M-Gurush mobile money transfers were created by the young people amongst other innovations.

CHAPTER TEN
FUTURE AND HOPES OF SOUTH SUDAN

Institutional Engineering in The Divided Society

After the political crisis and it's consequences, the failure of international community, the peace agreements and their slow implementation, the divided civil society and the failure of women and youth in forming South Sudan State as demonstrated in the empirical literature through weak institutions, an inherent lack of rule-of-law and culture to respect those institutions, institutional engineering is all necessary to eschew the state from collapse. This institutional design should inculcate a rule-of-law and a culture of respect towards institutions as showcased by the grounded institutional theory in the theoretical framework section of this book.

Another kind of institutional design is the surrendering of powers to the citizens through a practical political system that would enhance the accountability of the political parties, the political elites, the international community, the civil society, women's groups and youth groups. This could either be through the existing decentralisation or through the re-introduction of federalism. We begin this chapter through the examination of the two options. This is to discern a preferred political system in South Sudan.

The Decentralisation or Federalism in South Sudan's State Formation: Introduction

This section analyses the possible institutional engineering that could happen in a successful formation of South Sudan. It sets out the debates of rethinking South Sudan's institutional option for the governance in order to allow power and resources to be re–distributed for the citizens. The decentralisation and the federalism system of governance are critically analysed and discussed from the empirical literature perspective in order to discern the best option for South Sudan's state formation.

Decentralisation in South Sudan's State Formation

Decentralisation as a system of governance was first introduced by President Jaafar Nimeiri in 1976 in Sudan. He divided all of Sudan's provinces into two, namely, the northern and southern provinces. Regionalism was then introduced in the north in 1980, when the old northern provinces were reassembled as regions.[365] The powers of these northern regional governments were considerably less strong than the powers conferred on the southern region by the Addis Ababa Peace Agreement of 1972.

Upon the signing of the CPA in 2005, South Sudan established 10 states, 80 countries, 523 payams and 2200 bomas[366] and thus decentralised the service delivery. On the 2nd October 2015, President Kiir issued executive order 36 (#EO 36) decreeing the dissolution of the 10 states and broke them into 28 states, and again

---

365   Douglas Johnson, Federalism in the History of South Sudanese Political Thought (Rift Valley Institute Research Paper 1, 2014), 18

366   South Susan Statistical Year Book (Juba: National Bureau of Statistics, 2012,) 1

further into 32 states. On the 13th February 2021, the President of the Republic returned the country back to the 10 states, with the addition of three new administrative areas in Pibor, Abyei and Ruweng. As provided for in the Transitional Constitution 2011 as amended, South Sudan has three levels of governments: the national government, the state's governments and the local governments. These levels have either failed or are failing to provide public services to the South Sudanese citizens and therefore critical research is vital to assess whether decentralisation has done a better job or not in delivering services to the citizens of the nascent state.

The Concept of Decentralisation

Various scholars and policy practitioners have attempted to conceptualise the word "decentralisation" to make a case in this ever-changing world. Scholars such as Armin Von Bigdandy, Rudiger Wolfrum and others have endeavored to make sense of decentralisation. According to the two scholars, the term decentralisation is often used to describe legal and political structures that distribute power territorially within a state or beyond a state.[367] This broad notion of decentralisation encompasses confederations, federations and decentralised unitary states, since all of those systems distribute governmental powers to at least two levels. In addition, David De' Dau, a policy practitioner defines decentralisation as a transfer of authority and responsibility for public functions from the central government to intermediate and local governments, or

---

367   Armin Von and Rudiger, The principle of Vertical Separation of Powers: A Comparative Overview of Legal Concepts and Structures (Heidelberg: Max Planck Institute for Comparative Public Law and International Law, 2011), 13

quasi-independent government organisations or private sectors.[368]

Furthermore, Richard K. Mulla in his seminal piece entitled *'South Sudan: Federalism or Decentralisation?'*, defines decentralisation as the process by which the functions of and the decision making authority are transferred from the national government to the sub-national governments, or from one sub-national government to yet a lower one depending on the tiers of the government established in a particular country.[369] While Mohammed Kerre argues that decentralisation means increased efficiency, more equity, and greater participation and responsiveness of government to the demands of their citizens, it is, therefore, a political and administrative process that defines a shift in the focus of power (political and administrative) from traditional lines of command and control to a popularly-elected local level.[370] It involves the transfer of powers and functions from the centre to the lower political entities.[371]

Dimensions of Decentralisation

Decentralisation has political, financial and administrative dimensions. Political decentralisation involves the transfer of authority to the local level through an elected local government (perhaps as part of a democratic transition), electoral reform, political party reform,

---

368   David De' Dau, 'South Sudan: Decentralisation vis-à-vis Federation:' http://sudantribune.com/spip.php?article51448 (Accessed on 28th March, 2015)

369   Richard K. Mulla, 'South Sudan: Federalism Or Decentralisation?' http://www.southsudannewsagency.com/opinion/articles/south-sudan-federalism-or-decentralisation (Accessed on 28th March, 2015)

370   Ibid, 15

371   Ibid, 15

authorisation of participatory processes, and other reforms.[372] The financial or fiscal decentralisation involves regulating inter-governmental transfers of resources and giving jurisdictions greater authority to raise revenue. Administrative decentralisation transfers to the local level functional services, such as health care service, the operation of schools, the management of service personnel, building and maintenance of roads, and garbage collection.[373]

Decentralisation tends to be strongest when real political autonomy, significant administrative responsibility, and the financial resources to carryout primary functions have all been transferred to the local level. Parameters such as local autonomy and authority, local accountability, local resource availability and effective local institutions can therefore be used to measure the effectiveness of decentralisation.[374]

In unitary decentralised systems, sovereignty lies exclusively with the central government. This does not mean, however, that unitary states are governed entirely by the centre. Although final responsibility lies with the central government, many state functions are exercised on regional or local levels, closer to the people and their needs.[375] Regional or local authorities may exercise many administrative powers, but may design policies only insofar as the centre allows them to. Traditionally, local governments focus on providing local public services and implementing national welfare

---

372   Armin Von and Rudiger, 2011. The principle of Vertical Separation of Powers: A Comparative Overview of Legal Concepts and Structures, Max Planck Institute for Comparative Public Law and International Law, (Germany, Heidelberg), 13
373   Ibid, 15
374   Ibid, 15
375   Ibid, 14

policies.[376] Typical competences include economic development, local planning, social assistance, social housing, cemeteries, fire service, libraries and primary education. However, sub-national authorities in unitary states fulfil these functions only within the limits of the powers assigned to them by the centre.[377] Therefore, a well-functioning decentralised system depends on the goodwill of the unitary central government, instead of relying on existing constitutional divisions of power.

South Sudan and its Continuation of The Decentralised System

Since the independence in 2011, South Sudan has been questioning the suitability of the decentralisation system of government in its delivery of services. While most citizens think that the conundrum does not lie in the system of governance in South Sudan, but on effective leadership, others argue that decentralisation as a system of governance has concentrated the powers at the centre. Going by any of the arguments, the decentralisation system is on the sacrificial altar of South Sudan's state formation and failure. Decentralisation is a good option because it is what the people of South Sudan want, and has always been yearning to get, as the best form of governance.[378] However, the way it is expressed leaves

376   R Hague et al, 1998. Comparative Government and Politics-An Introduction, 4th Edition (London), 181

377   Armin Von and Rudiger Wolfrum, 2011. The principle of Vertical Separation of Powers: A Comparative Overview of Legal Concepts and Structures, Max Planck Institute for Comparative Public Law and International Law (Germany, Heidelberg) 14

378   Deng Riek, 'Decentralization: A best option of ROSS but Lacking Practicality (sic)' http://www.southsudannewsagency.com/opinion/articles/decentralisation-a-best-option-for-ross-but-lacking-practicality (Accessed on 28th March, 2021)

a lot to be desired. For example, the system is lacking practicality and political will from the government.[379] It is commonly believed that decentralisation is closely linked to democracy as it empowers people to have a say in their affairs, particularly, how they would like to be governed.[380] This way, they feel a sense of dignity and sense of self-worth.[381]

However, the periods of decentralisation (1972-1983 and 2005-2021) can be considered as failed attempts.[382] The main problem has been constant interference and undermining of lower level governments by the respective presidents.[383] Numeiri first did those actions in 1980, 1981 and 1983 when he dissolved the regional governments in South Sudan in order to achieve his objective of controlling and marginalising the Southern Region.[384] The self-government Act of 1972 (the then Constitution for the Southern Region) was abrogated; it broke down and the SPLM/SPLA war of 1983 started. However, given the independence of South Sudan, the trend in the respect to the decentralisation system did not change. Richard K. Mulla argues that President Kiir has followed the same footsteps of President Nimeiri; he has never respected any constitution fully since he took power in 2005.[385] He appointed the ministers, members of the national legislature, senior civil servants, senior officers of the organised forces and the judges

---

379   Ibid, 6
380   Ibid, 6
381   Ibid, 6
382   Ibid, 7
383   Richard K. Mulla, 'South Sudan: Federalism Or Decentralization?' http://www.southsudannewsagency.com/opinion/articles/south-sudan-federalism-or-decentralisation (Accessed on 28th March, 2015)
384   Ibid, 2
385   Ibid, 3

of the High Court, the Court of Appeal and the Supreme Court and also dismissed elected governors at his will amongst others.[386] Thus President Kiir and his government ministers have insisted on having a decentralised government amidst widespread cries for federalism in Equatoria and the Upper Nile States.[387] Though this has been the strategy, the real problem has, however, been the greed of those in power wishing to recentralise more powers with the aim of looting the country and marginalising the rest of the other communities.[388]

Besides, the administrative or financial decentralisation has not achieved much in South Sudan. What is lacking is a system that checks the corruption or how funds are spent in the states and counties. In Uganda for example, the government had introduced what they called a 'public expenditure tracking' system, which ensures that funds released to districts are accounted for by the respective recipients, either in districts or counties.[389] This method according to the Ugandan Government has ensured upwards accountability and thus tries to minimise the misappropriation of the transferred funds. This could have been borrowed in South Sudan to advance rewarding of administrative decentralisation.

However, a resident South Sudanese journalist named Ngor Garang Arol argues that South Sudan has been applying fiscal decentralisation as the political system in dispensing services to the citizens

---

386   Ibid, 3
387   Ibid, 4
388   Ibid, 4
389   Juma Mabor, Administrative Decentralisation: The Only Best Option for Governing South Sudan: http://www.southsudannation.com/administrative-de-centralization-the-only-best-option-for-governing-south-sudan/ (Accessed on 28th March, 2015)

without any tangible improvement. He argues for the alternative:

'In South Sudan, we have tried fiscal decentralization [sic] and the result is known to all of us. Much of the budget has always been spent in Juba leaving little to the states and explains why up to today interstate roads supposedly funded by the national authority are in a depilated state. So why not try another system and see how it will work instead of sticking to the same system we have tried in the past 10 years?'[390]

Instead of working for a consensus system of governance, President Kiir as argues elsewhere in this book issued an Executive Order Number 36 on the 2nd October 2015 further decentralising the existing country from 10 states into 28 states. He issued another order creating 4 more States, making a total of 32 states (plus Abyei).[391] On the 13th February 2021, the President via an Executive Order returned the country to 10 states, plus the 3 administrative areas of Pibor, Ruweng and Abyei. The President's move has been challenged as it contravenes the Agreement on the Resolution of the Conflict in South Sudan (ARCSS) and the Revitalised Agreement on the Resolution of the Conflict in South Sudan (R-ARCSS). He also violated the Transitional Constitution 2011 as amended. The Transitional Constitution 2011 as amended stipulates 10 decentralised states of South Sudan plus Abyei Administrative Area.

---

390   See Ngor Garang Arol on DPF Thread 'Breaking News: Son a Governor and a Member of National Security Service Has Joined Rebellion', 17th April 2015
391   http://www.sudantribune.com/spip.php?article61403 (Accessed on 16th January 2021)

Thus, the country is governed on the basis of a decentralised democratic system and is an all-embracing homeland for its people.[392] Confusion emerged on the notion of SPLM policy of "taking towns to the rural areas" and the introduction of federalism. The Executive Order Number 36 came as a surprise to many as the SPLM-IG had previously opposed the SPLM-IO's proposal of dividing South Sudan into 21 states.[393] Many view Executive Order 36 as taking troubles to the people in rural areas, not services as the architecture of the order had said.

The Origin of Federalism and the Demand of it from The South Sudanese People

The demand for federalism by the South Sudanese people go back to as early as 1947, known best as the Juba Conference. The Juba Conference was organised for South Sudanese leaders to deliberate and demand for federalism. A majority of the leaders that organised and agitated for the conference hailed from the Equatoria region, though the Upper Nile and Bahr el Ghazal regions were represented. Having failed to acquire it, the Southern Sudanese people demanded federalism again in 1954 and this intensified the debate as all chiefs and traditional leaders strengthened their positions. For example, Necodemo Gore raised the pertinent question, *'In case we receive federation, where shall we get our people to run it? How shall we finance it?'* Buth Diu responded with passion:

---

392   See Transitional Constitution of Republic of South Sudan, 2011 as amended, article 1, section 4.
393   Rens Willems and David Deng. The Legacy of Kokora in South Sudan. Briefing Paper, 2015. Intersections of Truth, Justice and Reconciliation in South Sudan (SSLS, University for Peace & PAX, November) 17

'May I draw your attention gentlemen, chiefs of all tribes, elders, and citizens present in this house? I should like to know whether you in this house want to be slaves or it will be better for you to be poor and free and happy [sic]? I would like to know whether you understand the meaning of 'Federation' as explained to you [sic]. Federation does not mean separation but internal law and order in the united Sudan, for you to be able to look after your affairs.... My honorable gentleman Necodemo Gore brought the question of management and finance of the Federation now under debate by Southerners. With regard to the first part of your question the present government must be bound to manage the federation of [the] South for fear of separation. If they cannot, we can manage to separate the Country. This I am quite sure the present regime has in mind. To conclude my dearest friend Mr. Necodemo Gore we are here for freedom and not money [sic].'[394]

However, Chief Abdalla of Torit–Katire in the Equatoria Province then broadened the debate about federation to include peoples from northern provinces; the Fur of Darfur, the Funj of Blue Nile, and the Nuba of Kordofan.[395] He declared that, *'I and my people strongly request federation to safe my fellow Blacks in the North.'* Musa Beshir, a non-tribal delegate from Khartoum repeated this call:

---

394   Minutes of Juba Conference 18-21 October 1954, NA FO 371/108326, and no.193; the spelling and punctuation of the original document have been retained.

395   Douglas Johnson, 2014. Federalism in the History of South Sudanese Political Thought, Rift Valley Institute Research Paper 1 (South Sudan, Juba) 11

'I am a delegate of 25,000 southerners in the North. This includes Nuba, Fur and Funj who carry the same idea of Federation [sic]. In this respect, I am not representing [a] tribe but I would prefer to say colour since the three communities referred to again and again [sic]. There are backward arrears in the North far too backward than the Southern Sudan [sic]. Therefore, I am speaking here for the Blacks who favoured your demands for Federation [sic]. Federation must go ahead to meet our demands in all our backward arrears namely Fur, Funj and Nuba Mountains.'[396]

Although the South Sudanese chiefs had differences on the demand of federation, South Sudanese politicians have had even stronger emerged differences at the Round Table Conference (its official title) convened in Khartoum on March 1965. Aggrey Jaden, William Deng's deputy, advocated for the principle of self-determination as the only means of solving the 'Southern Problem', and equating self-determination with independence.[397] Whereas William Deng supported the unity of Southern Sudanese with the North on the hope that Southern problems could be resolved within a given framework so as both Arab and black Africans can live together.

Thus, separatist southerners would use any opportunity to advocate for the federation of the region. For instance, 1969-1983,

---

396   Minutes of Juba Conference 18-21 October 1954, NA FO 371/108326, and no.193; the spelling and punctuation of the original document have been retained.

397   Douglas Johnson, 2014. Federalism in the History of South Sudanese Political Thought, Rift Valley Institute Research Paper 1 (South Sudan, Juba), 15

popularly known as Nimeiri period, was utilised by southerners to advocate further for federalism, which was craftily duped as 'autonomy'. However, differences arose between southerners and northerners. The first major disagreement between the two sides was over the very use of the term 'federal' to describe the role of the future central government.[398] Khartoum's delegation argued that the people's local Government Act of 1971 provided all the decentralisation needed for the proposed Southern Regional Government to run effectively.[399] However, in 1972, the Addis Ababa Peace Agreement that was signed was abrogated and the South Sudanese citizens continued with their quest for federal governance.

Federalism in South Sudan State Formation

After the independence of South Sudan, the idea of federalism as the system of governance surfaced, appeared ubiquitous and reached its apogee in 2013, particularly, after the December 15th 2013 political crisis. Discussions on a federal system of governance have polarised South Sudanese citizens. The debate in the independent South Sudan was complicated by the fact that the armed opposition in the current political crisis, precipitated by fighting in December 2013, adopted 'federalism' as a political platform while the government equated any talk of federalism with subversion and disloyalty.[400]

But if we were to learn anything from the past history of southern Sudanese political thought, it is that federalism means many

---

398   Ibid, 17
399   Ibid, 17
400   Ibid, 26

things. As the SPLM/SPLA warned at Abuja in 1992, *'no system is federal merely because it claims to be federal'*[401]; the term has been used to describe what we are, in practice, highly centralised systems of government, as well as more radical projects of devolution that remain untried.[402]

The Concept of Federalism

Pertinent scholars and policy gurus have attempted to define federalism. According to Richard K. Mulla in his ground-breaking piece *'South Sudan: Federalism or Decentralisation?'*, federalism is a system of governance whereby powers are divided in such a manner that the national government and the state government are each within a sphere of co-ordinance and independence.[403] To him, federalism is an equal to an ideology that combines shared rule with self-rule. Armin Von Bogdandy and Rudiger Wolfrum in their seminal work *'The Principles of Vertical Separation of Powers: A comparative Overview of Legal Concepts and Structures'*, define federalism as a political system whereby powers are divided between the central government and the numerous regional governments in which the central government cannot revoke these powers.[404] In other words, federalism means the 'coming together' of countries

401   See William Nyuon Bany 'Opening Address to the Abuja Peace Talks' 26th May 1992. Unpublished document collected by Yosa Wawa.

402   Douglas Johnson, Federalism in the History of South Sudanese Political Thought, Rift Valley Institute Research Paper 1 (South Sudan, Juba), 26

403   Richard K. Mulla, 'South Sudan: Federalism Or Decentralization?' http://www.southsudannewsagency.com/opinion/articles/south-sudan-federalism-or-decentralisation (Accessed on 28th March, 2015)

404   Armin Von Bogdandy and Rudiger Wolfrum, 2011. The principle of Vertical Separation of Powers: A Comparative Overview of Legal Concepts and Structures, Max Planck Institute for Comparative Public Law and International Law, (Germany, Heidelberg), 20

into one political system, mainly for the protection of their common interests and enhancement of their mutual benefits.

Federalism is defined as a form of government whereby the constitution provides that power be divided or shared between a central form of government and regional governments, like states.[405] Through laws and officials, both governments act directly on the people but also must agree on any changes to the constitution.

The division of power between the central government and its regional subdivisions may vary amongst different countries. In areas like defence and foreign policy, some regional governments may join the central government in making decisions. Some would say that federalism came about because too much power is concentrated on the central government and many regional governments wanted to retain local power and pride.[406] Others would say that the central government saw the need of providing services and public goods to the lower levels and thus surrender federalism to the regional governments. Whatever the case, this setup is particularly helpful in countries with large territories.

In any case, federalism is also seen as a possible solution to address differences amongst populations divided by cultural or ethnic backgrounds, but still seeking common law and order.[407] William Riker argues that the essential institutions of federalism are a government of the federation and a set of governments for the member units, in which both kinds of governments rule over the same territory and people and each kind has the authority to make some

---

405 See http://www.qwhatis.com/what-is-federalism/ (Accessed on 30th March 2020)
406 Ibid
407 Ibid

decisions independently from the other.[408] However, federalism could only be successful once there is strong accountable leadership at all levels of the governments.

The Dimensions of Federalism

Federalism has various dimensions and types when dissecting its concept. Although the dimensions have been contested by scholarly debates, political scientists and experts of government, political systems have been consented on a few dimensions. For the purpose of this book, some types of federalisms are analysed as follows, inter alia:

Firstly, we begin with 'fiscal federalism' that is associated with the allocation of resources to the sub-national levels of government thus reducing centralisation of resources at the national level. It has six building blocks such as the expenditure assignment to refer to the division of powers/responsibilities; the revenue assignment takes care of country-shared taxes, establishing the base rate and tax collection and transfers of funds to be done in cognizance of vertical and horizontal imbalance involving different types of transfer depending on the context and policy objectives.[409]

Secondly, there is 'territorial federalism' in which political power and resources are surrendered to the sub-national levels based on territory.

Thirdly, there is 'ethnic federalism' where political power and resources are surrendered to the sub-national governments based

---

408   See William H. Riker, 1964. Federalism: Origin, Operation, Significance (Boston: Little Brown & Company), 5

409   See Shawn Houlihan, 2015. Federal Systems Overview (Juba: Forum of Federations, January), 3

on ethnic cleavages. Although it was not originally designed as an instrument of ethnic conflict management, 'ethnic federalism' has become very popular today as a governance mechanism for 'holding together' multiple ethnic communities in a single, multi-level polity.[410] By combining self-rule for individual communities at the sub-federal levels with shared rule for all groups at the federal level, 'ethnic federalism' seems to provide the perfect formula for democratically maintaining unity in diversity in deeply divided societies.[411] Yet, this is not the case for all ethnic-federated states. 'Ethnic federalism' in practice has been described as a means by which the ruling party has divided the opposition along ethnic lines, making it difficult for a united opposition to rise and challenge its power.[412] The problem with 'Ethnic federalism' is not that it is insufficiently ethnic but that it is insufficiently federal, and it is possible that its emphasis on ethnicity is the source of that weakness.[413]

Lastly, there is 'symmetrical federalism' whereby all sub-national levels of the governments have the same constitutionally-embedded obligations and rights.[414] For example, the U.S, Germany, Austria, Switzerland, Argentina and Brazil practice 'symmetrical federalism'. What is more, 'asymmetrical federalism' refers to where

410   Larry Diamond, 1999. Developing Democracy: Toward Consolidation (Baltimore & London: Johns Hopkins University Press), 26
411   David Turton, 2006. Ethnic Federalism: The Ethiopian Experience in Comparative Perspective (Oxford: James Curry), 72
412   Douglas Johnson, 2014. Federalism in the History of South Sudanese Political Thought, Rift Valley Institute Research Paper 1 (South Sudan, Juba) 27
413   David Turton, 2006. Ethnic Federalism: The Ethiopian Experience in Comparative Perspective (Oxford: James Curry), 64
414   Armin Von Bogdandy and Rudiger Wolfrum, 2011. The principle of Vertical Separation of Powers: A Comparative Overview of Legal Concepts and Structures, Max Planck Institute for Comparative Public Law and International Law (Germany, Heidelberg), 29

special rights are provided to the distinct members in the federation.[415] For example, Canada's French-speaking Québec has a number of prerogatives in law, immigration and education that the French-English do not have. In addition, in India, special rights are given to the Kashmir and Jammu area and also to the Muslim minority.[416] This is the same to the Catalans of Spain who enjoy special rights from the Madrid government.

Federalism as Re-Institutional Engineering in The Divided South Sudan

The South Sudanese December 15th political crisis has triggered the debate of whether or not the state is considering federalism. Various scholars and policy practitioners have continued to reflect on the best option of institutional engineering to pull out South Sudan from the 'political mud'. Indeed, proponents of federalism argue that the South Sudan State should be re-engineered to surrender resources and power to the sub-national levels of the governments. However, the opponents of the federalism argue that the ongoing system, decentralisation, in critical observation, is already federalism in practice and thus there is no need to talk about any federalism per se. Hence, various divergences of federalism as the system of governance in South Sudan are analysed as below.

Federalism as a Panacea to South Sudanese Debacles

Many academics and policy practitioners have had frenzied debates of whether federalism was a panacea to South Sudan's political and

---

415   Ibid, 29
416   Ibid, 29

economic quagmires or not. Interesting debates stretched in this section include the timing of it, the perceptions that federalism, as Equatorians demand was a political hijack of the concept by the opposition group waging war against the government, as well as it being the purported type of federalism and the institutional challenges South Sudan faced regarding federalism.

We begin the analysis of the timing of federalism; many people believe that federalism is an overdue demand that has evolved from 1947 until now and thus it is a timely concept that the South Sudanese citizens and government must adopt and implement. The statistical intervention from Dr. Jafaar K. Juma titled *'Assessing Public Opinion Towards Federalism: What is the Proportion of South Sudanese in Favour of Federalism?'* reinforces the idea of timing and argues that federalism in South Sudan is immemorial, particularly in the Greater Equatoria Region, and thus the feelings of the South Sudanese people towards federalism in the whole country is practical and encouraging; nevertheless, the topic is sensitive and controversial following the 15th December 2013 political crisis.[417]

Moreover, the consultations done with the concerned Dinka (Jieng) community elders in Juba seem to be agreeing with the idea of federalism as an alternative political system to resolve republic conundrums. It argues that there was no problem with the federal governance except for the fact that the country was marginalised by the Khartoum and left without development.[418] Therefore, there

---

417   Jaafar Karim Juma , 2014. 'Assessing Public Opinions Towards Federalism: What is the Proportion of South Sudanese who Favor Federalism? Unpublished Paper (Juba: 5th July), 4

418   See D.M. Agok, 2014. 'Seeking Solution for Acceptable Administration to the People of South Sudan', Unpublished paper (Juba: 18th July), 1

was a need for the country to consolidate itself for some reasonable period of time to use available resources for equitable development until a suitable time to apply the federal system rose to the state without much difficulty.[419] But as things stand now, this step has to be skipped and the federal system must be introduced because the demand for it is a wish of the majority.[420]

Moreover, Santino Mabek Longar, a Canadian-based jurist views federalism as one of solutions for South Sudan's predicaments:

'I think federalism, though not surely the panacea for all the ills that have afflicted our nation can significantly reduce the level of tensions and domination that has plagued our nation. Without federalism, violent conflict, as a result of domination, both at the state and federal levels, will continue to define our political life for at least the next 30 years. Federalism also has the potential to serve as an engine of economic growth for South Sudan. This is because it improves economic efficiency (e.g. tax collection and competition) and helps the grassroots to identify their development priorities. It is federalism, no any other model of governance, is the best option we can have. I don't regret that I share this idea with Riek even though his motivations are entirely different.'[421]

However, President Kiir in many recorded speeches has been quite sceptical about the adoption of federalism as a political system

---

419   Ibid, 2
420   Ibid, 2
421   See Santino Mabek Longar (SAL), DPF on the Thread 'Dr. Riek Machar Position on IGAD Draft Agreement', 18th June 2015

of governance replacing decentralisation. In his speech on the 18th March 2015 at Dr. John Garang's Mausoleum while addressing thousands of SPLM-IG supporters, President Kiir wondered why the advocates want federalism when the ongoing political system, decentralisation, is federal in a nuanced sense. He says, '*I wonder what our people want, especially those who are advocating for federalism, the system we currently have is federalism in itself if you look at it closely.*'[422] James Adiok Mayik in his piece '*Why Federalism Must Wait?* jumped onto the presidential bandwagon and argued that federalism at this time in South Sudan shall disintegrate the country into tribal units (other than administrative units) and thus Adiok elucidates that tribal units can be a very dangerous tool for the somalisation of South Sudan.[423]

Nonetheless, South Sudanese tribes agreed in principle for the adoption of federalism as the system of governance. In a conference dubbed *as* the National Peace of South Sudan Tribes, under the theme 'Peace Now! South Sudan Tribes United Against War', conducted at the Nyakuron Culture Centre from the 17th to the 18th February 2015 resolved that a federal system should be the system of governance in South Sudan, that it should be part of the peace dialogue and that it should be a common and permanent solution to the war.[424]

As the South Sudanese continued to embrace the idea of federalism, the perception that it is the Equatorian's demand sent

---

422   President Salva Kiir Mayardit speech delivered on 18th March 2015 at Dr. John Garang De' Mabior Mausoleum in Juba.
423   James Adiok Mayik, 'Why Federalism Must Wait' http://www.sudantribune.com/spip.php?article51320 (Accessed on 4th April 2021)
424   See unpublished report of National Peace Conference of South Sudan Tribes held at Nyakuron Culture Centre from 17-18th February 2015

jittery feelings to the wider spectrum of South Sudanese society. The Equatorian's conferences conducted over the last few years have often resolved federalism as one of the systems of government that should be adopted as quickly as possible. This demand from Equatorians is seen as a solution to their socio-economic and political problems that are bedevilling the Equatoria region today. One of the concerns for the Equatorian citizens has been that the extravagance of other states, particularly the Greater Upper Nile and the Bahr el Ghazal regions, grew envious of the optimisation of resources for the development. The other reason has been tight centralisation of power and resources by the central government without any clear-cut development visions and paradigms. The Equatorians see themselves better off to be on their own on the development agenda and resources management than being drowned with others in sea of mismanagement of resources, coupled with a lack of a strategic and transformative vision. Thus in their quest for peace, the Equatorian governors signed a position paper on the IGAD Peace Talks in Addis Ababa and concluded that Equatoria accepts that during the transitional period, the TGoNU shall complete the permanent constitutional-making process of South Sudan, which shall determine the future structure of government and the full implementation of a federal system of governance.[425] Although the position paper stands for the Greater Equatoria region, citizens from this region have not been widely consulted.

Another interesting strand for analysis is the perception that

425   See Equatoria Position Paper on the IGAD Peace Talks in Addis Ababa, Ethiopia: Proposal on The establishment of the Transitional Government of National Unity (TGoNU in the Republic of South Sudan), 19th April 2015, Addis Ababa

the rebels known best as the SPLM in Opposition had hijacked the idea of federalism following the December 15th 2013 political skirmishes. The SPLM-IO has been calling for the restructuring of the state on a new basis using federalism. This state-of-affairs has been deepened by the SPLM-IO in their proposal of 21 states along the 1956 boundaries of the South's districts.[426] The SPLM-IO threatens to take the Ethiopian example to the extreme, creating weak states and unable to challenge or restrain whoever holds power in the federal government.[427] But is this going to restore stability in South Sudan when states are federalised on an ethnic basis? The answer is certainly no. We have homogenous former states such as Lakes, Northern Bahr el Ghazal and Warrap but the inter-clans' animosity, sectional conflicts and violence have been intensifying during pre- and post-independence times. This is due to compounded factors: cattle rustling and raids, high-level poverties, weak governance structures and a lack of reconciliations and restitutions amongst the communities. Thus, viewing ethnic federalism as an iota of peace, development and security is an assumed proposition that has been overlooked.

The focus of many South Sudanese has been on the creation of the federal states, rather than on the balance between federal and state governments.[428] The creation of a federal government goes hand-in-hand with the creation of federal states. The failure of past regional experiments in Sudan was that this principle was

---

426   See SPLM in Opposition 'Proposes 21 States with Ramciel as National Capital' 17th July 2014.
427   Douglas Johnson, 2014. Federalism in the History of South Sudanese Political Thought, Rift Valley Institute Research Paper 1, (South Sudan, Juba), 27
428   Ibid, 28

not adopted: the construction of decentralised states and regions was done primarily to protect the powers of those in charge of the central government.[429]

That aside, the institutional challenges of federalism range from levels of literacy that manifests as ethnic-based decisions. James Adiok Mayik asserts that South Sudan has recorded more than 70% of people that are illiterate that he argues is not fitting enough to help the masses understand the literal meaning of federalism.[430] With such a low level of human development, more than 70% of people being illiterate make ethnicity an impediment for a knowledge-based and creativity-based economic development that says federalism in South Sudan at this time will create villageism and savage belligerence amongst tribes.[431] We cannot plant federalism where the spirit of ethnocentrism is active not allowing federalism to come into view, into a formal split of South Sudan's nation into factional ethnocentrism governments that will start with rejection of those we view as trouble in our midst.[432]

Yet with federal institutional challenges, South Sudanese proponents of federalism argue that federalism is desirable for South Sudan. It is true that while our individual tribal nationalism is likely to set us against others, federalism in its crudest form has never been meant to promote any of the currently existing strong sentiments.[433] These regional sentiments are often sought after as a

---

429   Ibid, 28
430   James Adiok Mayik 'Why Federalism Must Wait' http://www.sudantribune.com/spip.php?article51320 (Accessed on 4th April 2021)
431   Ibid
432   See John Sunday Martin, 2015. 'Federalism: South Sudan in Dilemma', Juba Monitor, (Juba: Tuesday March 10th), 6
433   See Justin Ambago Ramba, 2015 'Federalism now, not later', Juba Monitor (Juba: Tuesday March 10th), 6

means of facing up to other regional blocks. But federalism is the opposite of prevailing regional political polarisations and antagonisms.[434] The survival of the country as a democratic nation would depend on its adopting federalism.[435] Although federalism can be ideal for post-conflict environments and building and accommodating diversities, the managing conflicts of diversity can be achieved through a federal system of administration that can avoid Dinka/Nuer conflict as happened in December 2013 or Equatoria/Dinka conflict as was the case in 1983 during 'Kokora'.[436]

Federalism and the Phenomenon of Kokora

South Sudanese scholars and citizens mask their faces with the myth that federalism is associated with Kokora, a local word in Bari referring to 'division or to divide'. Bari-speaking groups traditionally inhabit the Equatoria region and include Bari, Mundari, Nyangwara, Kuku, Kakwa and Pojulu. The simplest translation of Kokora into English is 'to divide' or 'division'.[437] This-state-of-affairs has continued to instil the fear of what this system of governance bring to the social cohesion of the country. Jacob K. Lupai in his seminal work '*Kokora: Often Misunderstood, Grossly Misinterpreted and Most Feared*', argues that the word is misunderstood and

---

434   Ibid, 6

435   Richard K. Mulla, 'South Sudan: Federalism Or Decentralization?' http://www.southsudannewsagency.com/opinion/articles/south-sudan-federalism-or-decentralisation (Accessed on 3rd April 2020)

436   Ibid

437   Rens Willems and David Deng, 2015. The Legacy of Kokora in South Sudan. Briefing Paper. Intersections of Truth, Justice and Reconciliation in South Sudan (SSLS, University for Peace & PAX, November) 4

misrepresented.[438] If that is so, it is not only that because of the way some in the three Equatoria states are reviving the anti-Dinka (or anti-jieng) propaganda in support of federalism,[439] but also because of the tribalistic way the advocates of the Kokora applied it at the beginning of the last civil war. Douglas Johnson argues that some of them who lived through Kokora-and were abruptly and brusquely told to leave their jobs and back to their home regions-have every reason to be suspicious of the advocates of the new Kokora, especially after reading the comment sections on articles posted on South Sudan News Agency and Sudan Tribune websites.[440] However, Douglas Johnson cautions South Sudanese on the myth of federalism:

> 'Let us be clear: Kokora is not the same as federalism. It did not create a federal state in Equatoria or any place else in Southern Sudan. It weakened the powers of regions while leaving the power of [the] central government in Khartoum untouched, enhanced even those who want genuine federalism are best advised not to adopt Kokora as their model.'[441]

---

438   See Jacob K. Lupai 'Kokora: Often Misunderstood, Grossly Misinterpreted and Most Feared', http://www.southsudannewsagency.com/opinion/articles/kokora-often-misunderstood-grossly-misinterpreted-and-most-feared (Accessed on 3rd April 2021).

439   Peter Kopling, MD's mistitled 'Peaceful Coexistence: How the Equatorians Got It Right', 29th June 2014

440   Douglas Johnson, 2014. Federalism in the History of South Sudanese Political Thought, Rift Valley Institute Research Paper 1 (South Sudan. Juba), 27

441   Ibid, 27

President Kiir echoes the same in his speech:

"Kokora 'will happen' if a federal system is introduced in the country. (…) The issue that people are raising now, that is the same issue that came in 1983, Kokora (sic). And Kokora should not again derail us from what we are doing."[442]

However, Kokora is not associated with federalism. Federalism as discussed thoroughly in this chapter is a system of the government that surrenders powers to the sub-national levels of governments. The type of federalism discussed is the territorial-based federalism that should be adopted immediately in South Sudan. The R-ARCSS has also indicated federalism as one of the political systems South Sudanese should adopt and that is why we have "Ministry of Federal Affairs" in the R-TGONU. Though federalism is a hope for South Sudan in reversing South Sudanese State failures and shocks, resilient South Sudanese are the hopes for South Sudan prosperity. Resilient South Sudanese, particularly, the youth are the hopes of this nascent State. As South Sudan celebrates its 10 years anniversary of the independence from Sudan, it is important that the youth are engaged in all the productive sectors, for instance, ICT innovations and particularly, agriculture, as South Sudan is a very fertile country. Thus, the R-TGoNU should earmark enormous resources to the Ministry of Youth, the Ministry of ICT and the Ministry of Agriculture. These three, together with federal system of government, led by quality leaders are the hopes of South Sudan.

---

442   See Radio Tamazuj 'Kiir raises fears of 'kokora' under federal system' https://radiotamazuj.org/en/article/kiir-raises-fears-%E2%80%98kokora%E2%80%99-under-federal-system (Accessed on 4th April 2021)

CONCLUSIONS

THIS BOOK HAS PROVIDED a strong argument on South Sudan's state formation, failures, shocks and hopes. It has done this through ten chapters. Chapter one introduced and brought out historical and modern theories of state formation, chapter two examined the independence of South Sudan, chapter three looked at South Sudan and the tasks ahead, chapter four process-traced the 2013 political crisis and its consequences through the mirror of political parties and political elites, chapter five appraised the role played by the international community, chapter six examined the 2015 and 2018 peace agreements and their implementations, chapter seven discussed civil society, chapter eight examined the role women played in South Sudan, chapter nine analysed the youth of South Sudan and chapter ten discussed the future and hopes of South Sudan through institutional re-engineering of the divided society.

The book argues the indicators of South Sudan's state failures and shocks and questions the reason why South Sudan could not collapse. It uses the analytical framework of *historical and modern state formation theories* for South Sudan's state failure and *Resilient of Citizen* for the survivability of the South Sudan State. The book notes that while the political parties, the political elites, the women, the civil society and the youth have contributed to South Sudan's state failure, the International Community, particularly, the troika countries and the United Nations (particularly UNDP and UNMISS) have contributed to both South Sudan's state formation and failure.

The re-institutional engineering in reversing South Sudan's state failure or prevention of South Sudan's state collapse was considered. The institutional theory was advanced to analyse the next institutional paradigm. The gist of the institutional approach is that the practicability of the institution is more important than having established institutions themselves. The choice between continuing with a decentralised system or introducing a federal system was argued and tested through literature reviews. The outcome that emerged was that a territorial federal system of governance is the most preferred option for reversing South Sudan's state failure as well as preventing South Sudan's state collapse and providing hopes to the South Sudanese people. Hence, the book has paraded a consistent understanding of state formation, failures and shocks and now institutional re-engineering of the state via federalism. Although federalism is a hope for South Sudan and is necessary to be instituted, the overall quality leadership to ensure that this federal system works to enhance strong regulated political parties, as well as patriotic political limited elites and non-partisan international community, a vibrant civil society, strong women and productive youth is far more imperative for successful South Sudan's state formation. Allocating enormous resources on the youth innovations and mass agriculture production is a hope for South Sudan prosperity.

BIBLIOGRAPHY

Books

Acemoglu, Daron and Robinson, James. *Why Nations Fail: The Origins of Power, Prosperity and Poverty.* London: Profile Books Publishers, 2012.

Amin, Gamal. *Egypt in the Era of Hosni Mubarak.* Cairo: American University in Cairo Press, 2011.

Asal, Victor. *Political Exclusion, Oil and Ethnic Armed Conflict.* New York: Oxford University Press, 2014.

Autesserre, Severine. *The Trouble with Congo: Local Violence and the Failure of International Peace building.* New York, Cambridge University Press, 2010.

Bennett, George. *Case Studies and Theory Development in Social Sciences.* Cambridge: MIT Press, 2005.

Borkenau Franz. 1936. *Pareto.* John Wiley & Sons, Inc. New York.

Bourdieu, Pierre. *Structures, Habitus, Practices: Pierre, The Logic of Practice:* Polity Press, 1990.

Brahimi Lakhdar & Salman Ahmed. *Seven Deadly Sins of Peace Making:* Reiner Publishers London. 2008

Brockmeier, Samuel et al. *The Impact of the Libya Intervention: Debates on Norms of Protections.* Taylor Francis Publication, 2016

Brubaker, Roggers. *Ethnicity Without Groups.* Cambridge: Cambridge University Press, 2004.

Burnell, Peter. "Building Better Democracies: Why Political Parties Matter?" *Westminster Foundation for Democracy*, London: WMFD, 2004.

Chayes, Sarah. *Thieves of State: Why Corruption Threatens Global Security.* USA: Norton and Company, 2015.

Commons, John R. *Institutional Economics And Its Place in Political Economy,* 1st Vol. New Brunswick and London: Transactions Publishers, 1934a

Dallaire, Romeo. *Shaking Hands with the Devil: The Failure of Humanity in Rwanda.* Oxford University Press, 2003

Daloz, Jean-Pascal. *The Sociology of Elites Distinction: From Theoretical to Comprehensive Perspectives.* London: Palgrave Macmillan, 2010.

Deng, Francis. 1995. *War of Visions: Conflicting Identities in the Sudan.* Washington: Brookings Institution Press, 1995.

Diamond, Larry. *Developing Democracy: Toward Consolidation.* Baltimore & London: Johns Hopkins University Press, 1999.

Douglas, Mary and Wildavsky Aron. *Risk and Culture: An essay on the Selection of Technological and Environmental Dangers.* Berkeley: University of California Press, 1983.

Draghics, Simone, 1989. *Max Weber: The Profession of Politics.* Washington DC, Plutarch, 1989

Edward, Thomas. *South Sudan: A slow Liberation. London.* Zed Books, 2015

Francois, J Bayart. 2009. *The State of Politics in Africa: The Politics of Belly,* 2nd Edition. Paris: Loners Publishers. 2009

Fukuyama, Francis. *State-Building: Governance and World Order in the 21ˢᵗ Century*, Washington: Palgrave, 2004.

Gellner, Ernest. *Nations and Nationalism*. Ithaca: Cornell University Press, 1983

Gurr, Ted. *Minorities at Risk: A Global View of Ethno-political Conflicts*. Washington: Institute of Peace Press, 1993.

Hague, Roggers, et al. *Comparative Government and Politics-An Introduction*. 4ᵗʰ Edition London, 1998

Hancock, Graham. *Lords of Poverty: The Power, Prestige, and Corruption of the International Aid Business*. New York Publishers, 1992

Hegley, John. *Elite Theory in Political Sociology*. University of Texas-Austin, 1999

Homes, Philips. *Retrogressive Cultures of Women Impediment*. Mamilian, 2019

Huntington, Samuel. *Political Order in Changing Societies*. New Haven: Yale University Press, 1968

Kimenyi, Mwangi. *Ethnic Diversity, Liberty and the State: The African Dilemma*. Massachusetts, USA: Ed-ward Elgar Publishing, 1997.

Konrad, Kai A. and Skaperdas, Stergios. *The Market for Protection and the Origin of the State*. Princeton, 2010.

Kombo, D and Tromp, D. *Proposal and Thesis Writing: An introduction*. Nairobi: Pauline Publications, 2006.

Knight, Jack. *Institutions and Social Conflicts*, Cambridge University Press, 1992

Kraxberger, Brennan. *Failed States: Realities, Risks and Responses*, Laxington: CreateSpace Independent publishing, 2012.

Kohari, Romir. *Research Methodology: Methods and Techniques.* India: New Age International, 2004.

Leki. Andrew. 2016. *African Union and Conflict in South Sudan.* Nairobi: Panguin Publishers, 2014.

Lewis, Bernard. *Historical Origin of Civil Society.* Princeton Publication, 1994

Malwal, Bona. *Sudan and South Sudan: From One to Two.* Oxford: Palgrave Macmillan, 2015

Marcoglou, Emmanuel. 1955. *Pareto and His Circulation of Elites.* University of Connecticut, USA

Melvern, Linda. *A People Betrayed: The Role of The West in Rwanda's Genocide.* Zeds Books, London UK, 2009

Migdal, Joel. *Strong Societies and Weak States.* Princeton University Press, 1998

Migdal, Joel. *Strong Societies and Weak States: State-society Relations and State Capabilities in the Third World.* Princeton, NJ: Princeton University Press, 1988

Modi, Richard. *28 States in South Sudan and Dinka Domination.* Blackstone Publisshers, Kampala, 2018

Mohammed, Nadir. Review of Mansour Khalid's Book 'The *Government They Deserve: The Role of the Elite in Sudan's Political Evolution'.* Kegan Paul Publishers: London, 1983

Mugenda, Abel and Mugenda, Olive. *Research Methods: Quantitative and Qualitative Approaches.* Nairobi, Acts Press, 1999

Myerson, Roger. The Autocrat's Credibility Problem and Foundations of the Constitutional State. *American Political Science Review 102* (February, 2008): 125-139. McNeill, William H.1982.

Ndulo, Muna and Margaret Grieco. *Failed and Failing States:The*

Challenges to African Reconstruction. London: Cambridge Scholars, 2010.

Nyaba, A. Peter. *South Sudan: The State We Aspire To*. Pretoria: CASAS, 2011.

Olson, Mancur. *Power and Prosperity*. New York: Basic Books, 2000

Orodho, A and Kombo, D. *Research Methods*. Nairobi: Kenyatta University, Institute of Open Learning, 2002.

Pareto, Vilfredo. *The Rise and Full of Elites: An Application of Theoretical Sociology*. New Jersey: New Brunswick, 1991.

Pitkin, Hanna. *The Concept of Political Elites Representation*. Berkeley: University of California Press, 1967.

Posner, Dan. *Institutions and Ethnic Politics in Africa*. New York: Cambridge University Press, 2005.

Prah, Kenneth. *The African Nation: The State of the Nation, Cape Town*. Centre for Advanced Studies of African Society. CASAS, Pretoria, 2006.

Pugh, Martin and Nathan Cooper. *War Economies in Regional Context, Challenges of Transformation*. London: Boulder, Co: Lynne Rienner, 2004.

Riker, William. *Federalism: Origin, Operation and Significance*. Boston: Little Brown & Company, 1964.

Risse, Thomas. *Governance Without a State? Policies and Politics in Areas of Limited Statehood*. New York: Columbia University Press, 2011.

Roberg, Robert. *When States Fail: Causes and Consequences*. Princeton: Princeton University Press, 2004.

Rothchild, Donald. *Managing Ethnic Conflicts in Africa: Pressures and Incentives for Cooperation.* Washington: Brookings Institution Press, 1997.

Skinner, Quentin. *The Foundation of Modern Political Thought.* New York. Cambridge University Press, 1988

South Susan Statistical Year-Book, National Bureau of Statistics, 2012

Tarimo, Aquiline and Paulin Manwelo. *Ethnic Conflict and the Future of African States.* Nairobi: Paulines Publications Africa, 2009.

Tesfaye, Tekele. *Ethiopia Relations with Greater Horn of Africa Countries.* London: Axum Publishers, 2015.

Tilly, Charles. *Coercion, Capital, and European States.* Cambridge. B. Blackwell, 1990.

Turton, David. *Ethnic Federalism: The Ethiopian Experience in Comparative Perspective.* Oxford: James Curry, 2006.

Uvin, Peter. *Aiding Violence: The Development Enterprise in Rwanda.* Westford: Kumarin Press, 1998.

Vanden, Harry and Garry Provost. *Politics of Latin America: The Power Game. London:* Oxford University Press, 2002.

Van de Walle, Nicolas. *African Economies and the Politics of Permanent Crisis.* England: Cambridge University Press, 2001.

Wellerstein, Immanuel. *The World-System Theory.* Cambridge Academic Press, 1974.

Wolff, Stefan. *State Failure in Regional Context.* London: University of Bath, 2005.

Zartman, William. *Collapsed States: The Disintegration and Restoration of Legitimate Authority.* London, Lynne Rienner Publishers, 1995.

Referred Journals

Acoco, Kaboré, and J. B. Maillart. "The Malian Conflict and International Law", *Journal of Global Studies* no 5(2013): 91-112

Becker, Gary. Conflicts and the Birth of the Nation State. *Journal of Economic History 33* (March, 1985): 203-211.

Berman, Bruce. "The Ordeal of Modernity in an Age of Terror." *African Studies Review* 49 no 1(2006): 1-14.

"Ethnicity, Patronage and the African State: The Politics of Uncivil Nationalism." *African Affairs* 97 (1998): 305-341

Brown, Michael. "Ethnic and Internal Conflicts, in C.A. Crocker, F.E. Hampson and A. Crocker,eds., Turbulent Peace: The Challenges of Managing International Conflict." *US Institute of Peace,* (2001): 209-226.

Carneiro, Robert L A Theory of the Origin of the State. *Science Journal. 169* (August, 1970): 733-738.

Chandra, Kanchan. 'Ethnic Parties and Democratic Stability'. *Perspectives in Politics* Vol 3, no 2: (2005): 235-252.

Why Ethnic Parties Succeed: Patronage and Ethnic Head Counts in India. Cambridge: Cambridge University Press. 2007

D' Agoot, Majak. 'Assessing the Utility of Risk Management Theory in the Governance of New States: Lessons from South Sudan'. *Journal of Risk Research:* (2019), 210-226

De Waal, Alex. 'When Kleptocracy Becomes Insolvent: Brute Causes of the Civil War in South Sudan'. *African Affairs:* 113/452 (2014): 349 (347-369)

Easterly, William. "Institutions: Top Down or Bottom Up?" *American Economic Review: Papers and Proceedings:* 98 (2) 2008), 262: 251-286.

Elaine, David. A Theory of the Size and Shape of Nations. *Journal of Political Economy* (1977), 85: 59-77.

Ference, Marko. "We Are Not a Failed State, We Make The Best Passports: South Sudan Biometric Modernity". *Journal of African Studies Review,* (2016), Vol (2): 113-132

Garrido, Luis. "Elites, Political Elites and Social Change in Modern Societies". *Revista De Sociology*, no 28: (2013): 31-49.

Grimm, Lemay-Hébert, N. and Nay, O. "Fragile States': Introducing a Political Concept". *Third World Quarterly 35* (2) (2014): 316-332

Idris, Amir, "Does ethnicity matter in South Sudan's conflict?" *The Citizen Newspaper,* January 19, 2015. Vol. 8. Issue 958

Korwa G. Adar, "Conflict Resolution in a Turbulent Region: The Case of the Inter-Governmental Authority on Development (IGAD) in Sudan", *African Journal on Conflict Resolution,* vol. 1, no. 2, (2000), pp. 43-46

Kadushin, Carl "Friendship Amongst the French Financial Elite." *American Sociological Review,* no 60 (2): 211 (202-221)

"Ethnicity, Governance and the Provision of Public Goods." *Journal of African Economies* Vol 15, no 68: (2006): 62-99.

Karine, Bannelier, and Theodore, Christakis, Under the UN Security Council's watchful eyes: military intervention by invitation in the Malian conflict', *Leiden Journal of International Law* 26: (2013) 855–874 (856)

Kasaija, Philip. "Explaining the (IL) Legal of Uganda's Intervention in the Current South Sudan Conflict", *African Security Review*, vol. 3, no 4 (2014): 1-26 (1)

Marieke, Schomerus. "They forgot what they came for: Uganda's

Army in Sudan", *Journal of East African Studies,* vol. 6, no. 1 (2012); 114-117

OECD. "Concepts and Dilemmas of State-building in fragile Situations: From Fragility to Resilience". *Journal of Development* 9, no. 3 (2009): 61-146.

Sally, Healy "Seeking Peace and Security in the Horn of Africa: The Contribution of Inter-Governmental Authority on Development," *International Affairs,* vol. 87, no 1 (2011): 132-156

Shaw, Malcolm. '*International Law',* 5th edition, Cambridge University Press. 2003

Vlassenroot Koen et al. "Doing Business Out of War. An Analysis of the UPDF's Presence in the Democratic Republic of Congo", *Journal of East African Studies,* vol. 6, no. 1 (2012); 236-245

Wassara, Samson "South Sudan: State Sovereignty Challenged at Infancy", *Journal of Eastern African Studies,* 2015.

Wippman, David. "Military Intervention, Regional Organizations, and Host-State Consent", *Duke Journal of Comparative & International Law* 7: (1996) 209–240.

Theses

Agok, Daniel. "Seeking Solution for Acceptable Administration to the People of South Sudan". Juba: *Unpublished Paper,* July 18, 2014.

Akech, Daniel. *Features of Self-Enrichment System in South Sudan. Unpublished,* 2015.

Equatoria Position Paper on the IGAD Peace Talks in Addis Ababa, Ethiopia: Proposal on The establishment of the Transitional Government of National Unity. *Unpublished,* April 19, 2015.

Garang, Ngor. "Breaking News: Son a Governor and a member of national security service has joined rebellion". *Development Policy Forum (DPF)*, April 17, 2015

Garang, Yach. "The Impacts of Inter-Ethnic Conflicts on National Security: A case of the South Sudan with a reference to Dinka-Nuer and Murle of Jonglei State". Grandfield University. *MSc Thesis*, July 2015

Houlihan, Shawn. Federal Systems Overview. *Forum of Federations,* January 2015.

Jovenale, L "The Implementation of the Sudan Comprehensive Peace Agreement: Opportunities and Challenges". Catholic University of Eastern Africa. Nairobi: *M.A. Thesis*, September. 2008.

Juba Conference, 18-21 October 1954, NA FO 371/108326, *Minutes* no.193. The spelling and punctuation of the original document have been retained.

Karim, Jaafar. "Assessing Public Opinions Towards Federalism: What is the Proportion of South Sudanese who Favor Federalism?" *Unpublished Paper,* July 5, 2014.

Kopling, Peter. 'Peaceful Coexistence: how the Equatorians got it right". *MD's miss-titled.* June 29, 2014

Nyuon, William Bany. "Opening address to the Abuja peace talks". *Unpublished document collected by Yosa Wawa.* May 26, 1992

SPLM in Opposition *Proposal of 21 States with Ramciel as National Capital,* July, 1, 2014.

Thapa, Manish. *Role of Civil Society & Political Party in Nation/ State Building Process in Nepal: New Dynamics of Development, Challenges and Prospects,* Nepal: CETS, November 2008

Unpublished Report of National Peace Conference of South

Sudan Tribes held at Nyakuron Culture Centre, February 17-18, 2015.

Newsletters, Magazines, Briefs & Reports

Adeba, Brian. 2015. 'Making Sense of the White Army's Return in South Sudan." Centre for Security Governance. *CSG Papers,* No. 1.

Aher, Martin Garang. 2014. The Dang And The Spear: Spiritual Warfare Over Leadership In South Sudan. *Personal blog,* February 5, 2014, accessed November 1, 2015.

Ajude, John. The Failure and Collapse of the African State: On the Example of Nigeria. *Fride,* September 2007.

Akuot, Ayuen. "Information Minister Threatens To Shut Down UN Radio Miraya". *The Citizens Newspaper,* Vol 8. Issue No. 983, Tuesday, February 17, 2015.

Amnesty International. 2000. Sudan: *The Ravages of War, Political Killings and Humanitarian Disaster.* New York: Amnesty International.

Akuot, Ayuen. "Information Minister Threatens To Shut Down UN Radio Miraya". *The Citizens Newspaper,* Vol 8. Issue No. 983, Tuesday, February 17, 2015.

Awolich, Abraham. "South Sudan's Fight Against Corruption: Are We Winning?" Weekly Review: *The Sudd Institute,* July 3, 2013.

Chol, Jacob. "White Army and Spiritual Mythology in South Sudan Political Violence". *APCG Newsletter.* Washington DC, 2016

Cristina, Paula. "Reforming the SPLM: A requisite for Peace and Nation Building". Policy Brief 63: *Institute for Security Studies,* Pretoria, August 2014.

Enough Project "War Crimes Shouldn't Pay: Stopping the

Looting and Destruction in South Sudan". *Sentry Report, September 2016*

Forest, James. 'Countering Terrorism and Insurgency in the 21st Century: International Perspectives, Combating the Sources and Facilitators.' *Westport, CT: Praeger Security International.* 2007

Fragile States Index. Published in *Foreign Policy*. New York, U.S, 2014.

Guigale, Marcelo. 'Director of Economic Policy and Policy Reduction Programmes for Africa.' *World Bank Briefing Report.* March, 1, 2012.

Hobley, Mary and Shields Dermot. 'The Reality of Trying to Transform Structures and Process: Forestry in Rural Livelihoods.' *Overseas Development Institute,* WP, 2000.

Ignatieff, Michael. "The Burden." *New York Times Magazine,* Washington: January 2003

Kioi, Joseph. "State and Nation Building in South Sudan after the Comprehensive Peace Agreement", *International Peace Support Training Centre, Issue Brief, No 4,* Nairobi IPSTC, 2012.

Kameir, El-Wahig and Ibrahim Kursany. 'Corruption as the 'Fifth' factor of production in Sudan.' *Nordiska Afrika Institute,* Research Report No. 71, Uppsala, 1995.

Martin, John. "Federalism: South Sudan in Dilemma". *Juba Monitor Newspaper,* March 10·2015.

Madut, Jok. "Diversity, Unity, and Nation Building in South Sudan". *Special Report,* United States Institute of Peace, Washington: USIP, 2011.

Mamdani, Mahmood. "South Sudan: The Problem and the Way Forward". *New Vision,* February 28, 2014.

Messener, James. "Fund for Peace Index'. *Foreign Policy Magazine,* January 2019.

Mach, Samuel. "Governor Criticizes UN Over Failure in War Torn Countries". *The Citizen Newspaper.* Vol. 8. Issue No. 921, Friday, November 28, 2014.

Mukisa, Farahani "Opposition blasts President over UPDF", *Daily Monitor,* 14th January 2014

Musisi, Fredric "UPDF came to Prevent Genocide in South Sudan", *Daily Monitor,* 9th January 2014

Oyet, Alphonse, UN Sanctions on President Kiir is A Regime Change. *The Juba Monitor,* Wednesday, January 27, 2016.

OECD Report. State Fragility. Belgium, Brussels, 2010.

Conceptualizing State Fragility. London, UK, 2012

Paul-Robert Juster & Marie-France Martin, Stress and Resilience. *Mammaoth Magazine,* 2013.

Perera, Suda. State Fragility, The Concept. *DLP Concept Brief No 3.* Washington, U.S, 2015.

President Kiir. Comments on *SSTV News Briefing* on Rumbek UN Impounded Weapons, March 30, 2014

Speech delivered at Dr. John Garang De' Mabior's Mausoleum in Juba at SPLM Rally, March 18, 2015

Speech during the 3rd Anniversary of Independence at Dr. John Garang De' Mabior's Mausoleum, July 9, 2014

Remarks at the Tana High Level Forum on Security in Africa, Bahir Dar, Ethiopia, April, 27, 2014

Ramba, Justin. "Federalism Now, Not later". *Juba Monitor Newspaper,* Tuesday, March 10, 2015.

Sentry Report. "The Nexus of Corruption and Conflict in

South Sudan", *Enough Project,* July 2015.

"Small Arms Survey, Pendulum Swings: The Rise and Fall of Insurgent Militias in South Sudan". *Small Arms Survey, Human Security Baseline Assessment.* Issue Brief No. 22, Geneva, 2013

Tadess, Medhane. "Turning Conflicts to Cooperation: Towards Energy led Regional Integration in the Horn of Africa". *ISS Report,* Addis Ababa, 2004.

Ting, Augustino. "A fallacy of Failed States Index: The Case of South Sudan", Weekly Review: *Sudd Institute,* October 18, 2013

Ugandan's Ministry of Foreign Affairs, *Press Release* 30th January 2014.

UNDP South Sudan Annual Report Juba, UNDP Compound, 2012

UNSC Report on Situation on South Sudan, April 25, 2014.

UNSC Report of Secretary-General on South Sudan. New York. June 20, 2013.

UN Security Council Discussed Sanctions for South Sudan: *Voice of America (VOA),* Day Break Africa News 7:30Am, February 25, 2015.

Willems Rens and Deng David. The Legacy of Kokora in South Sudan. *Briefing Paper.* Intersections of Truth, Justice and Reconciliation in South Sudan. SSLS, University for Peace & PAX, November 2015.

Internet Sources and Websites

Adiok, James "Why Federalism Must Wait" http://www.sudantribune.com/spip.php?article51320

African Union Commission of Inquiry on South Sudan Report,

2015 http://www.peaceau.org/en/article/final-report-of-the-african-union-commission-of-inquiry-on-south-sudan

Arinaitwe, Solomon "Minister Fails to Produce S. Sudan Letter seeking UPDF Intervention", Daily Monitor, 24 January 2014, http://www.monitor.co.ug/News/National/Minister-fails-to-produce-S-Sudan-letter-seeking

Chol, Jacob "When a Success Becomes a Burden: Challenges of Nations Building in Post-Liberation South Sudan' http://blogs.lse.ac.uk/africaatlse/2017/12/06/when-success-becomes-a-burden-challenges-of-nations-building-in-post-liberation-south-sudan/

De Dau, David. "South Sudan: Decentralization vis-à-vis Federation:" http://sudantribune.com/spip.php?article51448

Garang, e' Kuir "Jieeng Council of Elders, The Erosion of Jieeng's Values and 'Jieengization' of South Sudan", http://www.southsudannation.com/jieeng-council-of-elders-the-erosion-of-jieengs-values-and-the-jieengization-of-south-sudan

Guardian "South Sudan Peacekeeping Commander Sacked Over 'Serious Shortcoming'", https://www.theguardian.com/global-development/2016/nov/02/south-sudan-peacekeeping-chief-sacked-alarm-serious-shortcomings-ondieki

Gulf Today Article: "South Sudan Threatens Aid Workers' ':http://gulftoday.ae/portal/2a4d664d-bc8f-4049-a331-5ce031d33c10.aspx

Jok, Petero, "Toby Lanzer Expelled Over CNN Statements", http://www.newnationsouthsudan.com/national-news/toby-lanzer-expelled-over-cnn-statements.html

Kompass, Anders. 'Ethical Failure: Why I Resigned From the UN.' http://www.irinnews.org/opinion/2016/06/17/

exclusive-ethical-failure-%E2%80%93-why-i-resigned-un

Lupai , Jacob. "Kokora: Often Misunderstood, Grossly Misinterpreted and Most Feared", http://www.southsudan-newsagency.com/opinion/articles/kokora-often-misunder-stood-grossly-misinterpreted-and-most-feared.

Mabor, Juma. 'Administrative Decentralization: The Only Best Option for Governing South Sudan': http://www.southsudan-nation.com/administrative-decentralization-the-only-best-op-tion-for-governing-south-sudan/

Montevideo Convention on Rights and Duties of the States, 1933, article 1 https://www.ilsa.org/jessup/jessup15/Montevideo%20Convention.pdf

Mulla, Richard. "South Sudan: Federalism Or Decentralization?" http://www.southsudannewsagency.com/opinion/articles/south-sudan-federalism-or-decentralisation

Nation Building: http://www.wikipedia.org/wiki/Nation-building

Oren Dorell. "Corruption at root of South Sudan Violence: Analysts". USA TODAY, 27 Dec.2013, http://www.usatoday.com/story/news/world/2013/12/27/south-sudan-government-agreement/4218073

Press Statement by Jieng Council of Elders (JCE) rejecting im-position of peace on South Sudan: A clear message to the poten-tial perpetrators of South Sudan destruction http://paanluelwel.com/2015/04/01/jieng-council-of-elders-rejects-imposition-of-peace-on-south-sudan/

Radio Tamazuj, "First Batch of Regional Protection Starts to Arrive in Juba", https://radiotamazuj.org/en/news/article/

first-batch-of-regional-protection-force-starts-to-arrive-in-juba

'Kiir raises fears of 'kokora' under federal system' https://radiotamazuj.org/en/article/kiir-raises-fears-%E2%80%98kokora%E2%80%99-under-federal-system

Riek, Deng. "Decentralization: A best option of ROSS but lacking practicality (sic)'"" http://www.southsudannewsagency.com/opinion/articles/decentralization-a-best-option-for-ross-but-lacking-practicality

Status of Forces Agreement SOFA http://www.un.org/en/peacekeeping/missions/unmiss/resources.shtml

South Sudan Tribune: http://southsudantribune.org/news/states-news/128-unmiss-cargo-of-arms-destined-for-dr-riek-rebels-seized-by-security-forces-in-rumbek.

Sudan Post. "Ex-Defense Minister Kuol Manyang Juuk Says Government Killed, Failed Citizens": https://www.sudanspost.com/ex-defense-minister-kuol-manyang-says-govt-killed-failed-citizens/

Sudan Post. "Ex-Presidential Advisor Daniel Awet Akot Tells Kiir to Step Down": https://www.sudanspost.com/ex-presidential-advisor-daniel-awet-akot-tells-kiir-to-step-down/

Sudan Tribune, "SPLA top generals asked by anti-corruption to declare their assets", http://www.sudantribune.com/spip.php?article41727

'South Sudan: Four Years and Counting" http://www.sudantribune.com/spip.phd?article55684

"Foreign advisor to South Sudan's President flees Juba after disclosure of corruption letter", http://www.sudantribune.com/splp.php?article43641

"South Sudan's Kiir rejects deployment of extra troops in Juba". http://www.sudantribune.com/spip.php?article59615

"South Sudanese President Creates Four More States", http://www.sudantribune.com/spip.php?article61403

"UPDF Intervention in South Sudan" http://www.sudantribune.com/spip.php?article53378

South Sudan's Dinka Leaders and Their Community Have Failed Our Country. WES Governor at the Voice of Equatoria: http://www.upperniletimes.com

Tajuba, Paul "South Sudan Speaker Denies Writing Letter to Museveni", Daily Monitor, 27 January 2014, http://www.monitor.co.ug/News/National/South-Sudan-speaker-denies-writing-letter-to-Museveni/-/688334/2161502/-/b479 q0z/-/index.html

TVC News "Kenya Withdrew First 100 Peacekeepers from South Sudan". http://africa.tvcnews.tv/2016/11/11/kenya-withdraws-first-100-peacekeepers-south-sudan/#.WCbjMCN97ow

UN Principle of R2P: http://www.unr2p.com

INDEX

301

Severine 122-123, 283

Sexual 242, 244

Seyoum 148, 163

Shadong 25

Sharon 250-251

Shaw, Malcolm. 156, 291

Shawn 269, 292

Shilluk 201

Shumal 49

Simon 235, 238

Simone 17, 284

Skaperdas 7, 285

Skinner, Quentin. 2, 288

Sociological 105, 290

Sociology 1, 94-6, 114, 284-5, 287, 290

Solomon 158, 297

Somalia 139, 147-9, 250

Southerners 41, 61, 264

Sovereignty 2, 50, 111, 291

Spain 223, 271

Spiritual 76, 293

Statehood 1, 28, 30, 287

Stateless 5

Statesmen 236

Stefan 120, 288

Stergios 7, 285

Strayer 2

Subcommittees 43

Suda 27-28, 295

Sudan 14-17, 19-22, 24-6, 32-9, 41-2, 45-51, 53-61, 63-8, 70-1, 73, 75-81, 83-94, 97-100,

104, 106, 108-110, 112, 116-121, 123-9, 131-145, 147-169, 176-188, 190-4, 196-203, 207, 213-4, 217, 219, 222-5, 227-231, 233, 239-243, 245, 247-8, 250, 253-6, 259-267, 270-4, 276-281, 284, 286, 290-4, 296-300

Sudanese 16, 20, 26, 32, 35-47, 49, 51, 55-60, 67-8, 70-2, 75, 79-80, 84, 87-8, 90-1, 97, 99, 108-110, 114, 116-7, 127-9, 132-3, 135-7, 139, 147, 149-150, 153, 160, 162-6, 168-9, 176-9, 181, 185, 189-191, 196, 199, 201-3, 210-3, 215, 222, 224, 226, 228-9, 231, 240, 242-3, 246-7, 249-250, 255-6, 261, 263-7, 270-2, 274-281, 292, 300

Sudd 35, 108, 117, 293, 296

Sumbeiywo 148

Summa 221

Sunday 50, 277

Susan 185, 255, 288

Sweden 149

Switzerland 149, 270

Taban 57, 205

Tadess, Medhane. 147, 296

Taha 241

Tajuba 158-159, 300

Tallaway 234

Tamazuj 143, 280, 299

www.ingramcontent.com/pod-product-compliance
Lightning Source LLC
Chambersburg PA
CBHW041934260326
41914CB00010B/1289